Praise for *Winning Clients in a Wired World*

Visit www.winningclientsinawiredworld.com to read what others are saying.

Don't believe the title! This book doesn't include seven strategies; it's more like seven hundred! I loved it and it's now required reading for everyone in our firm.

> HAROLD EVENSKY
> Chairman, Evensky, Brown & Katz
> Author of *Wealth Management*

Kip Gregory does a remarkable job of showing how technology, instead of creating another headache, can free advisors for their real job—serving clients.

> EVAN COOPER
> Editor-in-Chief, *On Wall Street* magazine

One of the greatest challenges business leaders face today is figuring out how to effectively drive productivity and increase profitability. Gregory provides practical and actionable advice that any company, large or small, can immediately use to better compete and win in their marketplace.

> TIMOTHY MCMAHON
> CEO, Adams, Harkness & Hill, Inc.

The technology journey simplified and targeted to meet business goals. In today's competitive environment, you need an information advantage; this book gives it to you!

> JYLANNE DUNNE
> Executive Vice President, Relationship Management, BISYS

Winning Clients in a Wired World is packed with valuable business and sales management insights, woven together with practical uses of technology throughout. It's a real winner!

> JAY HOOLEY
> Executive Vice President, State Street Corporation

An excellent book you will find well worth your while! There are many useful techniques and activities that support the success formula: Revenue/Results = Activity × Effectiveness. I'm going to order it for my team and promote it in our workshops.

> PHILIP SIMENSEN
> Senior Vice President, Field Development, ING Advisors Network

A great reference for any advisor who wants to take fuller advantage of today's computer and Internet opportunities.

> RIC EDELMAN
> Chairman, Edelman Financial Services, Inc.
> Author of *The Truth about Money*

This book is the only one of its kind I've ever seen for financial professionals. Piece by piece, it eliminates the ceiling of complexity most of us encounter when trying to make better use of technology. The chapter on communicating with clients alone is worth its weight in gold. Thanks, Kip, you're going to make me look like a hero.

WILLIAM GREEN
Senior Vice President, Practice Development and Management, AXA

Lots of books stress the importance of leveraging technology and the Internet to operate more efficiently; this one outlines exactly how to get tangible economic benefit from what you've already invested in. Any financial services professional who is serious about improving their productivity should read *Winning Clients in a Wired World*.

JOHN HOWARD
President, Prudential Select Brokerage

Very few books get you talking to yourself, saying things like "Wow, I didn't know that!" or "*THAT* will be extremely helpful." This book is one of them. What makes it a must read for those of us in the financial services industry is that it's written for *us*. It's *full* of ideas for making our professional lives more manageable.

CHARLES KITTREDGE
Senior Vice President of Marketing, National Life Insurance Company

I only wish I had read this book *before* I became a financial advisor; I could have saved thousands of hours of research and frustration. I would not hesitate to recommend that others buy it. It is invaluable!

LEE PENCE
Pence Financial Advisors/The Strategic Financial Alliance (SFA), Inc.

This outstanding resource should be on every financial advisor's desk. It provides hundreds of proven technology solutions that would take years of searching on your own to find.

JOHN BOWEN
Chairman, CEG Worldwide LLC
Author of *Creating Equity*

Kip's book is a gift to the industry! Within minutes of picking it up, I was highlighting text, flagging pages, and implementing some very simple yet brilliant techniques. This is a must have resource for all advisors. Don't be left behind.

SHERYL GARRETT
Founder, The Garrett Planning Network, Inc.

Generating ideas is the easy part . . . moving them into action (execution) is the challenge. Kip tells you how structure and technology come to the rescue in getting that done.

REBECCA WINGATE
President, LifeMark Partners, Inc.

My list of ideas to implement from this book is a page long. The sections on Web searching and disaster contingency planning could save you the price of the book one hundred times over!

Kirk Hulett
Senior Vice President, Strategy and Practice Management, Securities America, Inc.

This is a cookbook of recipes for adding value to customer relationships. As a wholesaler, if you want to transcend the "product provider" role to become a partner who offers producers fresh ideas on growing and managing their business, learn and apply the strategies in these pages.

Larry Carr
Senior Vice President, Travelers Life and Annuity

This is a book *filled* with useful information. There is literally some idea or suggestion on every page that will save you time, help you serve your clients better, or help you build your business.

Norman Boone
President, Boone Financial Advisors, Inc

This must-read book for salespeople, relationship managers, and executives provides great step-by-step details on how to access and utilize software and Web sites to function more effectively. More importantly, it shows you how to couple those tools with proven management and leadership concepts to ensure success.

Gail Letts
Executive Vice President, SunTrust Bank

Winning Clients in a Wired World is an antidote to computer frustration, spelling out simple, practical ideas for using the technology you own together with the Internet to find more time and more business.

Myles Morin
Vice President, Wealth Management Sales, Manulife Financial

There is more help in these pages than any book I have ever read! I'm amazed at how much I did not know and could implement so quickly, and I have been using computers since 1981. I love it!

Ben Baldwin
Author of *The New Life Insurance Investment Advisor*

Kip Gregory tells you all you need to know to make better use of the Internet to serve your clients better, faster, and more efficiently. Kip's tips will improve your practice and simplify your life.

Don Philips
Managing Director, Morningstar, Inc.

Want to build more value into your business and gain greater leverage from your people, tools, and processes? Study this book. Chapter by chapter, it lays out how you and your team can get more from computers and the Web . . . in accessible, easy-to-follow language.

MARK TIBERGIEN
Principal, Moss Adams LLP

This book succinctly divulges the how-to of working smarter not harder. It's become a major component in the process of taking my practice to the next level.

RAYMOND CARTER
Vice President, Investments, R. W. Baird & Co. Inc.

In today's rapidly changing business environment, effective use of technology is more critical to success than it's ever been. In *Winning Clients in a Wired World,* Kip Gregory puts technology's power within your grasp—with tips and action steps you can implement immediately to strengthen your business.

CHIP ROAME
Managing Principal, Tiburon Strategic Advisors

Looking to simplify your life, increase your earnings, and significantly increase your level of productivity? Read this book. Kip does a brilliant job in eliminating the trepidation advisors feel in utilizing technology. His tips are useful, practical, and easy to apply.

KEITH GREGG
First Vice President, Wachovia Financial Securities Network

I'm implementing your strategies across the board in my practice and am certain that they will improve my effectiveness in marketing to higher net worth clients, communicating with existing clients and managing my business.

TOM RICKS
Sagemark Consulting

Kip Gregory has taken the tenets of client-building skills to a new level.

KAREN ALTFEST
Co-Director, Investments Program, The New School
Author of *Keeping Clients for Life*

This remarkable book on how to build a financial services practice shows you, in bite size pieces, how to harness the power of technology and the Web to create meaningful relationships with your clients. Gift yourself a copy.

LISBETH WILEY CHAPMAN
Author of *Get Media Smart!*

You can open this book to any page and get at least one good, *quick* idea to use immediately. Kip makes connections with the financial industry so that you forget you're reading about "technology" and start thinking of ways to use your computer and the Web just like any other business resource-to produce.

Winning Clients in a Wired World provides concise, easy-to-implement strategies for advisors and their teams looking to use technology more efficiently in growing their practices. Even those who are technologically challenged can benefit from its easy-to-follow format.

A brilliant, hands-on instruction manual, packed with insight and business wisdom. Read a few pages, and you're guaranteed to find exciting ideas you'll want to explore and implement in your practice . . . some of the most exciting technology-based tips and ideas for financial services businesses I've seen.

Kip Gregory is easily the financial advice industry's leading expert on how advisors can use technology more effectively, and this book, the ultimate resource.

A must read for anyone who wants to grow their business using technology. I found some great ideas to help me.

A great tool; full of timesaving, practical, useful, helpful ideas.

The handwriting's on the wall for those who want to survive in financial services: how and why we get paid has changed dramatically. Many of the old ways of doing business are obsolete. In these days of digital communication and do-not-call lists, Kip Gregory's book tells you how to harness computers and the Internet to do everything from organizing your ideas and streamlining your systems to what we all want most—finding good prospects and providing great personal service to our clients.

WINNING CLIENTS IN A WIRED WORLD

Seven Strategies for Growing Your Business Using Technology and the Web

Kip Gregory

WILEY
John Wiley & Sons, Inc.

Published by John Wiley & Sons, Inc., Hoboken, New Jersey

Published simultaneously in Canada

For general information on our other products and services, or technical support, please contact our Customer Care Department within the United States at 800-762-2974, outside the United States at 317-572-3993 or fax 317-572-4002.

Wiley also publishes its books in a variety of electronic formats. Some content that appears in print may not be available in electronic books.

Library of Congress Cataloging-in-Publication Data:

Gregory, Kip.
    Winning clients in a wired world : seven strategies for growing your business using technology and the Web / by Kip Gregory.
        p. cm.
    ISBN 0-471-24975-0 (CLOTH)
    1. Internet marketing.   2. Selling—Technological innovations.   3. Internet advertising.   4. Electronic commerce.   5. World Wide Web.   I. Title.
    HF5415.1265.G74   2004
    658.8'72—dc22

                                                        2003018289

10 9 8 7 6 5 4 3 2

Two roads diverged in a yellow wood, and I—I took the one less traveled by, and that has made all the difference.

—Robert Frost

For Garrett and Catherine, two daily reminders of the blessings of life— Have faith. Share your gifts. Go where they lead you. Enjoy the adventure. A.M.D.G.

And for Donna— In a word . . . thanks.

Contents

Getting Started

From Confusion to Competence

Even if you're on the right track, you'll get run over if you just sit there.
                                                        —Mark Twain

There are thousands of titles on marketing and selling, and millions of manuals and Web sites on sharpening your computing skills. But there's never been a book that laid out, in plain English, the essentials of using technology you already own to find, win, and keep clients—faster, cheaper, and more effectively.

Until now.

If you've been looking to exploit the box on your desktop called a computer to be more productive and to create a sustainable competitive advantage, this book is for you. It lays out practical advice that I have culled from a 20-year career in sales.

I'm the first to admit computers can be frustrating, especially for sales people. Having raised $1.5 billion in assets, I can identify with the pressure of "meeting the numbers." And I'm all too familiar with how much technology promises to improve life, and how frequently it comes up short. But I also know that, in a world where success increasingly hinges on the ability to turn information into advantage, your survival depends on smarter use of technology and the Web. Accept that and get on board, or risk getting left behind.

The information in this book will help you overcome any fears. It won't turn you into a technological guru (you have better things to do), but it will

1

help you take the tools already at your disposal and harness far more of the power they offer.

When you finish, you will be able to do a better job for your current clients, get in front of more of the right kind of prospects, and take greater control of your day-to-day routines. In short, by investing a little time in reading this book and implementing its suggestions, you'll free up more time to improve your business and enjoy your personal life.

Think of what's here as a buffet, not a ten-course meal. Digesting everything in these pages would be daunting to even the most die-hard computer user. Focus on the sections that address your most pressing challenges and go from there. And by all means, make this book your own: highlight and annotate it. It's meant to be a reference you refer to often.

Here's what we will be talking about.

- *Chapter 1: Keep What's Critical at Your Fingertips.* With so much to keep track of, you'll learn how to organize and manage the knowledge you and your team possess—easily, in one place.

- *Chapter 2: Achieve Breakthroughs Systematically.* You want to succeed with intent, not by accident. This chapter presents a simple approach to formulating and implementing improvements in any facet of your business.

- *Chapter 3: Work the Web for All It's Worth.* Here we will look at how to uncover what's valuable on the Web quickly and easily, and use it to your advantage.

- *Chapter 4: Build Relationships Through Better Communication.* One of the biggest challenges sales people face is keeping in contact. We'll see how you can use technology to create regular, meaningful conversations with customers, clients, prospects, and others.

- *Chapter 5: Present Yourself Professionally.* With technology, you don't have to be a showman to convey a professional image to your audience. We will cover tips and tools you can use when you're presenting in person, in print, or over the Internet.

- *Chapter 6: Automate Time-Consuming Tasks.* This chapter will show you how to create free time, or more selling time, by completing routine tasks faster.

- *Chapter 7: Get the Help You Need to Succeed.* Sometimes you need a real person, not a program, to get the job done. Learn how to find people to help you solve problems and improve your overall effectiveness.

- *Chapter 8: Assembling Your Toolkit.* When it comes to equipment, there's must-have and nice-to-have; we'll look at both. We will also explore which resources to tap to keep up with changing technology and where to go for help in resolving technical troubles.

- *Chapter 9: The Chat Room.* This chapter offers advice on taming technology from others who have been there and done that.

- *Chapter 10: Where Do I Go from Here?* Sometimes the end is really a beginning. Some parting suggestions on what do to next.

A TRULY INTERACTIVE TOOL

You're going to read about hundreds of outstanding Web sites in these pages, but you only have to remember one address: http://www .winningclientsinawiredworld.com. From there, you can link to every site in this book, and others, all broken down by chapter. While at the site, you can sign up to be notified of any changes in that list by e-mail, get periodic free tips on marketing and managing (also via e-mail), purchase the forms and worksheets included in Appendix B, and learn about a variety of other resources that can help you build your business.

 TIP: Take a minute now to register at the site. You'll receive an update of what's new since "Winning Clients in a Wired World" was published.

Some Explanations

Since *Winning Clients in a Wired World* is directed primarily at financial services professionals, throughout the book you will see terms such as *financial advisor, sales assistant, wholesaler, branch manager,* and *senior executive.* But you can apply its strategies, tactics, and tools just as well to other businesses, especially service-oriented ones. And it isn't only about sales and marketing; systemizing across your business is the key to creating more time for selling and marketing, so we'll look at ways to improve virtually all aspects of what you do.[1]

CASH IN THE DOWNSTREAM DIVIDEND

This book is primarily about helping you in *your* business. But sharing ideas from these pages with clients, prospects, and others you work with can be a great way to strengthen your reputation as a problem solver and trusted advisor.

That's especially true if you target corporate executives, entrepreneurs, self-employed professionals, or those in sales. Like you, people in those positions are constantly looking for ways to operate more efficiently and effectively. Show them a path to greater productivity and profit, one that leverages tools they already own, and watch your value to them soar.

I call it the "downstream dividend" of learning what's here. Make sure you capture it!

Where instructions are provided, I suggest you walk through them while sitting at your computer. Trying to absorb them by reading alone is like listening to someone describe how it feels to ride a bike: it's not the same thing as hopping on and trying it for yourself.

On many pages, you'll see phrases like *"Shift + Ctrl + Alt + . . . ,"* *"Ctrl + Alt + . . . ,"* and the like. What they mean is "press and hold those keys down while you press the last key in the sequence." They are keyboard shortcuts, and they can save you lots of time in getting things done. (The ⌨ icon also flags useful keyboard shortcuts.)

Similarly, you will notice words with one letter underlined, a signal that you can activate that command using your keyboard. When the command is on the main menu of a program (File, Edit, View, etc.), or within the small *dialog boxes* that open when you select certain commands, you activate it by pressing and holding the Alt key and then the underlined key. When the command appears on a submenu, pressing the letter alone will trigger it.

Finally, when you see words in bold italic text scattered throughout these pages (like this: ***winning clients***), you're supposed to type them on your computer as instructed.

And Some Encouragement

If you've ever felt as if you're missing a technology gene, or that you just don't get what everyone else does, let me put your mind at ease: It's not you; it's the "culture" of technology. Developers focus on *features* (what the program does); users care about *benefits* (what the program can do for them).

To be fair, the people developing these tools are only responding to user demand for more and more functionality. But in the process, programs have been loaded with layers of labyrinth-like menus whose features, in most cases, remain undiscovered and unused. Left to themselves to figure it all out, most users get confused and frustrated.

That said, you don't need to become a Bill Gates or Steve Jobs, you just need to master a few processes and procedures—and then implement them. As you do, realize you're not alone. Everyone wrestles with technology. Others have faced your problems and found solutions. Later on, I'll show you how to connect with them.

Let's get started.

What to Do Right Now

Before doing anything, take a few minutes to review what you're already equipped with. Make a quick list of the programs installed on your computer. Having a list like that is the first step toward leveraging what you own.

If you work with an assistant, have him or her take stock of what's in your toolkit using the *Software Inventory Summary Worksheet* in Appendix B. Having that inventory will help you avoid buying the same thing (or very similar things) twice, it will save you time in tracking down information if you have to call someone for assistance, and it will make upgrading or reinstalling software easier, by putting what you need to know in one place.

TIP: Open up your Programs menu (by clicking on the Start button) to see what's installed on your machine. You can sort the list alphabetically by right-clicking on any item on it with your mouse and choosing "Sort by Name." Windows will arrange the list contents from A to Z, first by folder, then by individual program.

TIP: When your inventory summary is finished, print out and keep a copy of it handy. Also, backup the file onto a diskette or CD-ROM—just in case.

What to Keep on Doing

If you're serious about leveraging technology, you need to develop an explorer's mind-set. That's the best way to learn what capabilities you possess; starting with the programs you use most often (probably tools like Microsoft Word, Excel, PowerPoint, Outlook, and Internet Explorer). I'm not suggesting you need to become an expert in them; you just need to get competent on the basic "drive the car" knowledge that lets you function in them self-sufficiently. The rest you can delegate, outsource, or ignore.

How do you build that skill? Take a few minutes before the morning kicks into high gear, during downtime over lunch, or after the market closes to open up any program you use often and poke around. Keep a list of useful features you discover along the way (use the *Program Feature Worksheet* included in Appendix B).

 TIP: One place to start your exploration is the shortcut section in Chapter 6. It outlines fast ways to complete dozens of tasks in programs you use every day.

You will find the exploration easier if you disable the personalized menus feature in newer versions of Windows and Office, which hide menu commands you don't use frequently.[2] To do that, you will need to make a quick change in two places: on the Start menu and within Microsoft Word (which will adjust the rest of the Office programs, too).

To make all the Start/Programs menu options visible, right-click in a blank area of the Taskbar (the area at the bottom of the screen, where the "Start" button is located; a menu of options (called a *shortcut menu* will appear); click on "Properties"; uncheck the box next to the bottom option "Use Personalized Menus," as shown in Figure 1.

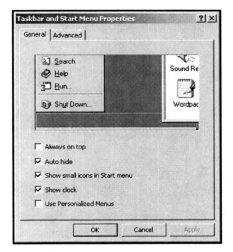

FIGURE 1   Taskbar and Start Menu Properties

To modify how Office program menus are displayed, open Word, select Tools, then Customize, then the Options tab. Check the box next to "Always show full menus" (see Figure 2).

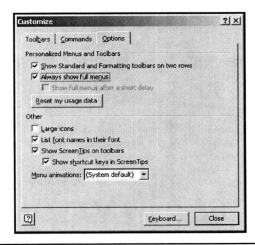

FIGURE 2   Customize

If you want to know what a particular feature in any Microsoft program does, try pressing the *Shift + F1* keys simultaneously (a small question mark will appear next to the mouse arrow). While in that "Help Select" mode, you can click on a command, check box, or drop-down list and (usually) read a description of what it does.

The Most Important Thing to Keep in Mind

Here's the last point. More important even than knowing what you own and learning what it can do for you, is having a handle on what you do. If you want to be more successful, start thinking of your business in terms of *process:* how you market, prospect, sell, service, trade, whatever. What's a process? A sequence of actions that leads to some result.

If you want to figure out where technology can help you, identify what you spend your time doing. What are the steps you follow? Is each necessary? Who performs them? Can they be automated? Can they be eliminated? *Understand the process.*

You want to build a more successful business? Determine the things you have to do day-to-day to get there. Not just you personally, you the business. Then, lay out a game plan, because there's no way you're going to make it without one.

The next two chapters describe the perfect place to put your plan together and how to go about doing it.

Notes

1. Some employers, particularly those in financial services, may restrict or prohibit the use of certain tools mentioned in this book, especially those relating to Web-based communication (i.e., e-mail and instant messaging). If you work for a regulated company, review your firm's policies or consult with your compliance supervisor/manager before utilizing such tools.

2. When the feature is enabled, the full menus of commands are not visible unless you click on the down arrow at the bottom of each menu (something many people consider an annoyance).

Keep What's Critical at Your Fingertips

Leveraging Knowledge and Time

The most meaningful way to differentiate your company from your competition, the best way to put distance between yourself and the crowd, is to do an outstanding job with information. How you gather, manage, and use information will determine whether you win or lose.

—Bill Gates, *Business @ the Speed of Thought*

Did you know . . .?

- Over 50 percent of the average knowledge worker's time is spent *looking for information.*
- Up to 20 percent of employee time is spent *replicating answers for others.*
- Over 80 percent of the knowledge available to most companies *is never actually utilized.*[1]

Any way you slice it, a big chunk of productivity is lost in the search and retrieval of information. If you're in sales, it's especially painful because every minute spent digging for something means less time for cultivating clients or calling on prospects.

So what if you could designate a single spot for capturing, organizing, and storing all your critical information: sales ideas, your marketing plan, phone scripts, proposal content, procedures, the things you currently carry in your head, scribbled on a notepad, or stuck on a Post-it? Suppose you could have instant access to that information any time you wanted—indexed so you could scan a list of topics, and immediately jump to what you needed.

Imagine you could use that very same indexing technique to professionally format documents and reports you wanted to share with clients or prospects: quarterly or annual account reviews, or a proposal to do business. Wouldn't that be a tremendous productivity boost and a potentially huge competitive advantage?

Now, what if I told you it wouldn't cost you a cent to obtain that tool because you already own what you need to create it, software you use every day; would you be willing to invest a few minutes in learning how to use it?

The Knowledge Journal Concept

What I'm describing is called a *knowledge journal*, a file created in Microsoft Word for organizing and leveraging what you know about acquiring and servicing clients, and running every facet of your business, more effectively. A knowledge journal is a bible of business processes, mission and values, goals, challenges, brainstorms, and anything else you want to refer to regularly.

Here's an example. You return from a conference with a notepad full of improvement ideas. You're excited about putting them to work, but you're met by a mountain of voice mail and e-mail demanding your attention. The urgent need to clear the backlog trumps your enthusiasm and, reluctantly, you put your notes aside. Other things come up; the notes get buried. Months later, cleaning off your credenza, you find them and think, "Gee, there was a lot of good material here, but now I can't remember what I wanted to do with it."

Sound familiar?

Keeping a knowledge journal is a simple, effective way to increase your return by keeping important information easily accessible.

 TIP: If you want to see what a knowledge journal file looks like once it's been created, you can download a sample from this book's companion site, http://www.winningclientsinawiredworld.com.

Getting Set Up

You can be up and running with your knowledge journal in fewer than five minutes if you complete the steps detailed here. They include set-up instructions and tips for dealing with issues you may encounter as you use your journal.

1. Start a Journal File

1. *Launch Word, press Ctrl + N to open a new document, and then type **My Journal** as shown in Figure 1.1.*

FIGURE 1.1 Starting a Journal File

2. *Press Ctrl + S to save the new document.*
    A small dialog box will open on screen (Figure 1.2). "My Journal.doc" should appear in the "File name" field; if it doesn't, type **My Journal** in it. Save it in your "My Documents" folder or someplace where you'll easily be able to find it later.

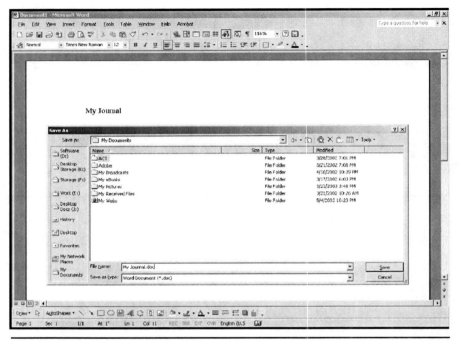

FIGURE 1.2 Saving Your Journal

2. Make a List of Section Titles

1. *In deciding what to put in your journal, six categories are musts: your ideal client profile, business plan, office procedures, sales ideas, conference notes, and software program features mentioned in the Introduction, "Getting Started." Other possibilities include best practices you've learned and newsletter article ideas and content. (You can review a more complete list of suggestions at http://www .winningclientsinawiredworld.com.)*

Type each section title on a separate line in your journal file. Keep the titles short so they're easy to read. Put a few extra lines between each title to leave room for the section content you'll add in a minute (if you haven't mapped out a business plan or documented office procedures, Chapter 2 will show you how).

2. *After typing a title for each section, assign it a Heading 1 style.*[2]

First, make sure that your cursor is placed somewhere in the section title that you want to change to Heading 1. Then press *Ctrl + Alt + 1* on your keyboard. When you do, the style of that line will change from "Normal" to "Heading 1." The size and font type of the text on that line will change, as illustrated in Figure 1.3.

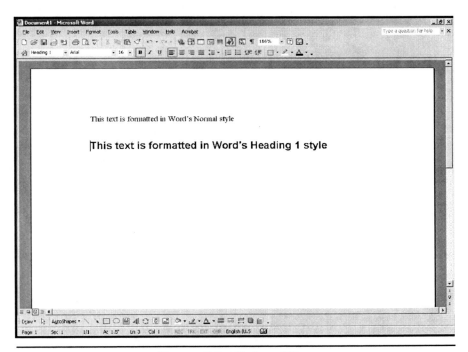

FIGURE 1.3   Styles of Text

3. Assemble Your Content

With the section titles in place, start filling in the spaces beneath them. Obviously you can type in the information, but if you already have your material stored somewhere electronically (e.g., on your hard drive, your network, or a CD), there are faster ways of entering it, including:

- Copying and pasting selected text.
- Inserting entire contents of text files.
- Setting up hyperlinks within your journal that point to files on your PC that won't easily fit in your journal (a spreadsheet, presentation, etc.).

TIP: If you can't remember where information is stored on your computer, press ⊞ + *F* to use the Windows' "Search for Files and Folders" feature to locate it.[3] You can search by the (full or partial) name of a file or folder, text contained within a file, date, or type of file (Word document, etc.). You can search for multiple files by typing a semicolon after each file name.

TIP: A number of programs available over the Internet will generate a list of files contained in any folder at the click of a button, another way to quickly put your hands on existing material for your journal. J-Walk's *Power Utility Pack*, discussed in Chapter 6 on page 187, is one of them.

To copy selected text from another source (file, e-mail message, etc.) into your journal:

1. *Open the file, message, or Web page containing the desired text and highlight that text.*
2. *Press Ctrl + C to copy what's highlighted to the Windows Clipboard.*
3. *In your knowledge journal, put the cursor under the section title where you want to insert the text and press Ctrl + V to paste it in.*

WHAT TO DO WHEN PASTED TEXT DOESN'T LOOK RIGHT

Sometimes text pasted into your journal doesn't look like what you type directly into it; that's because the pasted text has a different format (a situation that occurs most often when you are trying to copy text from a Web page). If you want it to match your journal text in appearance, use the "Paste Special" command on Word's Edit menu and select "Unformatted text" from the list of options in the "Paste Special" dialog box.

 To change the appearance of any text within a Word document to Word's "Normal" text format, highlight it and press *Control + Shift + N.*

To insert the complete contents of other text files directly into your journal:

1. *Place the cursor under the section title where you want the information inserted.*

2. *On Word's main menu select Insert then File.*

3. *Using the "Insert File" dialog box, locate and highlight the file whose contents you want to copy into your journal, and select "Insert."*

To include a hyperlink to files you don't want to (or can't) copy into your journal, such as a large Excel spreadsheet or a PowerPoint presentation file:

1. *Place the cursor where you want the link to appear in your journal.*

2. *Press Ctrl + K to open the "Insert Hyperlink" dialog box and then select the "Existing File or Web Page document" option.*

3. *Locate the file on your PC and select "OK."*

Note: The path will be displayed as a hyperlink in your journal. If you need more than the file path to remind you what the file's contents are, type in a phrase in the "Text to display" field at the top (see Figure 1.4).

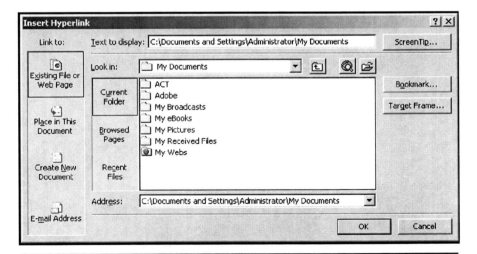

FIGURE 1.4   Inserting a Hyperlink

4. Insert a Table of Contents

The table of contents (TOC) is the key to leveraging the power of your knowledge journal. Without it, your journal is just another text file. When Word creates a TOC, each item in it hyperlinks to content somewhere else in the file, so you can click on any item and go instantly to that section, whether it's on page 2 or page 200.

Just like in a book, your table of contents should go at the very front of your journal on its own page(s), before any entries. To set it up:

1. *Put your cursor at the top of the file at the end of the line titled "My Journal" and press the* Enter *key to insert two blank lines under that title.*

2. *Move the cursor down to the beginning of the line where your first actual journal entry is and press Ctrl + Enter to insert a page break, then press the Up Arrow (↑) to move the cursor back to the first page of the document.*

3. *From Word's main menu, choose* Insert, *then* Reference, *and then* Index *and Tables (if you are using Word 2000 or earlier, then click on* Insert, *then Index and Tables).*

   An *Index and Tables* dialog box like the one pictured in Figure 1.5 will open on your screen; click on the "Table of Contents" tab, then click on OK. When you do, Word will create a table of contents using whatever text you flagged as "Heading 1." Each entry in the table will also include the page number where that heading can be found.

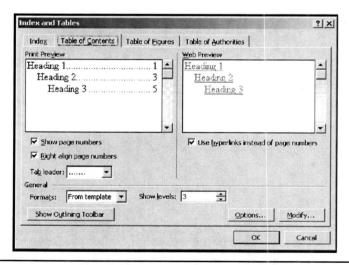

FIGURE 1.5   Inserting a Table of Contents

TIP: Once the TOC is created, click on any item listed in it; its hyperlink will take you straight to the related material. If nothing happens when you click, you may need to press *Ctrl + Click.* (Word can be configured to trigger hyperlinks either way. To see how it's set up on your PC, look under Tools, Options, Edit, for the box titled "Use CTRL + Click to follow hyperlink.")

TIP: To edit which styles get incorporated into your TOC, select "Modify" on the "Table of Contents" tab in the "Index and Tables" dialog box shown in Figure 1.5 (by default, any text assigned Heading 1, 2, or 3 is included).

5. Update Your Table of Contents Whenever You Make Changes

The first time you create a table of contents, you're going to feel like a magician. But if you don't learn how to update that table when information gets added to your journal later on, you'll end up a one-trick wonder. Here's how to keep it current:

1. *Type in a heading for each new entry to be added to the table of contents, changing its format to "Heading 1."*

2. *When you're ready to update your TOC, put your cursor anywhere in the table (one fast way is to press Ctrl + Home to move the cursor to the beginning of the journal file, then press the Down Arrow a few times until the cursor is blinking in the table's shaded area).*

3. *Press F9. The "Update Table of Contents" dialog box shown in Figure 1.6 will appear, offering two choices. Select "Update entire table."*
   Word will automatically adjust the TOC to reflect your changes.

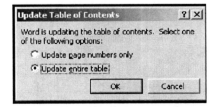

FIGURE 1.6   Updating the TOC.

To go right to the last place you worked in your journal, press *Shift + F5*, which will put your cursor where you made your last revision.

PUBLISHING PROFESSIONAL LOOKING PROPOSALS

Using heading styles and knowledge journal formatting is a great way to dress up documents you share with clients and prospects. Print them using *Adobe Acrobat* (http://www.adobe.com/products/acrobat/), discussed in Chapter 5, and you can send out the equivalent of an e-book with hyperlinks readers can use to jump from the TOC to the sections of the file they are most interested in. It's a fast, easy, effective way to make a good impression.

A Shortcut for Faster Access

How well you utilize your journal depends in part on how easily you can get to it; more than a click or keystroke to open it and you won't use it. Fortunately, Windows lets you create shortcuts to files and programs, which makes opening your knowledge journal a breeze.[4] You may not have realized it, but you use shortcuts every day. When you click on a program listed under "Programs" on the Start menu, you're using a shortcut to launch it. The same is true when you click a desktop icon to start an application or open a file.

To make your journal instantly accessible, you need to do two things: create a shortcut and then assign a keystroke combination that activates that shortcut. Here's what to do:

1. *Open the folder where you saved your "My Journal.doc" file.*
   If you saved your "My Journal.doc" file in the "My Documents" folder, click on the "Start" button, then on "Documents," and then on "My Documents."

2. *Right-click on the "My Journal.doc file."*
   A menu that looks something like Figure 1.7 will appear.

3. *Click on "Create Shortcut."*
   A new shortcut file titled "My Journal" will be added to the same folder "My Journal.doc" is saved to. You'll know which is the "My Journal.doc" shortcut file because it will be listed as "Shortcut" in the Type

| Open |
| New |
| Print |
| Open With ▶ |
| Quick View Plus |
| Quick Print |
| Quick Compress ▶ |
| Scan with Norton AntiVirus |
| WinZip ▶ |
| Send To ▶ |
| Cut |
| Copy |
| Create Shortcut |
| Delete |
| Rename |
| Properties |

FIGURE 1.7   Right-Click Menu

column (not as "Microsoft Word document"), and it will be 1 KB in size (see Figure 1.8).

Next, you have to move the shortcut file itself to your PC's desktop or to your "Programs" menu, otherwise you won't be able to activate the shortcut from your keyboard. Then you must assign a combination of keystrokes that, when pressed together, will launch it. Follow these steps to complete that process:

4. *Right-click on the "My Journal" shortcut file and select "Cut" to move it to the Clipboard.*

5. *Minimize any open windows to get to your desktop.*[5]

6. *Press Ctrl + V to paste the shortcut file to the desktop, and the "My Journal" shortcut will appear on it.*

7. *On the Desktop, right click on "Shortcut to My Journal" and select "Properties." A small window like the one in Figure 1.9 will open.*

8. *Click in the "Shortcut key" field and then press the following keys simultaneously: Alt + Ctrl + Shift + J (for journal).*

9. *Check to be sure the file path shown in the "Target" field is correct.*
   The information in the "Target" field tells your computer where to look for the file that the shortcut points to. If you saved your knowledge journal on the hard drive of your PC, the path should be correct. If your journal is saved on a network drive, you may have to adjust the path to ensure that the shortcut functions properly.[6]

10. *Press "OK."*[7]

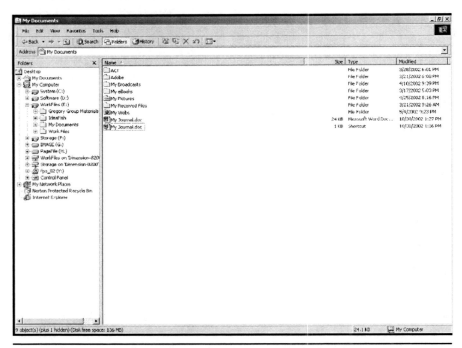

FIGURE 1.8   Shortcut Listing in "My Documents"

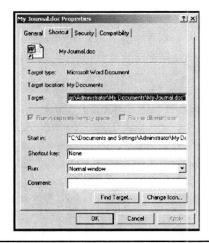

FIGURE 1.9   Shortcut Properties

Now anytime you need access to your journal file, all you have to do is press *Alt + Ctrl + Shift + J* to launch or activate it.

 TIP: If you ever move your knowledge journal to a different spot on your hard drive, remember to update the "Start in" path in your shortcut with the new location or the shortcut won't work.

Working Your Journal

Digitizing your thoughts so they can be easily rearranged, organized, and shared with others is almost as important as writing them down in the first place. But good ideas aren't worth anything unless you act on them, and you can't do that if they are buried in a file cabinet. Get in the habit of regularly writing in, and reviewing, your knowledge journal. Here are several suggestions of how to do that.

Maintain a list of communication ideas for staying in front of your target audiences throughout the year. Sometimes you have a good idea, but its timing isn't right. Without a tool like a knowledge journal to capture it, the idea is usually lost. Smart marketers bank that creativity somewhere, knowing they'll likely have a chance to apply it again. The "10¢ Idea That's Really Worth Using" presented in the accompanying box is an example of what I mean. It was the subject of my first *Kip's Tip* several years ago.

A 10¢ IDEA THAT'S REALLY WORTH USING

Here's a wonderful, inexpensive gesture to show clients you're thinking of them.

This morning, UPS delivered my latest order from Amazon.com. In the box I found a windowed envelope with a sheet of ten 1¢ stamps showing through, accompanied by this note:

Dear friend,

From the start, one of our primary goals at Amazon.com has been to make the lives of our customers easier. But recently, it struck me that

(continued)

despite all of our hard work there are still many inconveniences we haven't yet addressed.

We can't wash your dishes.
We can't pick up your dry cleaning.
We can't change the little light bulb in your refrigerator.
We can't make your tuna salad just the way you like it.

Then I realized there was one thing we could do that we've never done before—spare you the hassle of an extra trip to the post office! First-class postal rates went up a penny to 34 cents on January 7, so enclosed you'll find ten 1¢ stamps—a necessity for using up your old 33-centers. Sure, we're only talking about 10 cents in value, but hopefully the time you'll save will be worth much more.

Jeff Bezos (CEO of Amazon)

Why not use that terrific idea yourself? A brief note and a quick trip to the post office for stamps, and you've got a thoughtful, timely gift to add to your client mailings. Easy, economical . . . and smart. Give it a try.

TIP: If you would like to receive my *Kip's Tip* e-mail newsletter, visit http://www.kipstips.com to sign up. (Did I mention it's free?)

Create an operations manual for your business. How often have you heard that documenting procedures is critical to success? The reason so few ever actually do it is that so many find the task overwhelming. A knowledge journal makes the job easy.

Megan S. works for an investment advisory firm in Corvallis, Oregon. She learned about journaling in a workshop I gave at her broker dealer's National Education Conference. She later told me: "I got home and immediately implemented the idea for our operations manual, which is constantly changing and being updated. Setting it up was simple. Now anyone on our staff can find whatever they need just by clicking on a section title in the Table of Contents."

If you're not able to do it all at once, document one process a week, or a month, and very quickly you'll create a manual that lays out how things get done (which will make finding the right people to do the work much easier).

> **TIP:** When you are working in your journal (or *any* file), get in the habit of saving your work regularly. That way, if your computer freezes unexpectedly, you won't lose what you have created. Don't rely on the "AutoSave" feature built into Office and other programs. Press *Ctrl + S* to save your file every few minutes.

If you are a product wholesaler, record a new sales idea every day for two to three months. Not sure where to start? Here are some suggestions:

- Ask your colleagues around the country what's working in their regions.
- Read newspapers and industry magazines (in print or online).
- Review your firm's Web site.
- Check out competitor sites.
- Any time you visit with, call, e-mail, or write to share your ideas with advisors in your territory, ask about, listen to, and write down what's working for them.

Many conferences include a breakout where top producers share their secrets of success. Sit in and record the best ideas, or at least buy and listen to a tape of the session. Walk the exhibit floor; you'll pick up a ton of good stuff from talking with those in attendance. Once you start asking and looking out for those ideas, you will find them all around you. Put what you learn into your journal's "Sales Ideas" section.

Imagine what a source of creativity you'll be to clients, prospects, strategic partners, or potential employers after a few months of cataloging the material you find; your best ideas, at your fingertips—digitized, indexed, and ready to be shared at the touch of a button. You'll be a marketing powerhouse.

TIP: Sharing the knowledge journal concept with clients, prospects, and others is a great way to build a reputation as someone who really *knows* how to add value to a relationship and differentiate themselves competitively.[8]

TIP: Review your knowledge journal monthly (ideally weekly) to make sure you're on track with the goals and schedules, and to keep sales ideas fresh.

TIP: If you have a Palm or some other type of personal digital assistant (PDA), get the Premium Edition of *Documents To Go* (http://www .dataviz.com/products/documentstogo/). It allows you to use your knowledge journal file, including the hyperlinks, on your handheld.

Organizing Content

As your knowledge journal expands, you're going to want to rearrange its contents. You can manipulate, move, and manage your material in any of the following four ways.

1. Use Different Heading Styles to Divide Your Journal into Subsections

Word provides nine heading styles. The top three (Headings 1, 2, and 3) should give you enough to work with (think "chapters, sections, subsections"). To apply them, use *Ctrl + Alt + 1* (for Heading 1), *Ctrl + Alt + 2* (for Heading 2), and *Ctrl + Alt + 3* (for Heading 3). The label in the "Style" box in Word's "Formatting" toolbar will change to reflect the new style, as illustrated in Figure 1.10.

FIGURE 1.10 Word's Formatting Toolbar

Headings can be promoted or demoted by pressing *Alt + Shift +* →/← (→ is the *Right Arrow* key, ← the *Left Arrow* key).

2. Cut and Paste Text

To cut text from one location and paste it to another:

1. *Click on and highlight the text you want to move.*
2. *Press Ctrl + X to cut that text to the Windows Clipboard.*
3. *Move your cursor to where you want to insert the text and press Ctrl + V to paste if from the Clipboard back into your journal.*

 You can quickly select full paragraphs in Word by placing your cursor at the front of a paragraph, holding down the *Ctrl + Shift* keys and then pressing the ↓ (*Down Arrow*).

3. Sort Your Journal Entries Alphabetically (by the Heading 1 Titles) in the Outline View

You may just want to keep your entries sorted A to Z so you can scan through them quickly. To arrange them that way, follow these steps:

1. *Switch from "Normal view" to "Outline view" (Alt + Ctrl + O).*
2. *Collapse the text by pressing Alt + Shift + A.*
   If the outline is partially collapsed (i.e., some of the heading styles have a + sign, others a − sign), press *Alt + Shift + A* twice to expand and collapse the full outline.
3. *If there are different level headings (2, 3, 4, etc.) throughout the document, press Ctrl + A to "Select All," then Alt + Shift + _ to collapse them one level at a time.*
   You will need to repeat this step to collapse each Heading level, starting with the lowest. So for a document containing Heading 1, Heading 2, and Heading 3 styles, you'll need to do it twice to make all of the Heading 2 and 3 text invisible.
4. *Choose Table, Sort, Sort by Paragraph, Ascending (i.e., A–Z).*
   The contents will sort automatically, all of the collapsed text remaining with its associated Heading 1 text.

4. Use the Document Map on the View Menu to Shift Text Around Within a Document

The Document Map outlines the contents of your knowledge journal (or any other file), using the heading styles incorporated into the file. Use your mouse to highlight sections of your journal in the Document Map, then move them up or down in the document by pressing *Ctrl + Shift +* ↑ or ↓.

 You can move highlighted text up or down in a document in any "View" by holding the *Alt + Shift* keys and then pressing the ↑ (*Up Arrow*) or ↓ (*Down Arrow*) keys.

Can you create multiple journals? Absolutely! I have separate ones for diary entries, my business plan, useful Web sites, and this book. Each has a keyboard shortcut assigned to it for fast access. However, I suggest that you start with one file divided into sections, and break it into separate files only if it becomes too difficult to manage as a single document.

 TIP: Periodically purge journal contents to keep it clean. Delete or put a line through items you no longer need. To line out text, select the text, press *Ctrl + D* to open the "Font" window, then *Alt + K* to select "Stri̲kethrough Effect." ~~It will look like this.~~

Building a Group Knowledge Bank

Hopefully by now you're envisioning all kinds of ways to use your knowledge journal. Sharing and aggregating ideas with others may be one of them. *If you are a manager, I cannot encourage you strongly enough to start using the concept of sharing within your group.* Sharing knowledge within teams is what leads to breakthroughs and competitive advantages. Banking that collective knowledge is how individual core competencies become corporate ones. But like anything that's new, people may be reluctant (even resistant) to use it, no matter how great it sounds. Following are some concrete ways you can champion the change.

Institute a contest for the best ideas captured during a given week. If you belong to a study group or producer council, collect members' meeting notes into a single journal and distribute it to each contributor. If your team regularly attends industry meetings with concurrent breakouts, have members take notes on different sessions and then consolidate, publish, and distribute them after the meeting.

Sharing knowledge is a powerful management tool you can implement immediately and at virtually no cost. How often can you say that about technology? Don't pass it up.

TIP: Have your team save their journals on a shared drive on your office network. If you're not all in the same location, those who are off-site can e-mail their files to you as attachments. Either way, you can insert their contents wherever you want in your journal by following the instructions under Step 3, "Assemble Your Content," on page 13.

DEALING WITH INFORMATION ON (AND OFF) THE WEB

Figuring out how to retain valuable content found on the Internet is a universal challenge. Your knowledge journal is a solution for pieces of text, but it doesn't work well for saving entire Web pages and their graphics. Programs called *off-line browsers* solve that problem. They let you permanently save a Web page or an entire site on your hard drive, so that even if it vanishes from the Internet, you still have a copy to refer to.

Off-line access to information (i.e., the ability to open and view Web pages without being connected) is also useful when you don't have access to a Web connection but want to read articles or reports that have been published online or when you're meeting a client or prospect and want to show them something from the Web.

The off-line browser I use is called *SurfSaver* (http://www.surfsaver .com). It lets me title individual pages, type in notes about the page (e.g., why I wanted it in the first place), and assign keywords to it (e.g., names of clients who might be interested in what I found). SurfSaver comes in two versions: one free, the other paid (called Pro). The Pro version allows you to save multiple Web pages at once (versus just one at

(continued)

a time), store your folders on different drives (e.g., to a CD), and share your folders with other users across a network (instead of limiting access to a single machine).

TIP: Microsoft offers a handy, free plug-in called *Web Accessories for Internet Explorer 5* (http://www.microsoft.com/windows /ie/previous/webaccess/ie5wa.asp). I use its highlighting feature all the time to mark key text selections on pages in bright yellow before saving them with SurfSaver.

TIP: If you work for a large firm, corporate information technology (IT) standards may prevent you from altering your browser configuration. Check with your help desk to see what, if any, restrictions are in effect before attempting to install any browser plug-in. (Just what's a plug-in? Think of it as you would an accessory for a car.)

While SurfSaver is good for saving individual pages or small batches of pages, for bigger jobs, I use *WebWhacker* (http://www.webwhacker .com). WebWhacker can copy an entire site and give you an index of the site's contents that you can scroll through to find what you're looking for. You can use it to give someone a walkthrough of a site without ever worrying about having to connect to the Web. There's even a version of the product that lets you display saved sites on your palmtop.

Now that you've built a mechanism for harnessing your accumulated expertise, let's talk about a methodology you can use to apply that expertise to achieve even greater success. That's the subject of Chapter 2.

Notes

1. Source: AskMe Corporation (http://www.askmecorp.com).
2. A "style" is a set of formats that you assign to text—the font type, its color and size, whether it is italicized, bolded, or underlined, and so forth. Usually you work in what Word calls its "Normal" style, but there are dozens of other styles you can apply including "Header," "Footer," and "Hyperlink" (the style that's automatically applied when you type out a Web site URL like http://www.winningclientsinawiredworld.com).

3. The ⊞ key (referred to as the "Windows logo" key) is standard on newer keyboards and is usually located on the bottom row of keys to the left or right (or both) of the spacebar.

4. If you have trouble setting these up, ask your internal PC help desk if there are any restrictions on creating shortcuts on your computer. Firms that have thousands of PCs often disable such features to maintain consistency across their user base. (Can you blame them for wanting to establish certain standards?)

5. You do this by clicking on the ▬ button in the top right-hand corner of the Word window and any other open program windows, or press ⊞ + D to minimize all open windows at the same time.

6. Talk to your network administrator/PC support help desk if you need help resolving problems with setting up shortcuts to files stored on a network drive.

7. In some cases, you may have to restart your computer for the shortcut to take effect. When the restart sequence is completed, press *Shift* + *Ctrl* + *Alt* + *J* to make sure the shortcut works.

8. If you are a product or service provider selling through financial advisors, read *Using Technology to Build a Better Sales Force* in Appendix A for more ideas on marrying technology and distribution.

2

Achieve Breakthroughs Systematically

Mapping Your Route to the Next Level

The road to success is always under construction.

—Arnold Palmer

Insanity: continuing to do things the same way and expecting a different result.

—Unknown

Well-run businesses are more productive, profitable, and just plain enjoyable. So why don't more of those who run them take time to evaluate how theirs can be improved? Or if they do, to follow through and make changes? Generally because they think it takes too much time, it's too hard, or it's just not their "thing." Their role is bringing in the assets, playing rainmaker, being the idea guy. The details are someone else's responsibility.

That attitude isn't lost on clients and prospects. They sense it when they walk in the door, they see it in an assistant's eyes or hear it in a tone of voice, and they feel it in the "vibes" and how well follow-up occurs. And if all that is apparent to outsiders, how do you think the people on the inside feel?

I'm all for delegating; but abdicating is a different story. There's a great passage in *Execution: The Discipline of Getting Things Done* by Larry Bossidy and Ram Charan that describes what I'm referring to:

> There's an enormous difference between leading an organization and presiding over it. The leader who boasts of her hands-off style or puts her faith in empowerment is not dealing with the issues of the day. She is not confronting the people responsible for poor performance, or searching for problems to solve and then making sure they get solved. She is presiding, and she's only doing half her job.
>
> Leading for execution is not about micromanaging, or being "hands-on," or disempowering people. Rather, it's about active management—doing the things leaders should be doing in the first place. . . . leaders who excel at execution immerse themselves in the substance of execution and even some of the key details. They use their knowledge of the business to constantly probe and question. They bring weaknesses to light and rally their people to correct them.
>
> The leader who executes . . . puts in place a culture and processes for executing. . . . His personal involvement in that architecture is to assign the tasks and then follow up . . . making sure that people understand the priorities, which are based on his comprehensive understanding of the business, and asking incisive questions. The leader who executes often does not even have to tell people what to do; she asks questions so they can figure out what they need to do. In this way she coaches them, passing on her experience as a leader and educating them to think in ways they never thought of before. Far from stifling people, this kind of leadership helps them expand their own capabilities for leading.[1]

I think you want to be that kind of leader, one who executes. And obviously you believe in technology's potential to make the job easier or you wouldn't be reading this book. But my guess is no one has ever shown you a way to transition from where you are to where you want to be, at least not an approach you felt you could work with. That's what this chapter is about—providing a framework to identify and prioritize challenges, and showing you how to lay out a game plan to address them, one that's practical and easy to act on. The goal is to get you thinking about what you do as a business, as a system—a complete system—made up of processes that are mapped out, managed, and measured, so that they can be continuously improved.

Study successful salespeople in this or any other industry and you'll find that even though sales may be their first love, they realize that they run a business, and that if they don't run the business systematically, it won't be around long. That aptitude for seeing the big picture is part of what makes those people unique. But it's their willingness and ability to dive into the detail if needed, to work with their team to understand and sort out how things get done, and to identify how they can be done better that really sets them apart.

There's a lot of talk today about the importance of team building and establishing accountability—how to find the right people, equip them properly, give them the training they need, and set expectations of performance. Creating a cohesive team isn't as hard as it seems if you unite people around solving problems that not only make the business stronger, but make their work easier and more rewarding.

To create a cohesive team, you need a few tools, some questions to get you thinking, a method for surfacing and prioritizing challenges, and a way of mapping and implementing improvements. You also need a mechanism for ensuring that the changes you envision actually happen. Most importantly, you need desire and discipline; if you're satisfied with the status quo or not willing to see things through to completion, then the suggestions outlined here may be of little use to you.

RECOGNIZE THE RESOURCE(S) YOU HAVE

For many advisors, the business consists of two people: themselves and their assistant. A small team, yes, but a team nonetheless.

Real leaders (as opposed to managers) share a common trait: they bring out the best in people by seeking, listening to, and acting on the ideas and input of those they work with. They ask questions of their team such as, What would you differently? How can we do better? What would make this a better place to work?

Others have a different, potentially fatal, attitude. They think they are the only one who understands the business, its problems, and how to solve them. To them, support staff is just there to handle the small stuff.

Be smart: whether you work with one person or a hundred, leverage their brainpower in identifying ways to improve results. If you don't, you're making a serious mistake.

Identifying Opportunities

You can start laying out a game plan in as little as an hour or two. The following exercise will help you do that. It's a perfect item to put on your next off-site strategic planning agenda. When you're done, you'll have a clearer sense of what you do, how you do it, and where technology might help you do it better.

The exercise involves four steps: choosing a question (best done in advance), generating ideas, categorizing those ideas, and mapping out how to make improvements. Get a supply of 4 × 6 sticky note pads, markers, some easel paper, and masking tape. (You can order everything you need from *Staples* (http://www.staples.com) or *Office Depot* (http://www .officedepot.com).) Tape a few blank easel paper pages on the wall of your office or conference room, pass out a pad and marker to each participant, and you're ready.

1. Decide on One or More Starting Questions

When trying to solve complex problems, knowing which questions to ask can make the difference between getting to a solution that works and spending all your time talking about where to begin. One obvious question is, "What challenges do we face in growing this business?" Some others worth considering are:

- What are our advantages? How can we more fully exploit them?

- Who is our ideal client? How can we do business with more of those people?

- What are the most time-consuming things we do? How can we do them faster?

- Why do we win certain accounts? Why do we lose others?

- What sales and marketing opportunities are we missing?

- How do we communicate with our clients? How can we do it better?

- What is our sales process? How can we shorten it?

- How can we improve our bottom line?

- What does our competition do better than us? What can we learn from them?

ACTION STEP: FRAMING YOUR STARTING QUESTION

Write down three questions you want answers to.

1.

2.

3.

2. Brainstorm a List of Responses

With your question(s) in hand, turn to generating ideas and identifying solutions. Here's a simple approach that has never failed to produce a workable action plan.

1. *Take 10–15 minutes (more if needed) to jot down answers.*
   Every idea counts. Don't bog down in evaluating each thought as you write; concentrate on getting as many ideas on paper as you can. There will be plenty of time to judge what you've written when you're done.

2. *Write each idea legibly and in large letters on a separate sticky note.*
   Putting one idea on a page makes reviewing, rearranging, and organizing your thoughts easier later on.

3. *When finished, review your work to clarify points and eliminate redundancies.*
   Scan what you've written and, if needed, edit your content to clarify any confusing thoughts (trash any notes that express the same idea).

4. *Post your ideas on chart paper on the wall.*
   Put each note on the chart paper separately so it can be viewed and repositioned easily.

TIP: If you want to avoid the step of transcribing handwritten notes later, consider using *Inspiration* (http://www.inspiration.com) software to capture, display, organize, and rearrange ideas right on your computer. Your ideas can be imported directly into your knowledge journal in Word when you're finished.

3. Organize and Categorize the Responses

1. *Review the ideas and arrange those that are related into groups.*

   In reviewing others' ideas, something may hit a nerve; don't debate it. At this point all you are striving for is to identify and group like items together, so sort as quietly as possible. Look for and discard duplicates (if an idea is expressed repeatedly, note how often). It's OK for ideas to stand alone if they don't fit easily into one of the larger groups.

2. *Label each group with a summary or header that everyone agrees with.*

   Look for central ideas/themes (prospecting, client management, new business processing, servicing, etc.). Make sure everyone agrees to the terms used. Divide large groups into subgroups if necessary, with subheaders.

4. Pick the Most Important Topics

If you want your group to feel fully invested in this work, give them a stake in the outcome and a role in deciding what to tackle first. Give each participant a set of three cards printed with the numbers 1, 2, and 3. Each person gets to vote for his or her top three topics, which they cast as the list of headings is reviewed. Tally the votes. The top three vote-getters become the highest priorities.

BOUNCE IDEAS OFF YOUR COMPUTER

Every year businesses spend millions on consultants to help them solve problems. Imagine having a team on call 24/7 to pose questions, analyze your thinking, uncover key themes, and offer suggestions. That's *Idea-Fisher* (http://www.ideafisher.com), a one-of-a-kind, patented software program that mimics the human thought process.

IdeaFisher consists of two parts: the IdeaBank (for brainstorming) and the QBank (as in "Question") for consulting. The IdeaBank contains 65,000 words and phrases cross-referenced and categorized into groups of related concepts. The result is a database of more than 1.5 million associations—what someone has called a "thesaurus on steroids." Want to discuss feelings people have about money and investing in turbulent markets in your next newsletter? In seconds IdeaFisher can give you dozens of terms related to "feelings, investing and volatility," all grouped by category.

IdeaFisher's QBank piece contains different modules of questions, some part of the basic product, others available for purchase separately. Each module's questions are tied to a theme (strategic planning, advertising and promotion, new product/service introduction, etc.). You choose the ones that are relevant to your situation and type your thoughts into an "Answer Notepad." The program can even analyze your answers and tell what common threads run through them.

IdeaFisher even lets you add terms and questions to its database to customize the program with words, associations, or questions that are meaningful to you, making the program even more valuable.

While the program is terrific at stimulating ideas within a team, it's priceless if you work alone and don't have others around to bounce thoughts off of. Get it!

 TIP: Visit http://www.winningclientsinawiredworld.com to download a Checklist of Challenges: the most frequently cited issues people face in getting their business to the next level of success.

Three Steps to Improvement

With your priorities identified, it's time to consider how to improve results. For example, answering the earlier question, "What challenges do we face in growing this business?" might generate the following (oversimplified) result.

Client Service

1. Focusing on profitable clients
2. Staying in touch
3. Retaining clients

Marketing

1. Targeting a niche
2. Raising visibility
3. Generating leads

Staffing

1. Finding good help
2. Defining job duties
3. Training

Technology

1. Leveraging the Internet
2. Automating procedures
3. Managing information

Time Management

1. Getting organized
2. Setting priorities
3. Sticking to a schedule

Pick your top priority and ask yourselves, "How can we do a smarter job of. . . ?"

1. Write Down the Activities the Process Involves, One per Sticky Note

If you're auditing an existing process, note the steps the job currently involves. If it's something you'd *like* to be doing (but aren't yet), put down how you *think* it should be done.

2. Evaluate the Activities as You Sequence Them

Step back from what you do to look at how it's done and you'll begin to uncover problem areas; the places where processes break down because transitions aren't clear or certain tasks take too much time. Identify the steps that are critical, eliminate those that don't clearly add value, and flag whichever ones you think can be automated.

3. Complete a Work Flow Worksheet

Creating work flow worksheets is the last step in this phase, and the first one in building a business operations manual. Physically, these worksheets are nothing more than tables built in Microsoft Word (there's a sample of one in Appendix B). It's what goes in them that's important. They have three essential ingredients:

1. The name of the process.

2. The sequence of activities that comprise that process.

3. The person responsible for each activity.

Additionally, they include space for how much time is required to complete each activity, the cost of each activity, any tools you use (technology, forms, etc.), the "owner" of the process, and the date the process was (last) reviewed.

TIP: An electronic version of the work flow worksheet template (and other templates) can be purchased at http://www.winningclients inawiredworld.com.

Thanks to your brainstorming and organizing, you already have the process, the activities it consists of, and the sequence in which those activities are done; responsibility for individual tasks is easy to identify: who actually does the work?

The question is whether the person performing the task currently is the one best suited to continue doing it. If your tendency is to do everything yourself (including scheduling appointments, drafting correspondence, developing proposals, reviewing mail), you're paying a steep price; the same is true of an assistant who could function at a higher level if a junior staffer or intern was made available to handle certain tasks. (Chapter 7 covers where to find good people.) Completing the worksheet makes identifying those tasks you *can* delegate easier and positions you to place responsibility for them as low in the organization as possible, so you are free to do what only you can do.

Knowing the time and cost of completing each activity helps prioritize what changes to make first. The section titled "The Money Value of Time" later in this chapter can help you get a handle on what your time, and everyone else's, is really worth, and "Technology's Role," which follows immediately, will give you some suggestions on how to reduce the time needed to complete tasks through smarter use of available tools.

Finally, don't overlook the importance of establishing who is the process owner, the one ultimately responsible for the process as a whole. Make sure that's clear, even if you work with only one other person. Otherwise you may have a problem if the process breaks down and no one is willing to take responsibility for fixing it.

> **TIP:** For basic tasks (responsibilities, sequence, etc.) your knowledge journal may be all you need to create work flow worksheets, but if you want to build detailed time lines or prepare status reports, you need project-management software. *Microsoft Project* (http://www.microsoft.com/office/project/) is the best-known program. *iTeam work* (http://www.iteamwork.com) and *Common Office* (http://www.commonoffice.com) are two low-cost Web-based alternatives.

Technology's Role

Suppose in your improvement efforts you decide to focus on client communication, specifically, sending birthday cards to clients. What do you need to make that happen? Their name, address, birth date, a card, a personal message to go in it, a stamp, and an addressed envelope. Not a ton of things, but enough to chew up significant time if each is put together individually from scratch.

Ask yourself this: How will you know in advance whose birthdays are coming up? How can you produce a personal message quickly? How can you get the card or gift out the door in plenty of time? Where can you easily get a supply of stamps?

A database of names and birth dates, with a monthly "Birthdays" report would be a big help; almost any of the contact management programs listed in Chapter 4 will give you that ability. Programs like *CardWare client birthday soft-ware* (http://clientbirthday.com) and sites like *Today in History* (http://www.todayinhistory.com) can help you generate a personal message. A supplier like *papercards.com* (http://www.papercards.com) can provide birthday cards by the box (purchased online so you don't have to go to the store). And you (or your assistant) can buy stamps over the Web, have them delivered to your office by the *Post Office* (http://www.usps.com), and never leave your seat.

You're literally surrounded by solutions just waiting to be discovered. But if you don't focus on one situation at a time, you'll never sort them all out. That's why dividing your business into processes and breaking each one down to look at individual activities is so important. Ask yourself (a) does this have to be done at all? and if so, (b) how can it be done better, faster, or cheaper?

TIP: Read the section titled "Where to Get the Inside Scoop" in Chapter 8 to find out which sites to visit for information on general computing and financial services–specific software.

Your first step should be to refer back to the "Software Inventory Summary" discussed in the Introduction, "Getting Started." Review what you have to determine if anything you already own can improve the particular process you're evaluating. Next, turn to the Web. Every one of the ideas just suggested can be found by typing a few keywords into a search site like *Google* (http://www.google.com). (We'll talk more about searching with Google in the next chapter.) It also helps to be able to tap publications and Web sites that specialize in identifying those resources; Chapter 8 covers which ones are best.

If you're concerned that you won't know what you're looking for online, use your circle of contacts. Find out what they use to solve similar problems. Describing your situation is easy now that you've built a work flow. Approach other advisors, product wholesalers, or vendors you buy from—anyone you think might help. Ask what hardware, software, and Web sites they use (or know of) that could make a given task easier.

If you belong to a study or networking group, make the process you're grappling with a discussion item on the meeting agenda. Chances are excellent that others would benefit from hearing what you're doing. If you belong to professional or trade groups, solicit ideas from selected staff people or post questions in their member discussion areas at their Web sites.

Don't overlook clients you're close to, especially the tech-savvy ones. They may have some useful suggestions. Equally important, they can tell you if and how much of what you're asking about matters to them from a customer standpoint.

AUTOMATING DIRECT MARKETING TO PROSPECTS

Consider the steps you take today in marketing and selling yourself: what you're already doing, and what you'd like to be doing. Direct mail is a good example. Lots of advisors use direct mail as a prospecting tool for seminar invitations and newsletters. The process traditionally involves a

(continued)

number of steps: shopping for a list, putting it into a database, developing a mailing piece, merging and printing letters, folding them, stuffing and stamping the envelopes, and getting the whole package out the door.

Did you know that every single one of those steps can be automated?

At *infoUSA* (http://www.infousa.com) and *Zapdata* (http://www.zapdata.com) you can build custom lists according to criteria you select. Your firm, or others, can provide a library of preapproved correspondence. And the post office can handle fulfillment, from mail merging through delivery to each recipient; all orchestrated by you using *NetPost Services* (http://www.usps.com/netpost/). You can complete a full-blown marketing campaign in under an hour if you know what resources to use.

But you won't find those solutions if you don't know what you're looking for. And you won't know *that* unless you understand the processes you follow.

Eliminating paper (or "going paperless") is another process improvement high on the wish list of many advisors. Here's how Betsy D., a service assistant for an independent advisor in the Midwest, and her colleagues quickly got a solution up and working, once they were clear on what was needed.

We use a product called *OmniForm* (http://www.scansoft.com/omniform/) to cut down on the paper we use. What got us looking at it was one of those "there has to be a better way than doing this by hand" situations—a periodic update done for 50–60 accounts that required completing four or more forms for each account. The advisor I work for had heard about the product from another rep at a conference 2–3 years before and stuck it in the back of his mind. Then he saw the product advertised in a magazine and decided to investigate it. We bought it, our computer guy installed it, and we taught ourselves how to use it . . . all in about 5 hours spread over a week or two. It was very easy to learn. One person in the office does the scanning, and all of us know how to create the forms. This relatively inexpensive package has saved us thousands of dollars in time and expense, and helped us avoid errors and the follow-up that they require.

Bill H. is a Massachusetts-based registered investment advisor who works alone. Here's how he's figured out where technology and the Web fit into his business.

> I use technology where and when it makes sense. My main considerations are: Does it work the way it is supposed to, will it help my business get ahead competitively, what's the cost, will it be synergistic with other technologies, is it scalable (can it grow with the business . . . I made a mistake with zip drives for data storage)? If I like the answers, I give it a whirl.
>
> Most of my marketing is referral based; I don't market via the Web (for me a Web site is great, but it's just part of an integrated marketing strategy, and delivery system). However, there are a lot of tire kickers out there; I send them off to the Web site. I also steer all marketing-related questions to my Web site, which saves me a lot of money on mail.
>
> I have never had a client find me through a search engine, seek me out, and become a client without any interaction. However, I have used technology to make delivery of services easier. It also lets me operate from virtually anywhere in the industrialized world (assuming I have my laptop, cell phone, and PalmPilot).
>
> Technology also helps me address the front-end capacity problem all advisors face (meaning the up-front work with new clients); having some of that done before the initial meeting cuts down on the time it takes to get clients set up. And after they come on board, I can e-mail them personalized reports using tools like Adobe (Acrobat).
>
> My vision is to build a company that runs automatically and seamlessly. It should be so easy to run that a monkey can do it. I'm just about there; I just can't get the monkey to put on a suit. I'm striving to create a Web-centric business that runs like an automated manufacturing plant (financial service professionals are, after all, manufacturing a product). I have customers all over the country; I can walk into almost any library in the United States and get information, produce reports, make trades, print out forms, etc. I travel a ton, and my clients don't need to know that, they just need to know I'm accessible.
>
> I believe investment in new technology is a never-ending cost of doing business and staying ahead of your competitors.

Reading his comments, you might think Bill spends a fortune on technology. Actually, he invests about $15,000 a year in it—less than the cost of a part-time support person.

The Money Value of Time

Everybody knows that time is money, but have you ever figured out what that really means to you? On the one hand, there's what you're worth, the fee you charge for an hour of your time: $100, $200, whatever. On the other hand, there's your earning rate—what you actually make for each hour you work (e.g., a $100,000 income spread over a year of 40-hour work weeks comes to, surprisingly, about $50 an hour).

And then, for most people, there's the gap in between—their productivity gap. One of my goals is help you close that gap by bringing what you earn up closer to what you're worth.

Think for a minute about things you routinely spend big chunks of your day on. The time adds up quickly. Did you realize that 45 minutes a day handling e-mail amounts to over 175 hours a year? If you're a $100,000 earner, that's almost $10,000! Reduce that time by just 15 minutes (I'll show you how in Chapter 6), and you'd put $3000 worth of time back into your day to invest in revenue-generating activity. That's "time is money" in real life, and it's just one illustration.

What "Time Is Money" Really Means		
Earnings/Payroll	Per Hour	15 Minutes/Day Saved
50,000	26	1563
250,000	132	7813
1,000,000	530	31,250

A TOOL TO TELL WHAT YOUR TIME IS WORTH

If you point your browser to http://www.winningclientsinawiredworld.com/time.html, you'll find a worksheet called "Time is money." Enter your total compensation, how many hours a day you work on average, and the number of days you take away from the office annually, and the worksheet will tell you your hourly earning rate. Calculate one for each member of your team to determine the real cost of the activities of your business.

> ⌨ If you ever need a calculator when working on your PC, but don't have one handy, press ⊞ (the "Windows" key) + *R* to open the "Run" dialog box. Type *calc* in the Open: box to launch the "Microsoft Calculator" program.

The Economics of Your Business

Once you identify what your time is worth, you'll start measuring everything you do. That's when the realization of technology's benefit hits home hardest, when you see the effect it can have on systemizing, standardizing, and simplifying the processes that drive your bottom line: how many sales calls you can make in a day, the time it takes to complete a sale, or the speed and frequency with which you are able to touch clients.

The secret to leveraging technology is to concentrate its use on those things that fuel growth in your business. Generally, they fall into four categories:

1. *Client acquisition* (sales appointments, referrals, seminars, direct marketing).
2. *Client retention* (frequency of contact, quality of service, speed of problem resolution).
3. *What you charge* (fees, commissions).
4. *What it costs to deliver service* (compensation, benefits, equipment, rent).

Creating a spreadsheet that shows the relationships among those items will help you see how changes in any one area affect results. You'll find yourself better able to plan your future when you know which variables affect your bottom line most.

Keep in mind that expenses can be driven (theoretically) to zero, not beyond. You can retain up to 100 percent of your clients, not more. Your pricing is determined largely by competitive pressure (and, in financial services, regulation). Acquisition of new business is the only place where the upside is almost limitless. Guess what? Only a fraction of most advisors' time gets spent on it. Why? Because people get too bogged down in all the other stuff. (Which is exactly why you need to understand the "process" of what you do, so that you are positioned to automate, delegate, and eliminate as much of the nonessential activity as possible.)

Inspecting What You Expect

When it comes to implementing changes, remember you won't succeed unless you complete the circle. Edward Deming is considered by many to be the father of modern-day business improvement methods. One of the things Deming was famous for was his wheel of continuous improvement: plan a strategy, execute, check your results, and adjust where necessary, continually. Plan–do–check–adjust (or PDCA for short).

Without the "check" and "adjust," you leave the door wide open to failed execution. That's why the first thing we covered was how to create a mechanism for organizing and managing the knowledge—the information—you need to do your job more effectively, so you would have an easy way of collecting and reviewing what is important.

Each member of your team should keep an up-to-date copy of the work flow worksheets they are responsible for, and e-mail you updates, at least quarterly (more frequently in the early stages). Save those attachments to a folder on your hard drive and then insert them into your master file using the instructions outlined in Chapter 1 on page 15.

Use the knowledge journal concept to organize that work into a digital operations manual. Make sure everyone gets a copy. Include your business plan and everyone will have a clear picture of what your goals are, how you plan to accomplish them, and a road map for actually getting it done. That kind of clarity is worth its weight in gold.

Growth, Change, and the Nautilus

If you do all the things I've just described, you are going to create leverage, a lot of leverage. You'll build a set of core competencies you can use to generate results at almost no incremental cost. And the great thing is that you don't have to be a Wall Street giant; the process works just as well if you're a plain old Main Street sole proprietor.

In many ways, you are better off being the little guy. Big companies are aircraft carriers; they take a long time to change direction. They invest big money on process improvement efforts because they know they'll never create economies of scale, much less a sustained competitive edge, by doing things differently every time. They have to get thousands of people on the same page to do it, and that doesn't happen overnight.

Not you, you're a speedboat. You want to make a change to "You, Inc."? Map it out today, implement it tomorrow. That's the power of being small and flexible.

I do have one note of caution, however. Don't try to tackle everything at once (remember the saying, "yard by yard the game is hard, inch by inch it's a cinch"). Break your effort into phases and complete what will have the greatest impact and what is easiest, fastest, and cheapest to implement first. Your odds of succeeding will skyrocket. It's called *graduated change* (I didn't say "gradual"). Doing so will build your and your team's confidence, which is so critical to create in the early going.

That notion of starting small and building on past results didn't originate in business; it's found throughout nature. The nautilus on the dust jacket, one of the world's oldest living things, is an example of building on what's come before—continued, balanced growth. Like the nautilus, your progress may appear to be small at first, but remember that you're setting the stage. Stick with it and the rewards will grow proportionally bigger: greater control, more time to focus on sales, and a more valuable franchise. Who doesn't want that?

TIP: Visit http://www.winningclientsinawiredworld.com to download a free "Self-Assessment Questionnaire" that can help clarify your goals, strengths, weaknesses, and opportunities for improvement by evaluating your current business structure.

Note

1. *Execution: The Discipline of Getting Things Done*, Larry Bossidy and Ram Charan, © 2002, Crown Business, New York, pp. 25–26.

Work the Web for All It's Worth

Claiming Your Share of the Internet's Hidden Riches

*If you don't know where you're going, you'll probably end
up somewhere else.*

—Yogi Berra

Most advisors barely scrape the surface of what the Web offers. They send and receive e-mail. They get news headlines. They check stock prices or portfolio values. Maybe they shop. Frankly, it wouldn't occur to them to do any more than that. *Use it as a prospecting tool?* How do you do that? *Client development?* Most wouldn't know where to begin.

Your competition's fear, confusion, or ambivalence about the Internet's possibilities presents you with a huge opportunity, a chance to gain an advantage that's not tied to your performance record or the fees you charge. And the smaller you are, the more it can level your playing field in competing with larger rivals. Regardless of your size, the more you aspire to run a family office, to engage clients in "life planning," or to offer concierge services, the greater the imperative to learn your way around cyberspace.

My excitement about the Web stems from a conviction that the real currency financial advisors trade in isn't dollars, it's information. Finding it, sharing it, leveraging it; it's part of what you use to build trust, it's how you decide whom to target, and who not to waste your time with; it's what makes improvements in how you operate.

But to use information well, you have to know what to look for, where to look for it, and which tools to use to reach it. That's what we are going to cover in this chapter. Specifically, we'll address:

- Prospecting online, including sites that can give you a bead on potential clients (and current ones), and what to look for when you visit those sites.

- How to set up a customized information retrieval system that puts the news you want in your hands as soon as it's available, for less than $100 a year.

- A review of the basics of Web search, and some of its finer points (in case you don't just want to be fed, but indeed want to learn how to fish).

- Some quick, one-time changes to your browser that will get you to the information you need much faster.

- A collection of search engines and directories you can utilize to find almost anything.

When we're done, you'll have the tools and ability you need to gather intelligence faster and more effectively than ever before, a capability you can employ to build a moat around current client relationships and a bridge to those you want to do business with.

Prospecting Online

Wanting to learn how to prospect online may be one of the biggest reasons you bought this book; it's high on the list for many advisors. There are at least two ways you can go about it. One is the approach mentioned in Chapter 2, using the Web to purchase names of those who meet your criteria. We're going to talk about that first.

The other is less obvious. It involves gathering intelligence first, then making contact. Visiting the sites of associations, companies, the government, the media, nonprofits, and other groups to uncover information that helps you strengthen relationships with existing clients and establish relationships with centers of influence, opinion leaders, and decision makers who can hasten your success.

Why spend time doing that? Because, according to the Financial Planning Association, personal referrals are *the* single biggest source of new business for advisors (53 percent)—more than all other sources combined.[1] Staying current on what's happening in the world your clients (or others who refer business to you) live in gives you a way of staying in regular contact with them. More contact means more opportunities to discuss who they know that could benefit from your services.

TIP: The Federal Trade Commission's Telemarketing Sales Rule, which went into effect in late 2003, makes cold calling prospects at home more difficult; all the more reason to cultivate relationships with those who can connect you directly with others who need your services and expertise!

Even if you're not even thinking about client retention, you should consider this: unless you're managing all the money for all your clients, you're leaving something on the table. Smart use of the Web sites mentioned in this chapter, coupled with the communication strategies laid out in Chapter 4, will clue you in to the challenges your clients face, equip you to offer them solutions, increase their trust in you, and position you as the only logical choice to manage everything they have. Isn't that what you're working for?

TIP: Looking for a deep reservoir of ideas on ways to approach prospects? Browse or search the archives of any of the advisor focused magazines mentioned in Chapter 8. Their articles can be a gold mine of sales and prospecting ideas. Use SurfSaver (the tool mentioned on page 27) to keep a copy of any articles that include ideas worth reading again.

Purchasing Lists

The Internet has opened up a world of possibilities for prospecting, starting with the ability to develop your own list of targeted leads right from your browser. It's amazing; you can choose your criteria, create your list, make any adjustments to it, purchase and download it while you're online, and import it into a database in minutes. Here are two sites where you can get that process started.

infoUSA (http://www.infoUSA.com). At infoUSA, you can build lead lists of businesses and consumers in the United States or Canada (http://www.infoCanada.ca). Business data (14 million records) include, among other items, choices for type of business, size, geography, job titles, contact name, fax numbers, and Web site addresses. Consumer information on over 100 million households can be selected using 30+ criteria including, but not limited to, geography, age, income, home value, phone number, gender, ethnicity, and Internet usage.

One critical factor when working with any list is the freshness of the names. infoUSA advertises that their database is updated daily through a process of phone calls and compiling lists. Pricing per name starts at 30 cents and increases depending on how much additional information you want about each record.

Zapdata (http://www.zapdata.com).   This Web site is an offering of Dun & Bradstreet's Sales and Marketing Solutions group. Like infoUSA, it allows you to create a targeted list using criteria on location, industries, demographics, and other specialty data. Unlike infoUSA, it does not offer any consumer data.

TIP: A good list provider can help you refine your selection criteria. Ask them for guidance on how to make the most of the information they offer.

TIP: If you'd like to find product-specific leads, try searching on the product(s) or type of prospects you're targeting together with the terms *lead* OR *leads lists*. The **Google Directory** contains a list of more than a dozen life insurance–related lead sites at Business > Financial Services > Insurance > Agent Resources > Lead Generation Services.

Seventeen Sites for Compiling Intelligence

Each of the sites in this section can be useful in uncovering information: names of highly qualified prospects, an overview of the challenges they face, the organizations they belong to, the current status of their retirement plans, movers and shakers in different circles, and much more. Some are one-time resources, others you'll go back to repeatedly. Remember, this is a buffet: scan the list and visit those that offer the type of information you're looking to obtain.

American Society of Association Executives (ASAE) Gateway to Associations (http://info.asaenet.org/gateway/OnlineAssocSlist.html). Industry groups can be very fertile ground for identifying prospects and centers of influence. The ASAE maintains a database of over 6500 associations worldwide (most in the United States and Canada), a directory that can be searched by name, industry category, or location. Make your choices and you'll get a list of links to all the associations that match your criteria. *If you concentrate in a professional or industry niche, this site should be your first stop online.*

 Instead of clicking on a link and loading the selected page in the same browser window, press *Shift + Click* on the desired link to open the page in a new window so you can toggle to the results list if you want to try a different organization.

American City Business Journals (http://www.bizjournals.com). The *Business Journal* is published weekly in over 40 cities across the United States. If you target small-business owners and corporate executives, use it to learn what's happening in your local business community. Registering at the site gives you access to a searchable archive of articles and e-mail alerts on cities, companies, or people you want to keep track of anytime they're mentioned in an article.

Bureau of Labor Statistics' *Occupational Outlook Handbook* (http://www.bls.gov/oco/). This publication, updated every other year, offers a snapshot of hundreds of careers/occupations including markets you can focus on. Browse the listing of various categories (starting with the top two: Management and Professional and Related), search by keyword or look through the index for what you want. The Bureau of Labor Statistic's *Career Guide to Industries* (http://www.bls.gov/oco/cg/) is a companion resource that provides valuable background on chosen niches. If you want to know which ones the government projects to be the fastest growing in the next few years, visit the Employment Projections page at http://www.bls.gov/emp/home.htm.

Corporate Information (http://www.corporateinformation.com). Corporate information (CI) is a useful tool if you prospect companies internationally. It offers one-stop research on more than 20,000 companies in 50+ countries worldwide. One of its best features is the country-specific list of Web-based resources it provides when you search by country. You can also search by company, by industry sector within a country, and by U.S. state.

TIP: Sign up at *PrecisionAlert* (http://www.precisionalert.com) to be notified via e-mail when a company you're interested in will be Webcasting a corporate event of some kind (e.g., a presentation to securities analysts or an annual meeting of shareholders).

TIP: If you prospect among public companies, *Yahoo! Finance* is a must for current news and company-specific data (http://www.finance .yahoo.com). You should also take a look at *Report Gallery* (http://www.reportgallery.com), where you can view annual reports for more than 2000 companies or read a Zack's summary on the firm for free. If you want a printed copy or a PDF version of an annual report, visit the *Wall Street Journal* (http://www.wsj.ar .wilink.com/), where you can order a free copy from selected companies quickly and easily.

GuideStar (http://www.guidestar.org).   If you target philanthropic organizations, either as asset management opportunities or for their links to wealthy donors, GuideStar's database of 850,000 nonprofits across the United States will help you identify groups that might need your services. A step-by-step tutorial walks you through what's available. You can search by name of the nonprofit, keywords, city, state, zip, category, type (public or private), or income range, and GuideStar will provide a list of organizations that meet your criteria. You'll get a report that lays out the group's mission and programs, goals and results, financial position, leadership and Web address. If a Form 990 is available, you'll see a link to it too. Icons in the report even tell you how current the information is.

The Foundation Center (http://www.fdncenter.org).   Here is another philanthropy-related site where you can track news of what's happening across the foundation world, check for upcoming conferences, research funding trends, and more.

TIP: Marketing to foundations can be a potent way to expand your business. But your interest in them has to transcend a mercenary motive to manage their money or you'll never get anywhere. Find a cause you believe in, and would support anyway, and put your efforts there.

First Research (http://www.firstresearch.com). First Research picks up where the *Bureau of Labor Statistics Occupational Outlook Handbook* site leaves off. The company publishes background information on more than 140 industries, many of which employ the affluent investors you're interested in. Individual reports cost $99 each (to buy single reports go to http://www .industryprofiles.1stresearch.com/); an annual subscription (for a single user) is $675. Reports are updated quarterly and include an industry overview, call preparation questions, a summary of business trends and industry opportunities, news and media information, financial information, Web site links, and a glossary of terms. The company even keeps annual subscribers alerted to changes in the profiles they've selected via e-mail. A few minutes digesting one of these reports and you'll sound like an expert in your chosen industry.

FreeERISA (http://www.freeerisa.com). FreeERISA provides free access to pension and benefit plan information. You can search for companies' Form 5500 information by state, zip code, business name, or any combination of the three. You'll also find a synopsis of financial and membership data on public pension funds and terminating plans. Detailed financial information on certain defined contribution plans is also available. To get up to speed quickly, read the *Prospecting & Sales Insight Monthly* archive of articles written by Rich White (http://www.freeerisa.com/Insight/). White's articles will teach you how to prospect in the pension market and give you step-by-step instructions for using FreeERISA's information to do it more effectively.

Hoover's (http://www.hoovers.com). Now owned by Dun & Bradstreet (which also owns ZapData), Hoover's provides snapshots of more than 300 industries categorized in 28 different groups—with profiles of the leading companies in each and a news feed of current stories that mention them, and *lots* more. While much of the information is free, you must be a subscriber to access Hoover's premium content. The basic package, Hoover's Lite, costs $49.95 a month or $399 annually. It provides access to in-depth company profiles, key officers and directors (and their biographies), competitors, and in-depth financials. The more expensive Hoover's Pro and Pro Plus subscription packages include more information and additional tools, such as e-mail alerts and customized lead lists.

HRLive (http://www.hrlive.com).   HRLive provides a weekly summary of layoff announcements gathered from news services across North America; this site is an excellent place for identifying money in motion (think "retirement plan rollovers"). You can view them all, or filter results using keywords, industry category, location, headcount, or when the announcement was made. For example, if you live in Los Angeles and your niche is engineers in Aerospace and Defense, check on companies that have announced a layoff in the past 60 days. Once you've identified a company, visit their Web site to get more information on who to approach, or do a search at Yahoo! Finance.

InfoSpace (http://www.infospace.com).   InfoSpace is one of the Web's most popular lookup sites. Use its "Find Neighbors" feature to get names, addresses, and phone numbers of residents in any neighborhood. To try it out, go to *Reverse Phone Lookup* http://www.infospace.com/info/revphone.htm and type in a client's phone number, then click "Find." If their information is publicly available, their name, address, and phone number should appear on the screen. Click on the link labeled "Find Neighbors" underneath it and you'll get a list of neighbors.

 TIP: During your next conversation with a client whose neighborhood is one you want to prospect in, ask if Joe Dokes around the corner would be worth talking to and would they provide you with an introduction.

Internet Prospector (http://www.internet-prospector.org).   Primarily directed at the nonprofit fund-raising community, Internet Prospector can be a gold mine of prospecting information on companies, foundations, and individuals. The site publishes a monthly newsletter that you can subscribe to via e-mail. Pay special attention to the "People" and "Corporation" sections.

GRAB PROSPECT DATA FAST

Copying and pasting (or worse, retyping) prospect contact information you find in directories on the Web is as monotonous and time-consuming as watching paint dry. Two tools can make the task of transferring that information into your database lightning quick: *ListGrabber* and *Address-Grabber,* both from eGrabber (http://www.egrabber.com).

ListGrabber lets you highlight contact information found on a Web page (for one or more people) and import it directly into the appropriate fields in an Outlook, ACT!, or Goldmine record (and a variety of other programs). You can even use it to load information into your Palm® via Palm's Desktop software. AddressGrabber lets you do the same thing with information contained in e-mail messages.

Both can be downloaded and used on a free trial basis for 15 days.

Primedia (http://www.primedia.com).   Primedia describes itself as the #1 special-interest magazine publisher in the United States, offering more than 250 titles, including *Seventeen* and *Motor Trend.* Its sites can give you valuable insight into personal or professional interests the people in your target markets have. Check out both their Business and Consumer publications.

Search Systems (http://www.searchsystems.net).   This site offers one of the Web's largest collections of links to searchable public records databases (over 17,000 as of early 2004). If you target a specific niche, invest two minutes in learning if there's an Internet site that lets you locate people in that group easily.

SEC Info (http://www.secinfo.com).   As an advisor, you may use SEC filings all the time to analyze investments, but do you realize how much intelligence on the markets, people, and individuals you're targeting those files contain? SEC Info gives you free access to that information: on insider trading activity (Forms 3, 4, 5, 144, and U-12); proxy statements (Forms 14A and 14C); changes in control, bankruptcies, and resignations (Form 8K); and a listing of IPO filings (Form S-1)—all in a searchable, sortable, (mostly) downloadable format. Use this site to look up information by an individual's name, industry, business name, SIC code, area code, topic, central index key (CIK), file number, date, or zip/postal code.

SEC Info gleans both U.S. (EDGAR) and Canadian (SEDAR) information (according to the site, the only place on the Web where you can get that information for free). SEC Info also lets you create e-mail alerts to be notified automatically of new filings. The Help information at the site is sparse and there's no tutorial, but if you're willing to work through some test searches, you should get the hang of it quickly. Other sites offering SEC information include *EDGAR Online* (http://www.edgar-online.com), a publicly traded firm that also maintains the *FreeEDGAR* (http://www.freeedgar.com) and *EDGARPro* (http://www.edgarpro.com) sites, and *PriceWaterhouseCoopers' EdgarScan™* (http://edgarscan.pwcglobal.com/servlets/edgarscan).

 If you want to jump directly to a section of a file or Web page, press *Ctrl + F* to activate the "Find" feature in Word or IE, type in your term(s), and press *Enter*.

Trade Show News Network (http://www.tsnn.com). If you exhibit at or attend trade shows in your market, Trade Show News Network (TSNN) is an excellent resource. Its database of events can be searched by industry, show name, city, state, country, or date. *Tradeshow Week Online* (http://www.tradeshowweek.com) is a similar site that lets you sort search results alphabetically or chronologically, something not offered by TSNN.

VertMarkets (http://www.vertmarkets.com). VertMarkets operates dozens of industry-specific "online marketplaces" in a variety of industries including information technology (IT), manufacturing, and food and beverages. Each site offers news, information, and other resources of interest to buyers and sellers within that market. Check to see if VertMarkets manages a site that covers your professional or industry niche.

 TIP: Use *HydraLinks* (http://www.hydralinks.com), a $30 add-in to Internet Explorer (IE), to create a single list of important pages found at any of these sites. Save the list and open it whenever you need to get the latest information on your chosen topic. When you find a page you want to hold onto, file a copy with *SurfSaver*.

MAKE YOUR CLIENTS LOOK LIKE HEROES

Scott Kimball is a top producer with one of the big firms in Atlanta. He's also the author of *Top Gun Financial Sales—How to Double or Triple Your Results While Reducing Your Book*. We met in the spring of 2003 when both of us spoke in front of the same audience.

One of Scott's guiding principles is "Make Heroes Out of Others." In his book he tells the following story to demonstrate what he means. It's a perfect illustration of connecting the dots, not just so you look good, but more importantly, so your clients look good.

> I have a client who is a treasurer of a corporation. I was thinking about his job, what he is required to do every day, and how I might help him become a hero at his company. In looking over his financial reports, I noticed that the company had an outstanding issue of convertible bonds trading for less than par. Interest rates had dropped quite a bit from the time the bonds were issued . . . I suggested a couple [of ideas] to him. He could buy back some of the bonds . . . lowering his interest expense and "retiring" outstanding shares of stock for reporting purposes . . . [which] could potentially raise earnings per share. He could also do an interest rate swap, trading his high fixed rate for a much lower floating rate, thereby lowering interest expense. Either of these ideas, when presented to his senior management team, would allow him to provide real opportunities for increasing earnings per share and structuring interest income and expense more profitably.[2]

Scott already had his client's company's financials in hand, but if he didn't, he could easily have gone to several of the sites mentioned, downloaded the reports, and been reviewing their content, all within about 30 seconds.

Think of your top clients. What can you do to help them? How can you position yourself as a problem solver? Dig beneath the surface to unearth opportunities to help them. Leverage the Web everywhere you can to get the job done.

What to Look For

Okay, you've found a site that caters to an audience you're interested in. You're wondering "What do I do next?" Use the checklist that follows to start drawing and connecting the dots of intelligence it offers. (There's a blank form in Appendix B you can use to record what you find.) I'm not suggesting you spend time locating content about *every* item on this list; pick and choose the ones that would be helpful to what you're trying to accomplish.

Site Map. After scanning a site's navigation buttons, the first thing to look for is a site map. A well-designed one provides a bird's-eye overview of what content is available, organized by category, and can help you quickly decide whether or not the site is worth your time.

Search Function. Next, check to see if the site lets you search its contents for keywords. Look for a small box, usually near the top of the home page (and often other pages as well), with either the word "Go" or "Search" next to it.

TIP: If a site doesn't have its own search function, use the Google Toolbar's "Search Within the Site" feature to look for your keywords. You can read more about the Google Toolbar starting on page 84.

Articles/Press Releases. Articles written by or about an organization can provide insights into its goals and objectives, financial status, new product/service initiatives, changes in leadership (including retirements, relocations, and promotions), announcements of strategic alliances, and more. In addition, press releases often quote people you would like to prospect or otherwise cultivate: CEOs, senior managers, or human resources directors. Tying your call to something they've said only helps.

Management/Leadership. Often, sites provide biographies of top management and board members. Those sketches may identify common ground (industries worked in, companies worked for, positions held, schools attended, publications authored, charities supported, etc.) that you and those you are targeting share. Don't overlook indirect connections through friends, clients, or strategic partners. Mentioning something you saw about a colleague, neighbor, or fellow association member you'd like an introduction to is a more relaxed alternative to the "One of the ways my clients help me is to provide good referrals . . ." approach that makes many advisors (and clients) uncomfortable.

What's New? As with articles and press releases, a "What's New" page can give you insight into current happenings within an organization.

TIP: One of the best ways to stay on top of content changes on "What's New" pages is to add their uniform resource locators (URLs) to a *QuickBrowse* (http://www.quickbrowse.com) account and request notification any time the content of the page changes (we'll talk about QuickBrowse and how to use it at the end of the chapter).

Staff Directory. Online (public) directories of company employees are rare, but many associations do publish theirs. Find and cultivate people in these four roles: head of education/programming (for speaking opportunities), head of membership (to offer help in recruiting, a chronic challenge for many organizations), publications editor (for writing opportunities), and Webmaster (to understand what's where and who's who).

TIP: Put whatever management, leadership, and staff contact information you uncover into your database (including e-mail addresses) and group them (e.g., CEOs, program chairs, magazine editors) so that you are positioned to communicate with them quickly and easily when the time comes.

TIP: Developing a dialog with the Webmaster of an association you're targeting can be a smart strategy. Send them a short e-mail message explaining that you're trying to understand the issues their members face, and ask their advice on where to focus at the site to gain that insight. Treated well, Webmasters can be a terrific information ally.

Locations listing. If you are visiting an association site, does it offer a list of regional, state, or local chapters around the country? With company sites, are branch or subsidiary offices identified, as well as people at those locations who might be prospects for your services?

Event Calendar. Knowing when and where a group meets is helpful in formulating any approach to them. Here are some questions to ask when reviewing a calendar of events:

- When do important meetings take place? Are they national, statewide, or local?

- Are agendas published online? Are past presentations archived and downloadable from the site?

- Which events should you target to attend, or present or exhibit at? Who chairs them? What is the theme of each?

- How are decisions made about program content? When are they made? By whom?

- What is the process the group follows in identifying and selecting speakers or writers?

If the group publishes a magazine, check for an editorial calendar that lists themes of upcoming issues, then contact the editor (whose name you got from the online staff directory or masthead of the printed version) about contributing an article.

TIP: Event speakers and exhibitors can be great prospects or referral sources. See if the site contains a roster of who they are (and a biography or background sheet on each presenter). If an event has already occurred, scan the trade publications or local media for a write-up on whichever speaker you are interested in pursuing. If you find one that is meaty enough, have reprints made or a copy of the article mounted professionally on a plaque and hand deliver it as a gift to that person. It's a great way to make an introduction and start a dialog.

Links/Resource List. Check to see if a company or trade group has cataloged other sites related to their audience's interests.

Message Boards and Discussion Groups. Reading message threads at well-trafficked boards (more likely to be found at association and special interest sites than at companies' sites) can help you quickly get a sense of what people in that group are thinking.

TIP: Interested in what's being said around the digital water cooler? Search *Google Groups* (http://groups.google.com), a complete archive of 700 million public discussion forum postings dating back to 1981. Though technology-oriented topics tend to be the most active, you can find information on virtually any subject.

Opt-in notification. Some sites let you sign up to receive newsletters and press releases as they are published. If you concentrate on a specific company or trade group, it's worth being one of the first to know what's happening with the organization.

Personalization options. Does the site let you select what information you see when visiting it? If so, set yourself up to get just what you want.

TIP: Use Google's "Similar Pages" and "Backward Links" features (discussed later in the chapter) to leapfrog to other pages related to the site you're visiting.

BE A HERO TO YOUR CLIENTS

Any of your clients work in sales? Own a company? Considering a job change or actively looking for work? Guess what? They have the same need for information you do.

Case in point: job search. Lots of highly paid white-collar workers are finding themselves on the street looking for work for the first time in their lives. That's an unsettling situation, made scarier for those used to relying on a staff to get things done for them.

(continued)

If you have a client (or prospect) in a career transition, show them how to research companies and opportunities they are interested in pursuing, or help them identify people who can plug them into those companies. Help them clarify their strategy and cut through the clutter to land the job they want and you'll win not only a client but a friend for life.

The same thing is true if your clients sell for a living, or own their own businesses. What would it be worth to them to know how to keep better tabs on customers, prospects, and competitors? Be the one to show them how.

Never stop thinking of (and acting on) ways you can help your clients succeed, financially or otherwise. You'll solidify your business base and have a lot more fun in the process.

Directories Worth Digging Into

Directories can save you an incredible amount of time, yet they often go overlooked, maybe because there are thousands of them online, and it's tough to know where to start.

The eight directory sites that follow are worth your review. A few minutes exploring them can save you hours of hit-and-miss searching for prospecting information, market research, business advice, or computer support. All are created and managed by human beings, not compiled blindly by computers crawling the Web in search of content.

About.com (http://www.about.com). This site is a collection of free information on hundreds of special-interest topics, each managed and led by an expert guide. Each subject area offers articles, forums for posting questions and exchanging messages, and scheduled chat events. Many of these listings contain links to other Web sites relating to the chosen subject. If you concentrate within a particular niche, check if it's covered at About. You can browse the 20+ channels on the home page, type in a few search terms in the "Find It Now" box toward the top of that page, or scan the alphabetical index of its site content.

Some About topic areas that relate to popular markets for financial advisors are:

- Divorce support (http://divorcesupport.about.com).
- Human resources (http://humanresources.about.com).

- Management (http://management.about.com).
- Nonprofit charitable organizations (http://nonprofit.about.com).
- Senior living (http://seniorliving.about.com).
- Small business (http://sbinformation.about.com).

If you find a potentially useful topic, follow these steps to quickly judge its value:

1. *Scan the Subject Listing on the left side of your topic's main page for relevant content.*
2. *Type* **links** *in the search box near the top of the topic's home page (make sure "In this Topic" is selected), click on the "Go" button, then review the list of results provided.*
3. *Click on the "Forums" link on the gray bar near the top (underneath "Your Guide to One of Hundreds of Sites") and then "Click Here for Guest Access" to see what sort of messages visitors are posting.*

 About.com is free because it's ad supported; anytime a browser window opens with an advertising message, press *Ctrl + W* to close it.

 TIP: Over the past several years, About has discontinued coverage of a number of topics. Before giving up on the idea that the one you're looking for isn't out there, try *Former About Guides* (http://www .formeraboutguides.com), a nonaffiliated site where you'll find nearly 90 of those discontinued topics listed.

The StartSpot Network (http://www.startspot.com/network/). This site is another collection of special-interest directories that can help in client development and relationship management. Do you have clients that are looking for a job, are dedicated to certain causes, like to go to the movies or theater, or just enjoy shopping or travel? StartSpot can provide you with ideas for communicating with them, or just give you a better sense of what they're interested in. Check these six first: HeadlineSpot, PeopleSpot, LibrarySpot, EmploymentSpot, GiveSpot, and TripSpot.

Hotsheet (http://www.hotsheet.com). This site is a one-page directory of useful sites. Though it doesn't offer descriptions or proprietary content like About or StartSpot, it is an excellent plain vanilla list of sites recognized by many as the best in their category. Content is divided into 11 categories, each divided into subsections. The site offers free personalization ("My Hotsheet"), allowing registered users to add their own sites and access that information from any PC.

CEOExpress (http://www.ceoexpress.com). This site offers a collection of 600+ links to sites of interest to senior managers. The content is organized into four categories: Daily News & Info, Business Research, Office Tools & Travel, and Breaktime. You'll find sections on locating statistics online, company research (both United States and international), newspaper directories worldwide, and a variety of small-business resources. For $49 a year, you can subscribe to CEOExpress Select and customize what you see when you visit the site. *If you work with business owners or corporate executives, be sure to share this site with them.*

Refdesk (http://www.refdesk.com). This is a free resource with thousands of links to helpful sites. At the top of its home page is a collection of "of-the-day" spotlights (site. . . , thought. . . , word. . . , etc.), which can serve as useful newsletter content. Other sections offering worthwhile prospecting or client relationship-management information include Facts Search, Facts-at-a-Glance, Current News, and some of the Subject Categories (business and career resources, seniors online, and women's issues, to name three).

Google Directory (http://directory.google.com). This site takes the Web's largest human-edited directory (the *Open Directory Project*, http://dmoz.org/) and prioritizes each of its entries based on the popularity of its content. The nearly one-half million topics are put in one of 16 categories: Arts, Business, Computers, Games, Health, Home, Kids and Teens, News, Recreation, Reference, Regional, Science, Shopping, Society, Sports, and World. The Google Directory's ranked lists are one of the first things I check when I want to find out what's available online on a particular topic.

News Directory (http://www.newsdirectory.com). This site contains a database of newspapers and magazines worldwide. You can browse newspapers by country, or magazines by region or subject, or search for either by title. Clicking on any item listed takes you directly to that site. Knowing where clients, prospects, and others get their information (i.e., what they read) is one smart, fast way to gain insight into the issues that concern them.

Topica (http://topica.com).   This is where to go to identify special-interest e-mail newsletters. Search the directory for specific terms or browse an index of list names. Clicking on any title in the list will trigger a short description of the newsletter's content and instructions on (or a link to) where to sign up for it. *Be aware that all mailing lists are not alike—some are invaluable, others a complete waste of time.* (And if you find a good one, don't start blasting away with marketing messages to the readers; you'll get bounced from the group as a spammer faster than you can blink, and you might kill a goose that could lay some golden eggs.)

 TIP: Read the instructions later in the chapter on setting up a secondary e-mail account to receive messages from sources like the ones discussed in this section before signing up for any subscriptions.

BECOME AN EXPERT IN YOUR MARKET

You may be thinking, "I don't have time to look at all that stuff. My job is to call on people, not play researcher." Fair enough, if you already know who you're targeting, how they spend their time, where they meet, what they read, the things they worry or dream about, and when and how to approach them about your services, then have at it.

The problem is very few sales people, especially advisors, have that strong a grasp of their market. Ask them who they target and they'll say "seniors" or "retirees" or "rich people." Those aren't markets, they're census classifications.

If you want to expand your business, start by identifying your natural niche. Use your knowledge journal to build an ideal client profile based on the top people you currently work with. Then leverage the Web and what it offers to get closer to them and those who look like them. That's the essence of affinity marketing.

(continued)

People (especially the affluent) like to do business with others like themselves who understand their world, their thinking, and their experiences. Private-client firms pay outside consultants handsomely to immerse their teams in "the client experience" so their people will appreciate what it feels like to live and travel in the world of the rich and famous. The Web can give you many of those same insights a lot less expensively, if you're willing to put the pieces together.

You can work harder (more cold calls, more appointments, more proposals), or you can work smarter (those same activities, but directed at a focused audience you relate well to). It's your choice. Just remember the saying: If it was easy, everyone would be doing it.

What You Need, When You Want It . . . Automatically

Knowing which sites can help you isn't worth anything unless you can exploit the information they contain, and that's not possible if you have to continually go back to them to harvest content. To have practical value, the information needs to be delivered to you, automatically, in one place, on a timely basis. Here are three suggestions for setting up an inexpensive intelligence-gathering system (check with your firm to make sure you can implement them before moving ahead).

1. Create a Personal Portal to the Web (Time Required: < 60 Minutes)

My Yahoo! (http://my.yahoo.com) lets you configure a customized online news and information service that draws from nearly 100 different Yahoo! services. With a free My Yahoo! account you can include up to 20 different modules of information, arranged as you want to see them (some charge a fee); for example, top stories from Reuters and AP, business and industry headlines from any of over 40 sectors, or financial updates from CBS MarketWatch, Briefing.com, and EDGAR Online.

Here are three specific ways you can leverage My Yahoo!:

1. *Track information on companies and people you work with using the News Clipper.*
    Monitor news stories containing keywords you select (people, companies, competitors, personal interests, etc.).
2. *Keep up with useful new sites related to niches you target with the Web Site Tracker.*

Watch sites in categories including Arts, Business, Computers and the Internet, Education, Entertainment, Government, Health, News and Media, Recreation, Reference, Regional, Science, Social Science, and Society and Culture.

3. *Learn about clients' online interests by helping them set up their own My Yahoo! account.*

Why not host an event to help clients you know go online make the most of that time? Make setting up My Yahoo!, *My Way* (http://www .myway.com) or another personal portal one part of the agenda, reviewing your firm's site and its benefits a second, and other useful online resources a third.

TIP: When signing up for any service like My Yahoo!, look for a check box regarding receiving marketing offers from the provider "and its partners." Either opt out entirely, or make sure any messages you agree to receive go to your secondary e-mail account (we'll cover how to set one up shortly).

One last feature of My Yahoo! worth mentioning is its Notepad, which lets you save notes to your account using any computer connected to the Web; I use it when I'm working on someone else's computer to record my thoughts and save them. Back at my PC, I can open the Note and put it on my "To Do" list or copy it into my knowledge journal.

TIP: Set your My Yahoo! page as your home page in IE, and anytime you launch your browser, the headlines and information you want will be right in front of you.

---

2. Get Important Information E-Mailed to You Automatically (Time Required: < 15 Minutes)

To get your My Yahoo! page or anything else sent to you like clockwork, take a look at *Quickbrowse* (http://www.quickbrowse.com), a subscription-based service that will collect and deliver content to you by e-mail from different sites—all on a single page. Follow these three steps to get started with it:

1. *Open an account.*

    You can start with a free, fully functional 14-day trial or buy a quarterly or annual subscription (less than $50).

2. *Customize your content.*

    You can create as many collections of sites as you like, either picking from 15 popular news sources listed at Quickbrowse, or adding Web pages of your own. Start with those you *know* you want to review regularly (you can add or delete sites easily later on). When you're done, click on the Quickbrowse button to scroll through and review your customized collection of sites.

3. *Set up a delivery schedule.*

    You can choose daily, weekly, or whenever a page's content changes.

Use Quickbrowse to keep tabs on news about top clients, press releases on target companies (like layoff, promotion, or retirement announcements), market commentaries from various analysts, your competition, and more.

BE FIRST TO GET BREAKING NEWS

Imagine someone scouring newspapers and magazines for stories containing terms you designate and delivering a summary of those headlines to you every day by e-mail . . . for *free.* You get the e-mail, click on the link to any story listed in it and, bang, the full article loads in your browser. *That's* Google News Alerts (http://www.google.com/newsalerts), a service Google introduced in 2003.

Subscribing to Google News Alerts is a great way to track news about, or of interest to, clients, prospects, companies, target markets, competitors . . . you name it. Stories are drawn from thousands of news sources and listed by category at Google News (http://news.google.com). If you're not familiar with how Google News search works, try typing *layoff OR layoffs AND announced* in the search box. Among the results you'll get will be stories on organizations that have announced they are letting staff go, an opportunity for anyone who targets retirement plan rollovers and is looking for companies and people to contact.

If you find articles included in that, or any other, news search result useful and want to see more like them on a daily basis, click on the "News Alert" link on the "Results" page and set up an Alert. Type in the e-mail address you want that alert sent to (yours or someone on your team) and you're on your way. There's no limit to the number of alerts you can set up.

To pinpoint highly *specific* information—for instance, narrowing your search of layoff announcements to just those in your state or appearing in your local newspaper or just within the past week—it pays to familiarize yourself with Google's Advanced News Search options (http://news .google.com/advanced_news_search). With those advanced options, you can filter results using any of five categories: keyword, news source, location, where the terms occur in the article (in the headline, in the body, anywhere), and date.

One way to win business is to uncover and act on useful information quickly. Google News Alerts makes that job easier.

 TIP: If you're willing to pay, Smart Online (http://www.smartonline .com) offers a service similar to Google News Alerts called Business Intelligence. With a monthly, quarterly, or annual subscription, you can choose from dozens of preselected industry and lifestyle topic categories or create your own search. Business Intelligence even lets you share what you find with others by e-mail at the click of a button. Check it out.

---

3. Set Up a Secondary E-Mail Account (Time Required: < 5 Minutes)

Microsoft's *Hotmail* (http://www.hotmail.com) is a perfect place to collect newsletters and general research. By steering that information to Hotmail, you keep your main mailbox clean, while being able to view potentially helpful business intelligence in one place when you're ready. Here's how to take advantage of the tool:

1. *Open an account.*
   You can choose a subscription-based or free account. Free sounds appealing, but there are limitations. Storage size is capped, and the account must be accessed every 30 days to remain active. Forget to check your account one month and all your messages get deleted. My advice: Pay for the peace of mind of knowing your data will always be there. Two other tips: (1) During setup, skip (i.e., don't check) the boxes for free subscriptions or MSN Featured Offers, and (2) make sure boxes that

include you in public e-mail directories are *unchecked*; otherwise expect a deluge of spam.

2. *Customize your mail-handling settings.*

   Look under Options to see how to set up filters to sort out messages automatically and to keep unwanted e-mail out of your Inbox, and how to create a "safe list" to ensure that messages you want to get won't be filtered out as "junk."

3. *Check for new messages periodically.*

   One of Hotmail's greatest benefits is its flexibility. You, or anyone you assign, can check messages from any computer, at any time. Ask your assistant or an intern to review content and compress the "need to know" stuff into a quick summary (statistics, factoids, names, and contact information of prospects from articles and news releases).

TIP: Hotmail integrates tightly with Outlook Express, the free e-mail software that's bundled with IE. Using Outlook Express, you can download messages from Hotmail to your computer for later viewing and follow up offline (i.e., when you may not be connected to the Internet, as when you're traveling).

TIP: If you're concerned that you'll forget to check messages in a back-up e-mail account regularly, check out *ePrompter* (http://www .epromter.com), which will monitor up to 16 different e-mail accounts simultaneously, tell you what's in them, and let you manage those messages from a single screen.

The Language of Search

So far I've been feeding you sites worth knowing. But to master the Web, you can't be dependent on me or anyone else to show you what's out there; you need to learn to fish for yourself. This section and the one that follows will teach you how. Yes, they are dense with instructions, but they are worth digesting. Like knowledge journaling, they are "learn by doing" opportunities. I'd suggest sitting at your computer as you work through them. I also recommend sharing them with your assistant.

Remember the movie *The Graduate*? What's the first thing that comes to your mind? If you thought, "plastics" you read my mind—the scene is a classic in film history. Dustin Hoffman has just come home from college and is talking to a friend of his parents. The man says, "Ben, I just want to say one word to you—just one word: plastics. There's a great future in plastics. Think about it; will you think about it?"

Fast forward to today's Internet era; I want to say just one thing to you—keywords. Keywords are the directions you give search engines on where and what to scan cyberspace for; they are what I have been calling search terms up to this point. Keywords fill in the blanks to questions like, "Where can I find. . . ?" "I wonder if there's a site that. . . ?" "Wouldn't it be great to uncover. . . ?" or "How do I. . . ?"

Mastering the use of keywords can make the difference between viewing the Web as an electronic newspaper and harnessing its power as an intelligence-gathering gold mine. They are the Internet's equivalent of knowing your ABCs. If you don't understand how they work, you're not going to get very far.

Like it or not, we live in a digital society. According to *How Much Information?*, published by two University of California Berkeley School of Information Management Sciences professors:

> The world produces between 1 and 2 exabytes of unique information per year, which is roughly 250 megabytes for every man, woman, and child on earth . . . Printed documents of all kinds comprise only .003% of the total . . . Magnetic storage is rapidly becoming the universal medium for information storage.[3]

Just what is an "exabyte"? Try 1,000,000,000,000,000,000 bits of data, or 10^{18}. That's one million Libraries of Congress. Five exabytes equal all the words ever spoken by human beings.[4] Keywords let you navigate the Web's ocean of data without drowning in it.

Why the Web Is So Overwhelming

Over 8 million unique Web sites

5+ billion pages of content

40 to 80 pages added every second

Average Web page life span: 100 days

Source: Online Computer Library Center.

Four Methods, Three Levels

There are a dozen different ways of using keywords to zero in on the information you need. The four basic methods are: *any keyword, all keywords, exact phrasing*, and *Boolean*. In addition to those methods, there are three levels at which you can search: *within an entire page, only within the page title*, or *only within the URL*. The following example illustrates how each works.

Picture yourself as a college student taking an Introduction to Investing course. Your assignment: a report on mutual funds, specifically ones specializing in value investing. In the old days, your first stop would have been the reference desk at the library. But today search engines and the Internet can play that role, instantly, right from your computer.

You begin by searching on the terms *mutual fund* at Google and get a list of 1.2 million+ results. You have just done an *"all" keyword search*, the default option of virtually every search site out there. With an all keyword search, only pages that include all of the keywords you typed appear in the results. It's like asking a reference librarian to pull a list of all the pages of their library's books that contain the words "mutual" and "fund."

Maybe, because of how smart Google is at interpreting your request, you find what you want. Great, but to illustrate the point, let's assume that's not the case, and you need to keep looking.

If you were talking to an actual reference librarian, you might say, "Okay, how about showing me just a list of pages that contain the term 'mutual fund'?" She'd understand that you wanted to narrow your scope to include only pages that contain the precise phrase "mutual fund." You can ask a search engine to do the same thing by putting the phrase you want in quotation marks (" "). That's called *"exact phrase" searching*. It's an easy way to cut down on the results returned when you are looking for something specific. In this case, an exact phrase search on *"mutual fund"* would reduce the total to less than 600,000.

But you can even go further than that. If you see a lot of results that include information on "growth" mutual funds, and you're only interested in pages on value funds, you can use *Boolean search* to omit any pages with the term "growth" on them. Boolean search uses the words (called "operators" or "connectors") AND, NOT, and OR to include combinations, or choices, of keywords you want or exclude those you don't (Google lets you substitute a "+" sign for "AND," a "-" sign for "NOT" and a "|" for OR).[5]

To get pages that include the terms "value mutual funds" but not those that also mention the term growth (as in growth funds), you type *value "mutual fund" NOT growth* (or *value "mutual fund" -growth*), which would reduce your total to just under 100,000, or less than 10 percent of what you started with.

TIP: Google and most other popular search engines cap the number of results they report (vs. how many they actually find) at 1000. But whether it's 1000 or 1 million, if you don't find what you're looking for in the first 100 items listed, try using different, or more, keywords to narrow your search focus and reduce the result count.

What about "any" keyword searches? *"Any" keyword searching* is for special situations because it delivers the largest possible universe of results. For example, doing an "any" keyword search on *mutual fund* would generate a list of nearly 6.5 million results, most of which wouldn't relate to what you wanted.

So what's a circumstance where you might want to use it? Remember earlier I mentioned there are three levels of content you can search on: These are *anywhere on a page, only in the page title,* and *only in the page URL.* Maybe you target dentists and orthodontists as clients. Do an "any" keyword search on page titles or page URLs for *dentist orthodontist* to see what pertains to them.

Returning to the library reference desk analogy, requesting a list of keywords in the title of a page or the page's URL is akin to asking a librarian to scan for book titles only, not their content, when looking for your terms. Narrowing the scope like that dramatically reduces the results returned. In the mutual fund example, a search of "page titles only" reduces the count to a little over 20,000; one that looks only "in the url of the page" gets even smaller, down to a bit over 1000.

Table 3.1 contains several more examples that highlight the variation in the number of results generated, depending on which types of searches you complete (your results may vary).

TABLE 3.1   Number of Results per Search Method

Method/Level	Number of Results
Keywords searched: **"wealthy"** *or* **"affluent"** *or* **"high net worth"**	
Any keyword search, anywhere on the page	900,000
Any keyword search, only in the page title	11,000

(continued)

TABLE 3.1 *(Continued)*

Method/Level	Number of Results
Keywords searched: **"wealth management"**	
All keyword search, anywhere on the page	1,600,000
Exact phrase search, anywhere on the page	138,000
Keywords searched: **"women-owned businesses"**	
All keyword search, anywhere on the page	200,000
All keyword search, only in the the page	650

A SUMMARY OF SEARCH METHODS

1. Any keyword: Returns pages that include any keyword in your search query.
   - Equivalent to typing OR between each term.
   - Broadest approach: delivers the largest possible universe of results.
2. *All keyword:* Returns only pages containing all keywords in your search request.
   - Equivalent to typing AND (or +) between each term.
   - The default search option for Google and most other search sites.
3. *Exact phrase:* Returns only pages that include a specified string of keywords.
   - Put quotation marks (" ") around the precise phrase you are attempting to locate.
   - Good for locating proper names.
4. *Boolean:* Returns and/or excludes specific combinations of keywords.
   - Uses AND (+), NOT (–), and OR (l) in combination.
   - Most precise approach: returns the smallest number of results.

TIP: At Google, clicking on "Advanced Search" on the home page brings you to a page where you can try each method; use them individually or in combination. Try combining keywords in different ways to understand how each approach works. If you want to learn more after that, click on "Advanced Search Tips."

KEYWORDS FOR FINDING YOUR NEEDLE IN THE HAYSTACK

Here are 20 useful keywords for developing intelligence on target audiences—who they are, what groups they belong to, what they read, what they like to do, and so on. Use them together with terms that describe the market you're researching to pinpoint information.

association	group	newspaper
conference	industry	organization
convention	links	publication
corporate	list	report
directory	magazine	resource
foundation	meeting	survey
guide	newsletter	

Here are a dozen *event-oriented* keywords/phrases that can help you catch money in motion, especially when used to filter news stories and press releases:

acquired
announced
appointed
awarded
elected
hire OR hired OR hiring OR "plans to hire"
layoff OR lay off OR laid off
merged
promoted OR "promoted to"
relocated
retire OR "will retire"
transferred

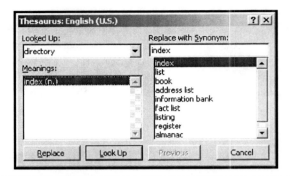

FIGURE 3.1 Word's Thesaurus

ACTION STEP: DESCRIBE WHAT YOU'RE LOOKING FOR

Take a minute to write down words and phrases that describe information you'd like to have on existing clients, prospects, markets, and so forth. Then search the Web using combinations of those terms to see what you can uncover.

TIP: Use a thesaurus to add terms with similar meanings to your list. You can find one online at http://www.thesaurus.com or use the one included in Microsoft Word.

 To use Word's thesaurus function, type a term in an open Word document, highlight it, and then press *Shift + F7*. A small window like the one in Figure 3.1 will open, giving you a list of terms related to the one highlighted.

Turbocharging Your Browser

If the Internet is the information superhighway, your browser (presumably Microsoft's *Internet Explorer,* http://www.microsoft.com/windows/ie) is the car you drive. Most people use IE to putter around the Web at a fairly slow pace. But with a few minor tweaks, ones you can make in less than an hour, you can turn IE into a Ferrari that rockets you right to the information you want in the blink of an eye. Follow the instructions below to take full advantage of IE's potential.

1. Organize Your Favorites (Time Required: < 15 Minutes)

You've undoubtedly bookmarked sites in what IE calls "Favorites." But if you're like me, after a while that list gets a little jumbled. Here's how to clean it up:

1. *Click on "Favorites" on IE's main menu, move your pointer to any one of the Web pages listed and right click; a small "shortcut" menu like that shown in Figure 3.2 will appear. Near the bottom of that menu, left click on "Sort by Name."*

   Your Favorites will sort from A to Z instantly, a much easier way to see what you actually have.

2. *Delete the ones you no longer want or need.*

   To get rid of Favorites that are no longer relevant, right click on them and choose "Delete." If you're reluctant to erase them entirely, create a folder called "Archive" and put all the links you don't plan to use in it.

3. *Check each of the links remaining in your list to make sure it still works.*

   "Dead" links (the ones that lead to a "Page Cannot be Displayed" message) only add to the clutter and confusion; delete them too.

 TIP: If you find a Favorite page no longer available, type its URL into the *Internet Archive's Wayback Machine* (http://www.archive.org) to see if a copy of the page still exists in its 10 billion plus page library. Save a copy in *SurfSaver.*

FIGURE 3.2   Sorting Your Favorites

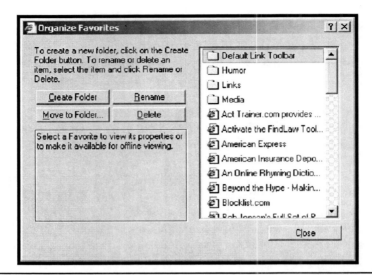

FIGURE 3.3   Organizing Favorites

4. *Move what's left into folders labeled "Products," "Clients' Interests," "News," "Competitors," and so forth.*

Create a new folder for each category by selecting F̲avorites, then O̲rganize Favorites. In the dialog box that opens (shown in Figure 3.3), click on "Create a folder" to add folders for each new category, then click to highlight each favorite you want to move and select "Move to folder" to put it in the new location.

 Press *Control + B* to open the "Organize Favorites" dialog box, then *Alt + C* to create a folder, *Alt + M* to move a selected favorite to a different folder, *Alt + R* to rename the favorite or *Alt + D* to delete it.

---

2. Make Your Most Frequently Visited Site Your Home Page (Time Required: < 1 Minute)

Do you have a "favorite" Favorite; one site you visit more than any other? If you're not seeing that page when your browser opens, here's what to do:

FIGURE 3.4 Address Bar

1. *Launch IE and type the URL of your favorite site in the Address box near the top of the browser window (http://www.cnn.com in Figure 3.4). Press* Enter *on your keyboard.*

2. *After your desired site appears, select Tools from the main IE menu.*

3. *Choose Internet Options at the bottom of the dropdown menu list: the window in Figure 3.5 will open.*

4. *Select the "Use Current" option under the "Address" box in the "Home page" section of the "Internet Options" window and click OK to finish.*

 In IE, press *Alt + Home* any time you want to load your designated home page.

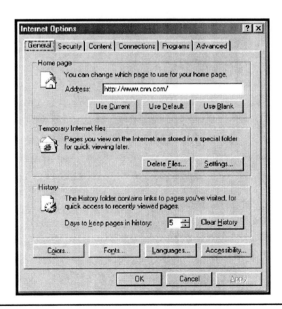

FIGURE 3.5 Internet Options

3. Make Google IE's Default Search Engine (Time Required: < 1 Minute)

Most people don't know that you can type search terms right into the Address bar in IE. When IE is first installed, MSN Search (Microsoft's search site) is set as the default search engine, which means any time you type search terms into the Address bar, IE will use MSN to locate the results. *Google* (http://www .google.com) is a better choice. Its knack for delivering incredibly accurate results at lightning speed have made Google the Web's top search engine. Here's how to make it yours.

1. *Launch IE and press Ctrl + E to open the "Search" pane on the left side of the browser window.*
2. *Click on the "Customize" button located on the right side of that pane near the top. A dialog box titled "Customized Search Settings" will appear.*
3. *Click on the "Autosearch settings" button in the lower left corner of that window (or press Alt + A) to open a second dialog box titled "Customize Autosearch Settings."*
4. *On the dropdown menu under where it reads "Choose a search provider for address bar searches:" click on "Google Sites."*

   Be sure "Just display results in the main window" is visible in the dropdown box below "When searching," otherwise Address bar searching won't work.

 TIP: If you install Google's Toolbar (covered later) you can make Google IE's default search engine by checking a box on the "More Options" tab in the "Toolbar Options" dialog box.

---

4. Leverage IE's Links Toolbar (Time Required: < 5 Minutes)

IE's Links toolbar provides one-click access to sites you visit frequently.[6] It's the place to store your remaining "favorite" Favorites. Things like:

Industry-related sites
Product sponsor sites
Key client Web sites

Address/phone number lookup

Custom content sites like My Yahoo!

Today in history/Joke of the day

Associations in target markets

Popular financial sites

Sites catering to clients' interests

The Wayback Machine

To move a Favorite to the Links toolbar, follow the instructions previously set out under Step 1.

ACTION STEP: CREATING A DASHBOARD OF YOUR "FAVORITE" FAVORITES

Write down up to five sites you visit often and add them to your IE Links toolbar:

1.

2.

3.

4.

5.

TIP: If you abbreviate the names of the Favorites you put in your Links toolbar, you'll fit more of them on it. Right click on any one of them and choose Rename.

TIP: You can assign keyboard shortcuts similar to the one you set up for your knowledge journal to sites in your Links toolbar or your "Favorites" list. To create a keyboard shortcut to a site in the Links toolbar, right click on it and choose "Properties." In the dialog box that appears, put your cursor in the "Shortcut" key field on the "Web Document" tab and press the combination of keys you want to use.

5. Install and Configure Google's Toolbar (Time Required: < 5 Minutes)

To make even better use of Google's capabilities, download the *Google Toolbar* (http://toolbar.google.com). The toolbar is a free add-in to IE that puts many of Google's powerful resources on a dashboard right inside your IE browser window (read "Harnessing the Horsepower of the Google Toolbar" on the next page to find out what they are).

To install it, click on "Get the Google Toolbar" and follow the prompts. (I suggest installing it *with* advanced features, but read the disclaimer to understand how those features work.) Click on "Yes" when you see the Security Warning that reads "Do you want to install and run Google Toolbar for IE. . . ?"

Once installed, follow these three steps to configure the toolbar:

1. *Select "Search Preferences Page" from the Google menu (click on the Google logo on the toolbar to access the menu). On the "Preferences" screen, change the "Number of Results" from 10 to 100.*

   This one adjustment will save you hours, especially if you access the Internet via a dial-up account and a regular phone line.

2. *Still on the Search Preferences page, check the box next to "Open search results in a new browser window."*

   This option allows you to view your list of results and the different sites on it in two separate IE windows. It's an easy way to cut down on browser drift, which is what happens when you go online looking for something specific, and "wake up" an hour later some place entirely different.

TIP: If you want to minimize time online, get a timer to tell you when it's time to quit—whether you're in the office or on the road. Today, many hotels charge by the minute for calls over a certain duration. Setting a reminder to disconnect before you cross that threshold can save you added expense. *Cool Timer* is one simple, free solution (http://www.harmonyhollow.net/ct.shtml). For other options, search Google on *free Internet timer.*

3. *Choose "Options" from the Google menu and check all the boxes listed under the "Options" tab except the one labeled "Open a new window each time you search," then click on OK.*

Making these changes will give you access to the toolbar's main features. Review the two other tabs titled "More" and "AutoFill" and decide for yourself whether any of them are worth including in your toolbar.

HARNESSING THE HORSEPOWER OF THE GOOGLE TOOLBAR

Accessing Google's powerful search engine no matter where you are on the Web (without having to go first to the Google home page to type in your terms) is the biggest reason to install the toolbar, but there are more than a dozen other ways it can save you time and effort. Here are the top seven ways I use it:

- Blocking out annoying pop-up ads;
- Finding out what Web pages link to the one you're viewing;
- Seeing what sites have similar content to the one you're viewing;
- Viewing Google Directory listings that include the currently displayed page;
- Navigating quickly from a page buried within a Web site to the site's home page;
- Highlighting search terms where they appear on the page in different colors;
- Jumping directly to each occurrence of any search term on a page.

You can also use the toolbar for:

- Searching for terms *within* a Web site (especially when a site has no map/directory, or offers no search capability of its own);
- Viewing a copy of a page that's been taken down from its original site;
- Going immediately to the top result listed by Google for your search terms;
- Searching Google's directory for categories related to your search terms;

(continued)

- Searching Google's News site for stories that include your search terms;

- Keeping a record of useful sites using a "blog" (short for "Web log");

- Advancing through sites returned in a list of results in a slideshow format;

- Searching 20+ years of newsgroup discussions (online special-interest groups);

- Conducting your search in over 40 languages.

To understand how these features can help you, test them out on a site that provides something you need: information on a client, a company you'd like to do business with or an industry you target. And keep in mind Google is continually adding new functions to the toolbar, so be sure to watch for new feature announcements.

 To put your cursor in the Google "Toolbar search" box (so you can type in your search terms), press *Alt + G.*

 TIP: You can highlight text on a Web page, then drag and drop it into the toolbar's search box so you can search for the highlighted terms.

6. Install and Configure Microsoft's Web Accessories for Internet Explorer 5 Toolbar (Time Required: < 15 Minutes)

The IE 5 Web Accessories toolbar mentioned in Chapter 1 offers a very useful feature called "QuickSearch." Like the Google toolbar, it eliminates the need to go to a search engine's home page to enter your search terms; you type your terms directly into IE's Address bar.

QuickSearch comes with built-in shortcuts to eleven sites, but you can add more. Three I recommend adding are *Yahoo! Finance*, for getting quotes and current headlines on stocks or companies you follow; *About*, for client and prospect hobbies and interests; and *Refdesk*, for potential newsletter article and message content.

Here's how to set it up. After you've downloaded and installed QuickSearch, find its icon on your Links toolbar (one will be put there during installation). Click on it; the window shown in Figure 3.6 will open.

Click on <u>N</u>ew and type in whatever shortcut letter(s) you want to use as a trigger (use the initials of the chosen search tool, for example *yf* for Yahoo! Finance). Next, in the Search box choose "Custom URL." Finally, type or paste in the URL for the sites search. Here's the URL to use to search on any ticker symbol at Yahoo! Finance:

http://www.finance.yahoo.com/q?s=%s&d=v1

To test it out, click on <u>T</u>ry it and type *ibm*, then select "OK." A new window containing current information on IBM from Yahoo! Finance should appear.
To add another search site to your list, follow these steps:

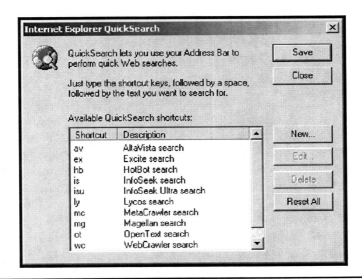

FIGURE 3.6   Internet Explorer QuickSearch

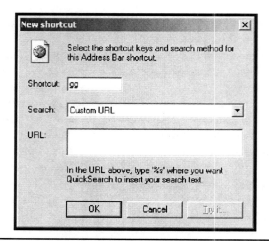

FIGURE 3.7 New Shortcut

1. *Go to the desired site and search the Web with it as you normally would (i.e., type in your search terms and then wait for the list of results to be displayed).*

2. *Look in the Address bar for the URL of the results list and find where your search terms appear in it. Highlight and copy the part of the URL* before *those terms.*

3. *Paste that partial URL into the "URL" section of the "New shortcut" dialog box in QuickSearch (see Figure 3.7).*

4. *Type %s where your search terms should be added.*

5. *Click on Try it . . . to test and make sure the shortcut works properly.*

Here are some QuickSearch shortcuts that can save you time in searching for information (the shortcut to use is in parentheses before the string of text you should enter into the URL field). *Note:* URL text should be entered as a continuous string with no breaks or spaces.

- Find out more about client hobbies and personal interests at About.com: (about) http://search.about.com/fullsearch.htm?terms=%s

- Research content for newsletter articles or broadcast e-mail messages at RefDesk:
  (ref) http://search.atomz.com/search/?sp-q=%s&sp-a=
  00020250-sp00000000

- Get intelligence on businesses you're targeting or competing with from YellowBrix:

  (ybci)
  http://infobrix.yellowbrix.com/pages/infobrix/coOverview.nsp?
  found=1&by_name=%s

- Look up meanings, spellings, and synonyms of words at Dictionary.com and Thesaurus.com:

  (def) http://dictionary.com/cgi-bin/dict.pl?term=%s
  (syn) http://www.thesaurus.com/cgi-bin/search?
  config=roget&words=%s

TIP: Check out *Ultrabar* (http://www.ultrabar.com), a cross between the Google toolbar and IE 5 Web Accessories. It's a free, very handy addition to make to IE.

---

7. Add an Address Bar to Your Desktop (Time Required: < 1 Minute)

Did you know it's possible to call up a Web page without opening IE first? Here's how you do it:

1. *Locate the Start button; the small bar that it's part of is called the "Taskbar."*

2. *Right click in a blank area of the taskbar.*

3. *Click "Toolbars," and then click "Address." An Address bar identical to the one included in IE will appear on the taskbar. Figure 3.8 shows what it will look like.*

Now type in the Web address (or *URL*) for the page you want to view in the box within your new Address bar and press *Enter*. IE will automatically open to that page.

FIGURE 3.8   An Address Bar on Your Desktop

> **TIP:** If you designate Google as your default search engine, you can type search terms into your desktop Address bar, press *Enter*, and IE will open to the list of Google results (and if you've installed Microsoft's "Web Accessories," it will work with other engines, too).

In late 2003, Google introduced a beta (i.e., test) version of a program called the Google Deskbar, which also allows you to search the Web using Google right from your computer's desktop without opening a browser window. Visit http://www.google.com/options/ for more information.

> The fastest way to open a Web page whose address starts in *www.*, and ends in *.com*, is to type the main section of the address in your browser's Address bar and then press *Ctrl + Enter*. The rest of the URL (*http://www.* and *.com*) will fill in automatically.

Beyond Google

I have talked about Google throughout the chapter. It's my first (and often only) stop when searching. But occasionally it doesn't provide what I'm looking for. Here are the other search sites I turn to when that happens.

Teoma (http://www.teoma.com), which means "expert" in Gaelic, is my first alternative. Teoma is every bit as clean and uncluttered as Google. It stands out because it interprets your search terms and can suggest ways to refine what you are looking for by adding more words to your request (in the "Refine" section of the search results page). It also provides a list of any link collections related to your search terms (under "Resources"). Teoma offers a free, downloadable search bar similar to Google's.

Vivisimo (http://www.vivisimo.com) groups search results in categories (folders) using the content of the pages it finds. For example, when I type in the words *lead lists*, the list of 200+ results is broken down into the categories including sales leads, consumer, mailing, and telemarketing lists,

American, and homeowners. You can look at a list of all the results, or click on any of the folders to review just a subset of results.

Clnet's Search (http://www.search.com) offers eight categories of specialized search (Business & Money, Downloads, People, to name three). Each, in turn, lets you choose from a handful of search sites relevant to that topic.

Dogpile (http://www.dogpile.com) and *Ixquick* (http://www.ixquick.com) are search sites that broadcast your terms to other search engines and display a list of the top results gathered from each.

> **TIP:** Add these search engine sites to your Web Accessories for IE QuickSearch list for faster access to the information they offer.

Now that we have looked at what the Web can offer and how to make the most of it, let's turn to setting up mechanisms and methods for leveraging the information you find online to build stronger relationships. That's the focus of Chapter 4—creating clear channels of communication with the audiences that matter most to you.

Notes

1. *The Value of Advice,* © 2000 Financial Planning Association.

2. *Top Gun Financial Sales—How to Double or Triple Your Results While Reducing Your Book,* D. Scott Kimball, © 2003, Dearborn Trade Publishing, p. 23.

3. http://www.sims.berkeley.edu/research/projects/how-much-info/summary.html.

4. http://www.jamesshuggins.com/h/tek1/how_big.htm.

5. The "l," referred to as the pipe or piping key, is usually found on the same key as the backspace (\).

6. If you haven't adjusted your browser since installing IE, you will find the Links toolbar compressed on the right-hand side of your screen next to the Address bar (the box where you type in Web addresses—look for the word "Links"). Stretch the toolbar's size by moving your mouse over the small vertical line to the left of where it says "Links" and then click and drag it to the left to make it as long as you want.

Build Relationships Through Better Communication

Using High Tech to Be in Higher Touch

"Information" and "communication" are often used interchangeably, but they signify quite different things. Information is giving out; communication is getting through.

—Sidney J. Harris, author

Do you make your living managing money or managing relationships? Too often advisors overlook the importance of communication in fostering and retaining loyal clients. They get caught up in the mechanics of the business and the "craft" of investing. They forget that well-cared-for clients are the key to referrals, the most important form of marketing there is.

A good communication system is built on three things: knowing your audience and the things they care about, having mechanisms for communicating with them about those issues, and delivering (ideally, exchanging) relevant content regularly.

In the last chapter, you discovered a variety of ways to mine the Web for useful information. In this one you're going to learn how to use that information and more to communicate more effectively with clients. Specifically, we're going to look at:

- How well you communicate with clients right now.

- Steps you can take to communicate even more effectively and consistently.

- ■ The role e-mail plays in a good client communication process.
- ■ How affluent clients and prospects are utilizing the Internet and the opportunities such use presents.
- ■ Innovative ways to work the Web to stay connected with the people you're targeting.

Follow the suggestions outlined and you'll build a powerful system for expanding your business by staying in closer contact with clients and others throughout the year.

How Good Are You?

Surveys show that clients like to hear regularly from their professional advisors-at least monthly and, ideally, more often. Think for a moment on your own experiences as a customer. Don't you expect people you buy services from to pay attention to your needs? What happens when they don't? At minimum, you're more open to the idea of taking your business elsewhere. And if things get bad enough, you actually do.

Your clients are the same way. In *Storyselling for Financial Advisors,* Scott West and Mitch Anthony point out that affluent clients are six times more likely to fire their advisors because of a poor relationship (87 percent) than because of investment performance (13 percent).[1] Lack of attention is often the reason why. What's worse, it's likely they will never tell you how they feel; they will just suddenly walk away from the relationship. On the other hand, staying in regular touch can pay big dividends. (Remember the Financial Planning Association study regarding referrals as the main source of new clients mentioned in Chapter 3?)

The message is clear: To get the business you want, concentrate on the business you already have, give clients the attention they deserve, and leverage those relationships into more introductions, more accounts, and more assets.

Take the following quiz to test the strength of your current connection (circle the appropriate answer to each question). Your responses will help you identify where you need to focus energy to get closer to your clients:

I have e-mail addresses for my top clients.	Yes	No
I know what their personal and professional interests are.	Yes	No

I read what they read.	Yes	No
I have sites bookmarked that cater to their interests.	Yes	No
I refer to those sites regularly to stay on top of current issues.	Yes	No
I contact clients routinely based on what I learn.	Yes	No
I can send mass-customized messages, letters, newsletters, and so on, at will.	Yes	No
I do so at least monthly.	Yes	No
Clients reciprocate in sharing information *they* think I and others I work with might be interested in.	Yes	No

Tally the number of "Yes" answers and interpret your results according to the following:

Total Yes Answers	*What Your Score Means*
9	Congratulations; you've created a solid system of client contact. Scan this chapter for ideas you may not have considered.
5–8	You're doing more right than wrong, but filling in the gaps in your communication could improve results. Use the planning process outlined in this chapter to map out a consistent schedule.
1–4	You are in serious danger of losing clients to an attentive competitor. Implementing the steps outlined in the next section should be your highest priority.
0	Consider another line of work that doesn't require much interaction with others.

Seven Steps to Improvement

If you didn't score as well as you'd like on the "connection quotient," all is not lost. Here are specific steps you can take to improve your results the next time around.

1. Get an E-Mail Address from Every Client Who Has One

These days, having clients e-mail addresses ranks with having their phone number and street address; you almost can't do business without it. If you don't have a current address for each client that uses e-mail, here are some ways to obtain one:

- Send out a self-addressed stamped postcard requesting it with your next mailing.

- Divvy up your client list among your staff and start making calls (or hire an intern).

- Ask every client who calls your office if their e-mail address has changed.

Before you convince yourself that your clients, all seniors, don't use the Web, realize that many well-off, well-educated seniors are active Internet users. (Why? They're retired, they have time to explore that others don't!) Don't dismiss that possibility with your clients without being doubly sure; you may be missing a golden opportunity!

2. Help Those Who Don't Have an Address Set Up One

When a client says they don't have e-mail, find out whether it's because they don't want it or because they don't know how to set one up. If it's the latter, offer to help.

Microsoft's *Hotmail,* described in the last chapter, is one easy option. Stay alert for opportunities to educate those clients about how to make smarter use of the Web generally (a number of ways are suggested later in the chapter); you may open your clients up to a world they never knew existed.

TIP: You can still find free e-mail accounts on the Web, but most have limitations. To see what's available, check the *Google Directory* under Computer > Internet > E-mail > Free > Directories and Guides.

---

3. Learn How Your Clients Like to Spend Their Time and What's Important to Them

While some businesses, in a manner of speaking, comb alley dumpsters looking for information on their customers, financial advisors frequently sit on an untapped gold mine of knowledge they don't use. Go back and review client profiles and completed product applications for your top group (those who gen-

erate most of your revenue, and so deserve the bulk of your time and energy).
Cull the following information:

Investment profile	Professional associations
Goals	Marital status
Concerns	Religious affiliation (if volunteered)
Date of birth	Clubs
Occupation	Hobbies
Industry	Interests
Employer	Education

 TIP: Whenever you're talking with a top client, make it your goal to learn and make note of two new facts about them. What you discover may enhance your understanding of who they are and what they need/want from you.

---

4. Manage That Client (and Prospect) Information in a Database

Customer Relationship Management (CRM) is a popular buzzword these days. It's a new term for an old idea: stay close to your clients. Used smartly, software can make that job much easier; the challenge in financial services is coming up with an industry standard. If you work for a large corporation, the system you use is likely dictated by your employer. Even if you're an independent, the products you offer will influence what kind of system you want. As a result, the "contact management" software continuum stretches widely, from off-the-shelf programs to one-of-a-kind solutions.

Space doesn't allow for a detailed look at each alternative, but here are five categories of products to consider if you're shopping for a solution. Realize there will be trade-offs to any decision you make. Popular generic software is inexpensive but likely won't meet your precise needs without modification. Custom solutions may give you everything you want, but at a much higher price. Before deciding which way to go, do your homework: ask other advisors in your area, study group, or your broker-dealer what they use, would they recommend it, and why (or why not).

1. *Commercial off-the-shelf e-mail software.* If you're looking for an inexpensive (free) way to manage basic information on a limited

number of contacts, one tool to consider is *Microsoft Outlook Express* (http://support.microsoft.com/support/ie/outlookexpress/win32/), bundled as part of Internet Explorer (IE). It lets you catalog essential contact information using the Windows Address Book. You can also create groups of contacts (e.g., top clients, prospects), which makes broadcasting messages easier. Of course, there's also Outlook Express's big brother *Outlook* (http://www.microsoft.com/office/outlook), part of the Microsoft Office suite, which will do those things and more.

2. *Commercial (generic) contact management.* Moving beyond e-mail programs takes you into the contact-management category. There are dozens of products to choose from. Some of the best known are:

- ACT! (http://www.act.com).

- Goldmine (http://www.frontrange.com/goldmine).

- Maximizer (http://www.maximizer.com).

- Salesforce (http://www.salesforce.com), a Web-based solution.

My view is that the similarities of these programs (and the benefits they can offer you) far outnumber their differences. More than which product you use, success is a function of learning the capabilities of the one you own, and then using it!

I do, however, have a suggestion if you work alone or in a small office. Give serious consideration to ACT!. It's reasonably priced, easy to customize, has a support network of hundreds of certified technicians, and a wide range of third-party add-on products. Its popularity (4 million+ users) means you will have an easier time hiring people who are experienced in working with and supporting it. The downside: it won't integrate with your portfolio management software or financial-planning program right off the shelf (though the firms below have addressed that issue).

3. *Generic contact-management programs that have been customized.* At least three companies have created customized versions of ACT that they market to financial advisors: *Act4Advisors* from Allied Financial Soft-

---

TIP: Check out *ACT! Addons* (http://www.actaddons.com) for software applications designed by third-party developers to enhance ACT! (you can find similar products for GoldMine at *GoldMine Add-on Store* (http://www.addonstore.com/goldmine/).

ware, Inc. (http://www.software4advisors.com), *Brokers*ACT* (http://www.brokersact.com), and *CyberBroker* from Max Pro Systems (http://www.maxprosystems.com). In addition, Frontrange Solutions has created a version of their *Goldmine* software that integrates with Financial Computer Support Inc.'s dbCAMS (http://www.dbcams.com) portfolio tracking and reporting software.

4. *Industry-specific contact management.*   As much as everybody wants it, I've yet to see a true one-size-fits-all CRM software solution for advisors. Who wouldn't love to combine financial planning, portfolio management, and client management into one program? The problem is finding one that covers all the bases, and the products, you need it to cover. The eight programs listed below attempt to address that challenge, or at least parts of it:

- Advisors Assistant (http://www.advisorsassistant.com)
- The Bill Good System (http://www.billgood.com)
- Brokers Ally (http://www.brokersally.com)
- E-Z Data (http://www.ez-data.com)
- Junxure-i (http://www.gowithcrm.com)
- ProTracker (http://www.protracker.com)
- Qube from Advent (http://www.advent.com)
- Text Library System (http://www.financialsoftware.com)

5. *One-of-a-kind, firm-specific solutions.*   Finally, there are the "enterprise" systems many large firms have implemented to meet their unique needs. If you fall in that category, I encourage you to take full advantage of the training and support your company offers to understand and exploit the capabilities of your particular system.

5. Develop Your Message Content

Beyond sending out quarterly reports, an annual account review, and a birthday card, most advisors struggle to come up with reasons to be in touch with their clients. That's why one of the first steps suggested was to review the information you already have on your best clients and organize it, so you're positioned to take action on it.

Knowing what topics your clients care about, being able to uncover information about those subjects online (thanks to what you learned in Chapter 3), and drawing from the suggestions in the final section of this chapter, you should have no problem coming up with additional reasons to be in touch. (You're aiming at a minimum of twelve "touches," so you need to come up with seven more.)

You don't have to be a professional writer to provide good content. There are many resources you can tap to develop it: preapproved materials, software templates, companies that specialize in ghostwriting newsletters and articles, and even media consultants.

Your first contact should be the marketing department of companies you work with, to see what materials they offer. Call the internal sales desk, or ask your wholesaler. Programs on targeting different audiences are widely available: women investors, business owners, retirees, minorities, the super affluent, and so forth. All of those can be sources of information worth sharing with clients.

In the software template category, check out:

- Sales LetterWorks (http://www.roundlakepublishing.com/SalesLW.htm)
- Text Library System (http://www.financialsoftware.com)
- WriteExpress Easy Letters (http://www.writeexpress.com)

For ghost-written publications, take a look at:

- Advisor Products Client Newsletter (http://www.advisorproducts.com)
- Newkirk Products (http://www.npi-opus.com)
- R&R Newkirk (http://www.rrnewkirk.com) (not affiliated with Newkirk Products)

 TIP: *CompanyNewsletters.com* (http://www.companynewsletters.com) offers a library of helpful articles if you're contemplating starting your own newsletter. Here's a good example: "Ten tips to make sure your newsletter gets read, not tossed."

Finally, if you want to construct a full-scale PR campaign, contact Beth Chapman at *Ink & Air* (http://www.inkair.com), who helps advisors and product providers raise their visibility with the financial services media, or read *The Guide to Financial Public Relations: How to Stand Out in the Midst of Competitive Clutter and Credibility Marketing* by Larry Chambers.[2]

6. Map Out a Communication Calendar

Having a good story to share is meaningless if you don't actually get the message out. There are two ways to do that: one spontaneously, the other scripted. We'll talk about spur-of-the-moment opportunities in the next step, but right now let's focus on how to coordinate a planned, prepared, and packaged communications campaign.

First, realize that there are a number of different ways to connect with your audience, 15 of which are highlighted in the following box.

---

15 WAYS TO COMMUNICATE WITH CLIENTS

Interactive	*Passive*
Face-to-face	Audio/video tape
One-on-one call	Live broadcast
Group phone call	Letter
Web conference	Voice mail
Web chat	E-mail
Survey	Article
Discussion Lists	Book

Your Web site

The challenge is marrying the message you want to share with the right medium to deliver it. Using the *Communication Planning Worksheets* in the Appendix B will make the task easier. Here's how to use them.

1. Start with the Client Communication Idea Calendar (worksheet 1). Fill in important happenings throughout the year that you already have anticipated: quarterly account reviews, annual meetings, birthdays, client anniversary dates, significant milestones, and so forth. Put each event in the column it relates to: financial, personal, professional, or family.

2. After you've written down all the things you can based on what you know about each group, use the list in "101 Ways to Get Closer to Clients" later in this chapter to supplement your list. Keep going until you've written down at least 30 to 35 ideas; you're aiming for at least 12

very good ones, so the more you come up with, the stronger your pool of ideas. Consider asking others for input; more people equals more ideas.

3. Use the Client Communication Matrix (worksheet 2) to record the topics you want to pursue. Strive to achieve a balance among each of the four categories on worksheet 1 in the items you write down on worksheet 2.

4. Go through your worksheet 2 list item by item and check off appropriate mechanisms for getting the word out, then take a second pass through the worksheet and circle the *best* method for each item.

5. Finally, use worksheet 3, the Client Communication Schedule, to finalize your plan. The form provides space for up to three items per month.

TIP: *Butler Webs* (http://www.butlerwebs.com/holidays/) offers one of the most complete calendars of holidays and noteworthy events you can find on the Web. Use it to brainstorm ideas for filling in any gaps in your calendar.

---

7. Keep Your Eyes and Ears Constantly Open for Useful Information

Not every opportunity can be planned ahead of time. Sometimes something pops up unexpectedly and presents a perfect opportunity to communicate with your audience. The 1-cent-stamp idea from Amazon mentioned in Chapter 1 is a good example.

Here's another. In late 2002, the FBI announced its largest identity theft arrest ever, involving stolen credit information from more than 30,000 victims. What better chance to remind clients of some simple precautions to take to reduce the chance of falling prey to the same fate? The *Kip's Tip* in the following box went out three hours after the headline broke on CNN.

HELP YOUR CLIENTS AVOID IDENTITY THEFT

Monday night's announcement of arrests in an identity theft crime involving at least 30,000 victims was shocking. News like that is a harsh reminder of the downside of living in a digital world; it leaves all of us feeling exposed and vulnerable. There are ways to reduce the risk of exposure, and now is an excellent opportunity to remind clients what they are. Here are three preventive steps anyone can take to stay ahead of identity thieves:

1. Order a credit report from the three major credit bureaus: *Equifax* (800.685.1111; http://www.equifax.com), *Experian* (888.397.3742; http://www.experian.com) and *Trans Union* (800.916.8800; http://www.transunion.com). The FTC recommends reviewing those reports at least annually to ensure your information is correct and to catch any unrecognized (and potentially fraudulent) transactions.

2. Before disposing of them, shred bills and other materials that contain account numbers or passwords, birth dates, social security numbers, or anything else that could be useful to someone bent on stealing from you. *Staples* (http://www.staples.com) carries dozens of shredders. Search on the keyword "shredder" to see what's available.

3. Be careful what you share via e-mail or at unsecured Web sites. Including personal data like what's mentioned above in regular (i.e. unencrypted) e-mail is only inviting a problem. So is typing that data into forms at sites that aren't secure. Check for "https" (not just "http") at the beginning of any Web page URL as well as a small padlock icon at the bottom of your IE window before providing anything sensitive.

Want to know more? One leading source of information is the *US Government's Site on Identity Theft,* run by the FTC (http://www.consumer.gov/idtheft/). It includes sections on how to minimize your risk, what to do if you're a victim, and how to file a complaint.

How can you be helpful to your clients? Here are five suggestions:

1. Put together and distribute an identity theft prevention checklist.

2. Deliver a talk on how to protect yourself at your next client appreciation event.

3. Send them an annual reminder to request fresh copies of their credit reports and offer assistance in reviewing the reports, especially to older clients.

4. Negotiate a discount with your local office supply company for clients who purchase a shredder from their store.

5. Ready a list/library of resources (books, articles, contacts, and phone numbers) to help clients whose identities have been stolen regain control. (One place to start is http://www.identitytheft.org.)

(continued)

According to an April 2001 Financial Planning magazine article, the FBI ranks identity theft as the fastest growing white-collar crime in America. Educating yourself about the issue enough to counsel clients on what steps they should take to avoid the problem is a perfect example of how to provide excellent value-added service. In this season of giving thanks, can you think of a better way to show how much you appreciate them than demonstrating your concern for their welfare?

When you find good content that's not immediately applicable, put it in a clipping file, either in your knowledge journal or *SurfSaver* (http://www .surfsaver.com). To better organize content, create separate sections/files (market-related information, hobbies/interests, trivia, factoids, etc.). Get others looking for valuable news, too; not only staff but study group members or people you cross-refer business with.

TIP: Remember, if you would like to receive the free *Kip's Tip* e-mail, visit http://www.kipstips.com to sign up.

The Pros and Cons of E-Mail

Of the 15 ways to communicate listed in the previous section, e-mail is by far the fastest, most cost-effective method. Still, it remains underutilized by most advisors. Poor writing (and typing) skills, lack of time, and absence of a systemized approach are a few of the reasons why. Add the hassle of compliance review and the reluctance to employ it is understandable.

Yet e-mail (when it's done well) offers a sense of immediacy, intimacy, and responsiveness that's tough to match. When time is of the essence and you just can't get to everybody individually, e-mail provides a bridge.

Here's a case in point. Norm Boone owns an independent advisory firm in San Francisco that works with high-net-worth clients (http://www.BooneAdvisors .com). Late on the evening of September 11, 2001, he sent out the following message:

To our clients and friends,

Tuesday's tragedy in New York and Washington stunned and shocked all of us. Our thoughts and prayers are with the victims and families of this violence. Many of us will have lost friends and our sympathies go out to each of you. If you can do so, we urge you to give blood, in support of those who will need this vital gift.

I know many of you have concerns about what actions, if any, you should take in response to possibly troubled markets. While it is too soon for any of us to have all the facts, we felt it important to communicate our perspectives to you as quickly as possible.

Events of this magnitude often have worldwide political and economic effects. It is very possible that the markets will be turbulent in the near term, once they reopen. But in the past, market upsets associated with major world events like this have been relatively short-lived. Selling in response to such events has rarely been a good long-term decision.

Major tragedies such as this are frightening and it is a normal first urge to want to seek safety for your investments. That being said, we strongly believe that the best strategy is to stay the course through what will undoubtedly be a turbulent market period. As events unfold and facts become clearer, we can discuss what strategic adjustments, if any, are appropriate. We will continue to share our thoughts in the days and weeks ahead.

We welcome your calls and the opportunity to discuss these events and the implications for your own lives with you.

Treasure each day those who are special to you.

Norman M. Boone, CFP

Brief, reassuring, and heartfelt, all in 275 words, less than a single screen of text. Of course, Norm and his colleagues were also making calls to selected clients, but his quick note went a long way in calming those who couldn't be reached right away.

Let me be clear: I am *not* suggesting that e-mail be your sole means of communication. It needs to be *part* of a coordinated communication plan that incorporates the other approaches already mentioned. At the same time you have to ask yourself, "What other mechanism allows me to deliver a personalized message to as many people as I want, instantly, at little or no cost?" Can you think of one? I can't.

TIP: Categorize your clients by how they use e-mail: obsessively, regularly, occasionally, or never. Users who use e-mail frequently probably prefer to get information electronically, as it minimizes interruptions, saves time, and allows them to respond when it's convenient for them. Users who use e-mail infrequently are just the opposite; they may be annoyed to get messages from you that they really wanted to be told about in person or by telephone. Match your communication method with your clients' preferences.

As good as e-mails can be, you still have to be careful with it. The two most common mistakes I see are *message dumping* and *poorly developed content*.

1. Message Dumping

Sending a message to a group where all the recipients' names are visible at the top is an unnecessary blunder. A "personal" note, no matter how well-written, loses luster when readers see it went to 50 people. Clients like to think they are the only one you're thinking of, even if they know you work with others. Why blow the chance to make them feel special? (And don't forget about confidentiality; many resent their address being made public without their permission.) The quickest fix is to put your own name in the To: field and recipients' names in the Bcc: (blind carbon copy) field - so the only name they see at the top is yours.

2. Poorly Developed Content

Before you broadcast any message, make sure it's something recipients *want* to see. Excessive e-mailing makes you look like a spammer. Be sure the "what's in it for me" in your message is clear to the reader. Show them how to save time, money, or aggravation, avoid worry, why a strategy you suggested still makes sense, or why you're recommending a change. Spell it out. Edit ruthlessly. Better yet, ask someone else to edit it for you.

TIP: To improve your writing skill, study what others write. To sharpen your sense of what flows well and what doesn't, analyze newspaper and magazine articles and study correspondence you receive that strikes you as especially effective.

Effective E-Mail Strategies

Here, in their own words, are three examples of ways people have used e-mail to broaden their base of business. As you'll see, these methods range from simple, straightforward situations to very sophisticated strategies.

Joe B.

The approach Joe uses, good old-fashioned drip marketing to clients, is earning him between $25,000 and $50,000 of additional income, and priceless points for staying in touch. Not a bad revenue stream, considering that his cost of getting the message out (aside from his time) is next to nothing.

> I try to obtain an e-mail address for every client and prospect. For instance, when we open accounts I ask people if they use the Internet; most do. If they say yes, I ask if I can get their e-mail address so that I can offer ideas or information to them without interrupting their business day.
>
> I do a lot of reading, especially Saturday mornings, and use the time to identify economic trends and where to invest to take advantage of them. Then I develop a list of clients who might relate to that theme, and drop them a note customized—maybe starting with a comment on their children, future career plans, etc. During the week, rather than cold call, I'll send out 3 to 5 different e-mail messages like that that discuss either specific investment ideas or general market concerns. During the past two years, I have found that these messages generated about $500 to $1000 per week in additional gross revenue.
>
> What the approach does is allow me to contact clients in a low threat manner. It's also helped me hang on to accounts when they've moved out of town. I use e-mail to stay in touch because it seems to get answered, while calls might not get returned. In one case, by staying in touch, I was able to get a $350,000 IRA rollover from a client . . . .

GIVE CLIENTS A SHORTCUT FOR REACHING YOU BY E-MAIL

Want to make it easier for your best clients to get in touch with you by e-mail? Put a shortcut on their PC's desktop that automatically opens a blank e-mail message addressed to you anytime they click on it.

Follow the steps below to set one up on your own computer, then share the instructions with your clients:

(continued)

1. On your desktop, right-click and select "New," then shortcut.
2. In the small wizard that opens (titled "Create Shortcut") type ***mailto:*** followed by your e-mail address in the field underneath where it says "Type the location of the item" (there should be no spaces in the string, for example, mailto:joeadvisor@aol.com).
3. Select "Next."
4. In the field underneath where it says "Type a name for this shortcut," type ***E-mail*** [your name] (i.e., E-mail Joe).
5. Select "Finish" and you're done. A new icon labeled "E-mail [your name]" will appear on your desktop.

Once it's in place, clients can double-click on that icon anytime they have a question that needs answering or they see something online they want to forward you; a blank message preaddressed to you pops open ready to be filled in by them.

Lynn M.

Cultivating relationships through regular communication may begin with clients, but it shouldn't end there. Here's how Lynn parlayed a monthly e-mail message into relationships with two media outlets in Dallas—and four different appearances on television, on the same day! (Wouldn't you like *that* kind of exposure?!)

After attending your session at (the FPA's) Success Forum 2000, we devoted part of our planning retreat later that year to considering the info you shared. We carefully created our e-mail groups, discussed places to look for appropriate "Interesting Facts" to send each month, and basically put the plan in motion. I used ACT! to set up groups of clients, prospects, and centers of influence, and began e-mailing them a monthly "Interesting Facts" message. We included the financial editor for the Dallas *Morning News* in our COI group, because I wanted to increase our exposure with the media.

In August 2001, she (the editor) was planning for a series of articles about recent layoffs and sent a broadcast e-mail through the FPA to the planning community asking for help. I replied and she recognized me from my messages. I provided her with the outline for her story and she quoted me three times! WFAA saw her story and wanted to run a similar series on their *Good Morning Texas* program and asked her whom she recommended to interview. She gave them my name.

Once I had established contact with the producer, I added her to my centers of influence e-mail group. She was then copied on everything that went out to our clients beginning the afternoon of 9/11. By 3:00 P.M. that afternoon I had a message out to all groups, including key media contacts. Because of swift action, our clients were calm and well informed throughout this tragedy, and I ended up being interviewed not once, but four times on different TV news programs.

The monthly e-mail messages cost us nothing, and networking expenses are minimal (I think I might have taken one PR contact to lunch and spent $50). After the initial planning, much of what happens on a day-to-day basis is being present and acting right away when opportunity arises.

TIP: Visit *NewsLink* (http://www.newslink.org) to find the links to news papers, TV, and radio stations in your area. Call each organization to learn who covers money and investing issues. Before making contact, Google each reporter's name to see what you can learn about them. If the organization's site includes a "Biographies" section, scan it for background. Read and study *Get Media Smart! Build Your Reputation, Referrals and Revenues with Media Marketing* by Beth Chapman (http://www.inkair.com) for expert advice on cultivating relationships with the media.

Andrew B.

Andrew works for a Toronto-based mutual fund group. We first met when his firm hired me to present a workshop on technology and the Internet to advisors across Canada. While a field wholesaler, Andrew created a communication system for keeping in front of advisors in his market using e-mail and the company Web site. Here's how he described it.

I create and broadcast a monthly e-zine for advisors, the *Wholesalers Notebook,* which I started doing on paper in 1998. Today, it reaches an audience of about 1000 electronically, and typically generates at least 6 inbound replies/calls within 24 hours (the record high is 44 replies). It's become a very effective tool for both lead generation and client-servicing.

The e-zine is actually published at the Web site; the e-mail broadcast gives the advisor links to check out various sections of it. I give a text file with the updated content to my assistant, and she uses EZMail to broadcast it out. I create it in a Word file template, then transfer to HTML using Dreamweaver. A paper version goes out by snail mail to any advisor in my database who doesn't have an e-mail address (and even then I'm trying to get one from them).

To me, having a Web site is part of being a "complete" wholesaler, who is just as good at marketing himself as he is at marketing his products. It's crowded out there, not just with products, but with people too. I needed a way to achieve superior positioning. The Web site and e-zine were the best things I could think of. Most of the evidence of the payoff for the extra effort is anecdotal (e.g., a top producer says "I recognize you, you're the guy with the Web site; make sure you stop by my office before you leave"). Usually it's the other way around, me knocking on his door like everyone else. . . . to no avail. The key question is "What do I do that causes a top producer to call me and ask me if I've got time to see him?" If I can answer that question correctly, I'll succeed in wholesaling.

He must be doing something right; not long after sharing his story, the company promoted Andrew to be its Vice President of National Accounts.

INSTANT MESSAGING: EXPRESS E-MAIL FOR YOUR BEST CLIENTS

One way to broaden the channel of communication with clients is to use instant messaging (IM). Remember Batman on TV and in the movies? Installing IM software on both your and clients' computers is like setting up a bat phone between you—a way to reach one another instantly via PC; like e-mail but faster, because your message doesn't go to a mailbox, it goes right to the recipient's (computer) desktop where it appears in a small window. (And don't worry, you control whether you appear online to others or not.)

IM's popularity has skyrocketed in the past few years. Total use across the United States exceeds 40 million, and many of your clients and prospects are in that group. Assuming the use of IM is permitted by your firm, here are five ways to exploit it as a client service tool:

1. Offer "after-hours" access to selected clients.
2. Save time by eliminating certain types of phone calls.
3. Archive exchanges for security and accuracy.
4. Share files with your team (in and out of the office).
5. Set alerts to remind you of certain events.

The best known IM services are *AOL Instant Messenger* (http://www .aim.com), *ICQ* (http://web.icq.com/), *MSN Messenger* (http://messenger .msn.com) and *Yahoo! Messenger* (http://messenger.yahoo.com/). *Trillian* (http://www.trillian.cc) lets you communicate with subscribers of all of those services using a single interface. There are also products designed specifically for corporate users: *FaceTime* (http://www.facetime.com) and *Jabber* (http://www.jabber.com) are two examples.

Whatever IM program(s) you use, be sure that copies of all conversations a regulator would consider correspondence are archived where they can easily be retrieved.

TIP: People who IM regularly abbreviate to speed things up: BRB (be right back), FWIW (for what it's worth), IMO (in my opinion), IOW (in other words), etc. (BTW, if U C something U don't recognize, look for an explanation at *Acronym Finder* (http://www .acronymfinder.com).)

Mastering the Electronic Medium

Whatever forms of electronic communication you use, here are seven things worth remembering to employ it more successfully.

1. Keep Messages as Brief as Possible

Mark Twain supposedly said, "Forgive me for the long letter. I didn't have time to write a short one." The more frequently you communicate, the shorter your messages should be. A good rule of thumb: limit their length to two screens of text or less.

2. Organize Your Message Content

When you have to write something longer, organize content into sections with different headings and put a table of contents at the top of the message; that way readers can scan and scroll to the section(s) they are interested in. You can also insert hyperlinks to more detailed information on the Web.

TIP: Hyperlinking to Web sites is not only a smart way to keep messages short; it can also help you avoid copyright violations. It's illegal to copy and share someone else's work verbatim without their permission, but you can summarize an article and include a link to it. For more information on what constitutes "fair use," visit the *Library of Congress Copyright Office* at http://www.copyright.gov.

---

3. Write a Compelling Subject Line

If you want to make sure your messages get read, give the recipient a reason to open them. Whenever possible, frame the header as a benefit statement for the reader. Write it after you've written your message.

4. Use Your Signature to Spotlight Your Services or Your Web Site

Most e-mail programs let you automatically insert standard text (called a "signature") at the bottom of every e-mail message you send. Use it. Include your phone number and your web site. Spice it up with a quote, a quick tip, or a Web site worth looking at, but be sure to freshen the information at least monthly. Two good sources for quotes are *Bartleby* (http://www.bartleby.com) and *The Quotations Page* (http://www.quotationspage.com).

5. Learn How to Send Mass Customized E-Mails

Mass customization means sending individualized messages to more than one person at the same time. If you have ever done a "mail merge" with a word processor, you have "mass customized" correspondence. The simplest way to mass customize an e-mail message is to put the recipient's name at the beginning of an otherwise uniform message. On the other end of the spectrum are situations where you want to pull multiple pieces of information from a person's record in your database and insert them into different sections of a template.

To find out if your e-mail or contact management program supports mail merging, open its Help function (by pressing the *F1* key from within the program) and type **e-mail merge** or **mail merge** in the Help index to see what comes up, or contact the product's technical support group for guidance.

TIP: There are Web-based e-mail programs that can make the job of personalizing messages easier. Three worth looking at are *Connecting Point* (http://www.romni.com), *Constant Contact* (http://www.constantcontact.com), and *Client Dynamics* (http://www.clientdynamics.net).

TIP: *Slipstick's Outlook and Exchange Solutions Center* (http://www.slipstick.com) is a great source of answers to questions on using Microsoft Outlook, such as how to use it to do mail merges.

6. Understand the Rules

Working in a regulated industry, you're responsible for knowing the ground rules on communicating. Throughout the book, I've encouraged you to make sure you're familiar with your firm's internal compliance guidelines. Another resource to consult if you are a registered rep is the *NASDR's Internet Guide for Registered Representatives* (http://www.nasdr.com/4040.asp), which includes sections on sending e-mail, as well as guidelines for communicating in chat rooms, on bulletin boards, and using an Internet home page.

7. Never, Never, Never Send Something Readers Will View as Spam

Once in a while someone asks about mass e-mailing prospects. My answer is always the same: Don't do it. Junk e-mail is a huge problem, and getting bigger. Is it worth risking your reputation as a highly regarded professional for the slim chance you might land a new client through blind e-mail marketing? Invest your time, energy, and marketing dollars instead in building a good opt-in e-mail program where the only people you send to are those that have asked to receive what you offer.

TIP: Think twice about forwarding jokes or other humorous e-mails you receive. Bad judgment has cost some firms millions of dollars in settlements. Be very careful; you wouldn't want what you wrote showing up on the front page of the newspaper, would you?

The Affluent + The Internet = Opportunity

Back when the Internet was a novelty, rich, well-educated consumers were the first to embrace it. They still do. Those same people are using it today for a variety of purposes. According to Forrester Research's *The Millionaire Online* report, the four most popular online activities among the affluent are e-mailing, searching for information, viewing stock quotes, and visiting financial sites.

What Millionaires Do Online	
Activity	*Participation Rate* %
Send e-mail	94
Use search engines	73
View stock quotes	63
Visit financial sites	38
Visit reference sites	35
Look for medical information	33
Read periodicals	29
Use directories/city guides	25

Source: Forrester Research.

Just like you, those people (your clients) are struggling to avoid information overload. You've got a wide-open opportunity to show them how to overcome the problem. Why not put together a client-appreciation event that shows them how to do it? As a relationship-builder, it's an appealing idea for several reasons:

- People always want to learn ways they can save time and money, or avoid frustration (and you'll get points for showing them how).

- Talking about it with clients will give you insight into their interests, lifestyles, and so on.

- It offers a chance to showcase your firm's Web site, how it can help, and how to use it.

At the top of Forrester's list is e-mail. Here are some common challenges clients encounter in working with e-mail, things you could help them solve in a well put together seminar:

- Setting up and maintaining distribution lists/groups of family, friends, and others (some people call them e-mail "trees").
- How to avoid spam.
- Protecting yourself from viruses.
- Working with (i.e., sending, receiving, and storing) attachments.
- Switching e-mail providers.

When it comes to working with the Web, here are things your clients would like to know:

- Which tools (browser, search engine, etc.) are best and how they work.
- How to find what they need and avoid what they don't.
- How to eliminate pop-up ads.
- How to view, download, and save files.
- Easy ways to keep track of and share useful sites.

Finally, don't forget teaching them the things *you* want to be sure they know:

- Where to find your Web site and what they should use it for.
- How to access their financial account(s) online.
- How to reach you by instant messaging (if you use it).
- How to open, read, and save PDF files you send them.

TIP: For more information on where to get presentation content on any of the topics just mentioned, visit http://www.winningclients inawiredworld.com

---

I even know of advisors who send interns to clients' homes to help those clients get investment accounts set up online or get a new PC up and running smoothly. Talk about customer service! What does that have to do with managing their money? Maybe nothing. But it has *everything* to do with creating loyal clients who love what you do and tell the world about it. The bottom line: If you're willing to think creatively, there's no limit to the ways you can get closer to clients and help them succeed.

101 Ways to Get Closer to Clients

Brainstorming a list of reasons to be in touch with clients and others can be fun, but it's time-consuming to create such a list from scratch. This final section is included to make the job faster and easier. Take what you can use and leave what you can't. Some of these ideas will hit home for you, and some may not fit your style. It's your call.

The first thing to do when using the Web to understand your clients better is to search on their name for what's published about them. Searching for information about yourself is called "ego surfing"; looking up what's there about your customers is just smart business. You may not get something on all your clients or even any of them, but you never know unless you try. The more visible and notable the person is within the community, the more likely you are to find information on them online.

 TIP: Create a "Background on Top Clients" folder in your IE Favorites for bookmarking search results pages that list results on top clients and prospects. Once saved, anytime you click on one of those pages, a fresh list of results will be generated. Reviewing those pages periodically is a good way to stay on top of what's being published about the people you're interested in.

A second thing worth knowing is how to find phone numbers, addresses, or e-mail accounts online. Calling 411 is a thing of the past. Today you can find all those things and more instantly at a number of sites. One is *The Ultimates* (http://www.theultimates.com). Just enter a first and last name, city, and state one time and select from a half dozen leading online directories to search for information you want in Infospace, WhoWhere, Switchboard, among other sites. You can find a specific business (or type of business) the same way, and many business listings also include a link to the company's site and e-mail.

TIP: Enter a name, city, and state abbreviation at Google, and at the top of the results list, you'll get phone numbers and addresses for people and businesses who match your criteria. Click on "More phonebook listings" at the bottom of the list if what you're looking for isn't displayed.

There are literally thousands of ways to use the Internet to get closer to clients. Below are 25 of them (the rest of the "101" list is at http://www.winningclientsin awiredworld.com). Some of these are investment related, some are not. I've included keywords you can use to locate other sites on the same theme, so that if the site mentioned disappears, you'll have a head start in finding a replacement.

1. Get clients' opinions on ways to improve your services. (http://www .zoomerang.com)   Keywords: *free feedback surveys*

2. Dispatch an intern to set clients up with online access to the financial accounts they have with you (and others). (http://www.monstertrak .com)   Keywords: *post college internship job*

3. Publish an opt-in (i.e., permission-based) e-mail newsletter. (http://www .becentral.com)   Keywords: *opt-in e-mail newsletter*

4. E-mail an electronic birthday or anniversary card. (http://www.blue mountain.com)   Keywords: *electronic greeting cards*

5. Create and send a collage of famous events on their birthday. (http://www.thehistorychannel.com, http://www.todayinhistory.com, http://www.biography.com, http://www.on-this-day.com, and http:// www.thehistorynet.com)   Keywords: *today in history*

6. Clue them in on what's happening in the place where they were born. (http://www.onlinenewspapers.com)   Keywords: *online directory newspapers*

7. Show them how to order/refill prescriptions over the Web. (http:// www.drugstore.com)   Keywords: *online prescriptions*

8. Point them to where they can get a free copy of their credit report. (http://www.freecreditreport.com)   Keywords: *free credit report*

9. Send them flowers on Valentine's Day. (http://www.proflowers.com) Keyword: *flowers*

10. Make a donation online to their favorite charity. (http://www.justgive .org)   Keywords: *find charity make online*

11. Assist them in finding information on medical conditions. (http:// www.webmd.com)   Keywords: *health medical*

12. Monitor news of their company or industry. (http://biz.yahoo.com/ industry)   Keywords: *online industry news sources*

13. Give them a hand in researching career opportunities online. (http:// www.rileyguide.com)   Keywords: *career guide*

14. Learn more about their religious traditions/beliefs. (http://www.beliefnet .com)   Keywords: *religions spirituality*

15. Show them an easy way to manage all their frequent flyer accounts in a single place. (http://www.myairmiles.com)   Keywords: *frequent flyer account status*

16. Help them shop for bargain airfares, hotel rates, and rental cars. (http://www.priceline.com or http://www.sidestep.com)   Keywords: *discount travel airfare hotels*

17. Point out how to renew their car registration at their state motor vehicle department. (http://www.carbuyingtips.com/dmv.htm)   *state motor vehicle Web sites*

18. Show them how to cut down the amount of junk mail they receive. (http://www.dmaconsumers.org/offmailinglist.html)   Keywords: *reduce junk mail*

19. Fill out change-of-address cards for them when they move. (http:// www.moversguide.com)   Keywords: *change of address*

20. Assist them in finding financial aid or scholarship money for college. (http://www.finaid.com)   Keywords: *college scholarship guide aid*

21. Set them up a golf tee time. (http://www.teemaster.com or http://www .teetimes.com)   Keywords: *golf tee time reservation*

22. Remind them when it's time to change the oil, rotate the tires, or replace the battery. (http://www.carcarecity.com)   Keywords: *car maintenance reminder service*

23. Give them a gift certificate to their favorite store or catalog. (http://www .giftcertificates.com or http://www.webcertificate.com)   Keywords: *online gift certificates*

24. Shop with them for a new car. (http://www.autobytel.com)   Keywords: *new used car pricing service*

25. Shop for a lower mortgage rate or home equity loan. (http://www .bankrate.com)   Keywords: *mortgage rate comparison*

THREE SITES TO SPARK YOUR CREATIVITY

One great way to come up with your own "101" list is to periodically review "best of the Web" articles in leading publications. Here are three worth consulting, not only for potential client communication ideas, but for ideas on improving your own business.

USA Today Hot Sites
(http://www.usatoday.com/tech/webguide/front.htm)
   Every day, *USA Today* publishes a list of five sites, along with a quick paragraph on each about what makes them interesting. You can scan these daily listings all the way back to 1996 to see what information might apply to people you do business with. You can even sign up for a free e-mail newsletter to have these Hot Sites (along with other stories from the paper's "Tech" section) delivered to you automatically.

> **TIP:** If you just want to see the newest Hot Sites, without the other stuff that's included in the paper's "Tech" newsletter, add the URL above to your QuickBrowse account.

PC Magazine's 100 Best Sites
(http://www.pcmag.com)
   For a number of years, *PC Magazine* has published a list of its hundred best sites. Today they publish "Classic Sites" and a group of "Undiscovered Sites." Both lists are worth reviewing, not only for client communication ideas, but because you may find some sites useful to you and your business. You can even download all the URLs into your IE Favorites so you don't have to keep returning to the site to check out the list.

PC World's Best of the Web
(http://www.pcworld.com)
   Like *PC Magazine*, *PC World* runs a story annually on the Web's top sites. They also devote an entire section of their site to different kinds of "Best of the Web" findings (you can get to it from the home page by selecting (in the section titled "Browse by Topic") Internet & Networking > Sites > Best of the Web.

TIP: To review lengthy articles faster, look for (and click on) the link labeled "Printer Friendly Version." You can scroll through the entire article in one screen, which makes digesting the information quicker and easier.

Notes

1. *Storyselling for Financial Advisors: How Top Producers Sell*, Scott West and Mitch Anthony, © 2000, Dearborn Financial Publishing, Inc., pp. 111–112.

2. *The Guide to Financial Public Relations: How to Stand Out in the Midst of Competitive Clutter and Credibility Marketing,* Larry Chambers, © 2002, Dearborn Trade Publishing.

5

Present Yourself Professionally

Rising Above the Crowd

*I've been in the business for 30 years, I'm too old to use
PowerPoint; besides . . . I like to be the #1 visual aid.*

—One advisor to another (overheard in conversation)

Sales may be a numbers game, but it's a people business. And there's no better way to connect in a hurry with lots of people who need what you offer than to develop a reputation as a first-class presenter. Unfortunately, it's a skill few advisors consciously work at improving.

Great presentations don't start with software or hardware; they're built around a clear message, a solid connection with your audience, and a compelling call to action. And while you don't need technology to accomplish those things, used well they can make a good presentation even better.

Of course, you can't mention the words "presenting" and "technology" without discussing PowerPoint. By one estimate more than 30 million presentations are delivered using the program every day. That's why much of this chapter is devoted to making the most of the software; it's today's standard for communicating your message to a group.

But before we get into PowerPoint and other resources that can enhance your delivery, let's look at how to develop your underlying content.

Plan Your Presentation

Contrary to what you may think, top-notch presenters invest hundreds of hours in developing and refining their material. The final product you see delivered so effortlessly doesn't just "happen," it's the result of lots of thoughtful planning, preparation, and practice. Here's what to keep in mind as you begin mapping out your next presentation.

Know What You Want.   Effective presentations are really a call to action, a plea to your audience to take a step in some direction. Good calls to action are emotional, playing on feelings of fear, hope, pride, achievement, and even greed, among others. If you want to be successful, start by developing a clear picture of what you want people to do with what you tell them and package the presentation around that outcome.

Understand Your Audience.   Your ability to be persuasive hinges in part on how well you answer the unspoken question on your audience's mind: What's in it for me? Put yourself in their shoes. Ask: "If I were one of them, what issues would keep me up at night? What goals would I be aspiring to?" Learn what challenges they (or people like them) are trying to overcome. Speak to those issues. Spell out clearly how you can help them.

Keep It Simple.   Don't overload your audience with too much information. Think in threes: three main points; three supporting points for each one of those. More than that and you risk losing your listeners. Problem—solution—result is an easy three-part approach to follow.

 TIP: You can give yourself room to cover more material in a PowerPoint presentation (for example, to respond to questions you anticipate from the audience) by using hyperlinks to "hidden" slides that are not part of your core presentation. View "About hyperlinks and action buttons" in the PowerPoint Help file to learn how to set up these slides and links.

Be Topical.   Has what you're talking about happened to you, or someone you know? Has it been in the headlines recently? Situations people can relate to personally make the strongest impressions, so highlight them in your talk. Do your homework by regularly browsing the newspapers and periodicals your audience reads. Clip stories in *SurfSaver* (http://www.surfsaver.com) that might make good presentation content. Use your knowledge journal to develop stories into vignettes that work for you.

Your audience probably doesn't understand your subject nearly as well as you do (that may be why they're there). Demystify it in language they understand and you'll be a hero. *IdeaFisher* (http://www.ideafisher.com), the brainstorming software tool mentioned in Chapter 2, is a great tool for finding the right terms and metaphors to get your point across.

TIP: *Storyselling for Financial Advisors* by Scott West and Mitch Anthony (©2000 Dearborn Financial Publishing), cited in Chapter 4, includes dozens of great suggestions on how to integrate stories into your sales process. Take a look at it.

A Quick Lesson in PowerPoint

Investing time clarifying what you plan to talk about is the essential first step to making a successful presentation. Step two is to begin developing your actual material. In the hands of a knowledgeable user, PowerPoint's ability to help you do that is impressive. But if you're among the uninitiated, the program can be an intimidating jumble of menu options and icons. This section spells out the stuff I wish someone had told me way back when.

Sketch Your Ideas in Outline View.   Like a new house, a new presentation moves through different stages: design, construction, and finishing work. PowerPoint's "Outline View" gives you a place to put your initial thoughts in order (and move them around) when you begin framing your presentation. To access it, click on the "Outline" tab in the left-hand pane of the "Normal View" window.

Here are some shortcuts that can save you time in moving information around in the "Outline":

- You can insert a new slide or a new line of text within a slide by pressing the *Enter* key.
- Demote or promote text (e.g., from a title to a bullet, a bullet to a sub-bullet, or the reverse) by pressing the *Tab* or *Shift + Tab* keys.
- Move contents around within your outline by highlighting text and then pressing *Ctrl + Shift + the up or down arrow keys* (↑↓) to relocate it.

Construct Your Slides with Placeholders. People talk about PowerPoint "slide shows," but unlike traditional 35-mm slides, PowerPoint slides don't consist of a single image. Rather they are a collection of *objects* (text, pictures, shapes, etc.) that taken together create an image. Each of one of those objects—their color, size, location, and movement—is controlled using settings found under the Format, Draw, and Custom Animation menus.

The fastest way to incorporate objects into a slide is to use one of PowerPoint's preset slide layouts. Those layouts, which you can find listed on the "Slide Layout Task Pane" in recent versions of PowerPoint, include placeholders for each type of object.

Using the preset layouts to build your content is smart for two reasons. First, the placeholder objects built into them shift automatically when you select a different slide layout (objects you create from scratch using the Draw menu don't), which means you can rearrange the appearance of your content quickly without having to manually adjust each object on a slide. Second, any text (e.g., bullets) you type into the placeholder is displayed (and can be manipulated) in the "Outline View" (text in text boxes created using the Draw menu isn't).

TIP: To see which "Slide Layouts" will work best for your content, play with the choices on the "Slide Layout Task Pane."

Use Templates to Save Time. Templates are prefabricated "packaging" you can apply to your content, a color scheme and a set of "master" layouts you can use to dress up your slides. There are thousands of PowerPoint templates to choose from, starting with those installed on your hard drive. Here are three suggestions for finding one that's right for you:

- Look under File, New, From Design Templates (in the task pane on the right of the screen).[1]

- Ask your product and service providers what templates they make available.

- Contact a firm like *Template Central* (http://www.templatecentral.com) that builds custom-designed templates for a fee. Template Central also sells thousands of templates that can be purchased and downloaded directly from the site. You can also check out the Web sites in the

"Resources" section later in this chapter or try Googling *custom-designed PowerPoint templates*.

Chapter 6 presents more about templates and how to use them.

Stick with a Consistent Color Scheme. By default, each PowerPoint file uses an eight-piece color scheme, with different assignments or "slots" for each of eight components of your slides: Background, Text and Lines, Shadows, Title Text, Fills, Accent, Accent and Hyperlink, and Accent and Followed Hyperlink. Here each color has been carefully selected to work well with the others in a well-designed color scheme.

Anytime you create a new object on a slide, PowerPoint uses the default colors in that file's color scheme. For example, if the "Fills" default color is blue, any shape you create will have a blue fill. If the "Accent and Hyperlink" default color is dark red, any Web addresses you type in will automatically be colored dark red. Change any of the default colors in the color scheme and every object created using that default will also change.

PowerPoint gives you the flexibility to select and use other colors as well, but unlike objects created using the default color assignments, those objects don't change color automatically if you change the underlying color scheme. (It's akin to how placeholder objects and those you create using the Draw menu behave when you change between preset slide layouts.)

Presentations get messy when you apply the colors in the color scheme indiscriminately to objects on your slides; in other words, when you focus the color itself instead of the slot in the color scheme the color occupies. The situation is complicated further if you select additional colors beyond the eight in the default color scheme.

The key to avoiding problems is to be consistent with the colors you use and to associate the right color scheme slot with each object on the slide. If you want to make changes, do it before you get too far into your presentation. To make them, click on "Edit a Color Scheme" at the bottom of the "Slide Design— Color Scheme" task pane and select whichever of the eight categories you want to adjust (see Figure 5.1) and then selecting Change Color.

TIP: Once you finish making your changes, add your new color scheme to the Standard Scheme menu so you can easily apply it to other files.

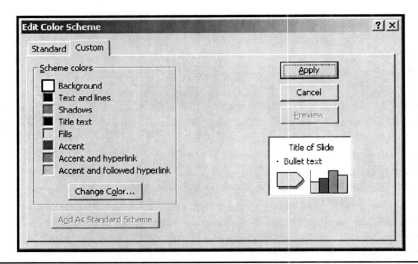

FIGURE 5.1 Edit Color Scheme

TIP: For fast, free help in selecting compatible colors for your slides and other materials, visit *Color Schemer Online* (http://www .colorschemer.com/online.html) or buy the software program the online tool is based on at http://www.colorschemer.com. For a good, quick overview of the importance and use of color in Power-Point, visit *Color Voodoo* (http://www.colorvoodoo.com) and buy a copy of *Color Logic for PowerPoint.*

Learn How Masters Work. Want to quickly add your logo or company Web address to the bottom of every slide or handout page? That's one of the things PowerPoint Masters can do for you. Every PowerPoint file contains a separate master for the slides, handouts, and speaker notes associated with that file. Those masters are like minitemplates; they dictate which fonts, text sizes and styles, colors, and object positioning should be used as defaults on the file's slides, handouts, and notes pages.

To see what each of the masters looks like in a particular presentation file, open that file, select Ⓥiew, then Ⓜaster, and then either Ⓢlide Master, Handout Master or Ⓝotes Master. A "Master View" toolbar will appear on which will be several icons, including one for the "Master Layout."

By default, each Master contains the following placeholders (you can access the "Master Layout" by clicking on its icon on the "Master View" toolbar that appears when you first open the Master):

Slide	*Handout*	*Notes*
Title	Date	Slide image
Text	Page Number	Body
Date	Header	Date
Slide Number	Footer	Page number
Footer		Header
		Footer

You can move, resize, or exclude any or all of the placeholders (for instance, you can resize the Title placeholder on your slides so that longer titles appear on one line, not word wrapped on two).

To enter text in the date, page/slide number, and header or footer placeholders, select "View," "Header and Footer," and then select either the "Slide" or "Notes and Handout" tab.

Older versions of PowerPoint (2000 and earlier) allow for only two slide masters within a presentation file: one for the title slide and one for all the other slides. Starting with PowerPoint XP, you can create and use *multiple* slide masters, which means you can have distinct slides or whole sections of slides within your presentation with different backgrounds, color schemes, fonts, or other standard information in each.

To create a new slide master, select View, Master and then Slide Master. Click on a slide in the Slides tab in the left-hand pane of the "Normal View" and press *Ctrl + M*; a new master will be inserted. Give the new master a name to distinguish it from other masters in the file (by right-clicking on it and selecting Rename Master) and you're ready to use it.

To apply a different master format to one or more slides in the file, close the "Master View," select the slide(s) you want to change, and then click on "Slide Design—Design Templates" on the "Task Pane." Select which design template you want to apply from those listed: "Used in This Presentation," "Recently Used," and "Available for Use."

For more information on working with multiple slide masters, read the page titled "About the slide master" in the PowerPoint Help file.

TIP: Take a look at *"Free Microsoft PowerPoint Training and Tutorial Resources"* at http://www.educationonlineforcomputers.com/links/ Free_Microsoft_PowerPoint_Training/ for a comprehensive list of free online PowerPoint tutorials.

TIP: If you don't want to learn all the finer points of creating PowerPoint files, you can turn the whole job over to *Source Productions* (http://www.sourcepro1.com) which will build you a presentation from scratch or fix an existing one.

Design Dos and Don'ts

As you lay out your slides, keep these guidelines in mind; following them will make your material more attractive.

Work with Fewer Fonts, and Make Sure They Are Readable. Select one for the title and one for the text (all the text), and stick with them. Don't overload slides with a variety of fonts; use bold, italics, or different colored text when you need to highlight important points. Sans serif fonts like Tahoma and Arial look best; they are also standard on most PCs, which means if you ever need to present your material on someone else's computer, you won't be scrambling to make a font substitution. Body text should be at least 28 points in size to be clearly readable at the back of the rooms.

Follow the 6 × 6 Rule. Use no more than six lines of text, six words per line on a slide, preferably less. Put key points in short phrases. If everything you intend to say is on the slide, what does the audience need you for?

Avoid Complicated Graphs or Tables. I've seen presenters show slides containing dozens of trend lines and hundreds of numbers, and not just on one slide, but throughout the whole presentation! Don't make that mistake. Remember, it's not an eye test.

TIP: *Ibbotson* (http://www.ibbotson.com) markets a set of individual PowerPoint presentation modules on 13 different investment-related topics for $800, or $100 each. Take a look at the Sales Presentation System section of their Web site for more information on what's available.

Employ Animations and Slide Transitions Sparingly. Overused animation and transition effects can be distracting and annoying. Pick a basic, uniform slide transition such as "Blinds," "Dissolve," or "Random Bars" and use it consistently. Add in others occasionally for emphasis. Avoid the "Random Effects" option; you want predictability not surprise in your delivery.

If a slide contains a bulleted list of text, set PowerPoint to reveal those bulleted items one by one. Introducing them all at once only gives your audience the chance to read ahead and tune you out. Keep control of the information and the pace by bringing up each point individually. Experiment with the custom animation settings on the "Slide Show" menu to see what works best for your content.

The same is true of graphs that incorporate two or more sets of data. It's easier (and often more dramatic) to demonstrate the contrast between numbers and trends if you build up that difference by introducing each series separately.

TIP: Opening and closing credits of movies and TV shows can be a great source of animation ideas for PowerPoint. Keep an eye out for effects you can apply to your slides.

Be Judicious in Your Use of Images. Professional-looking artwork enhances your material, but cheap artwork can diminish your message. Although the Web is full of free clip art and pictures, most of what's out there isn't appropriate for serious business presentations. One exception is Microsoft's *Clip Art and Media Gallery* (http://office.microsoft.com/clipart/), which provides very good images you can download directly into the *Clip Organizer* that's part of Office.

One of the hidden advantages of working with clip art from Microsoft (versus other sources) is that the images can be modified to match your color scheme using the Recolor button on the Picture tab of the "Format Picture" dialog box.

Another reason I like Microsoft's site is you can choose images by theme and color scheme. *Screen Beans* are a good example. You'll find more than 100 of them on Microsoft's site (search on the keywords "screen bean" within the site); additional images are available from *a Bit Better corporation* at http://www.bitbetter.com.

Here are sources of affordable photos, clip art, and other images that are suitable for business presentations:

- Cartoon Bank (http://www.cartoonbank.com).
- Comstock (http://www.comstock.com).
- Corbis BizPresenter (http://www.bizpresenter.corbis.com/).
- CrystalGraphics (http://www.crystalgraphics.com).
- Digital Juice for PowerPoint (http://www.digitaljuice.com).
- Hemera Image Express (http://www.hemera.com/image/).

Critique Your Work with a Fresh Set of Eyes.   After creating your slides, ask someone else to look at them and give you candid feedback on content, flow, and clarity. At minimum, set them aside for a day before reviewing them yourself. Be a ruthless critic; constantly challenge yourself to make your point with fewer slides and less text.

 TIP: *Design Sense for Presentations* (http://www.designsense-cd.com/) is a tutorial for businesspeople who need practical guidance on design principles. Its modules cover slide layout, working with type, creating visuals, and the smart use of color. You can either buy it on CD or access it by subscription over the Web.

TIP: Visit http://www.winningclientsinawiredworld.com to see examples of both well-designed and poorly constructed slides.

Using Screen Shots

It's 11:00 AM. You're scheduled to make a 12:30 luncheon presentation to hundreds of people and an out-of-town friend calls and mentions an article he just read that you realize would provide a perfect lead-in for your talk. Faxing it won't work; it wouldn't be big enough or look very professional. Pick up a copy of the paper? You don't have time. Here's your solution: Go to the newspaper's Web site, capture a screen shot of the headline, and paste it into your opening presentation slide.

Screen shots are easy to build into your material and don't cost you anything. If you have a Web page or Web site that you want to highlight or documents you'd like to use as props, screen shots let you show the audience what they look like.

Here's how to create them.

Push the Print Screen Button

1. *Open the program you want to take the picture of to the appropriate screen. Press the Print Screen button (usually found on the top row of your keyboard) to copy the image in your monitor to the Windows Clipboard.*

2. *Open PowerPoint and select a blank slide (or insert a new blank slide into an existing presentation).* If you're working in the multipane "View," be sure to click on the slide itself, not the smaller image of the slide on the "Slides" tab to the left.

3. *Press Ctrl + V.* The image will be pasted from the Clipboard onto your slide.

 To snap only the currently active window, not the contents of the whole screen, press *Alt + Print Screen.*

Enlarge the Image

If you're presenting to seniors or working in a large room (or both), you want your screen shot images to be easy to see. Lowering your screen resolution settings before hitting the "Print Screen" button is a quick way to blow them up. Figure 5.2 below was snapped in 1280 × 1024 resolution (common on today's

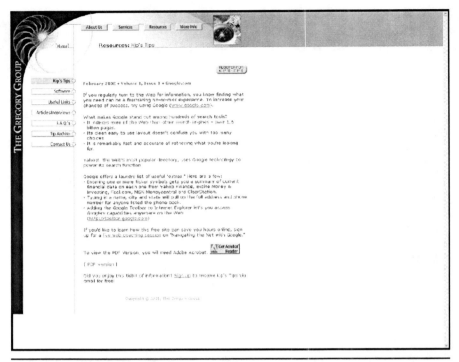

FIGURE 5.2 Higher Resolution Setting, Full Screen View

high-end monitors), while Figure 5.3 was snapped at 800×600 (the "standard" setting). Which do you think would be easier to read at a distance?

Not only is the type in Figure 5.2 much smaller, there's a large area of blank space on the right side of the picture frame. That's because most Web sites are built to be viewed at 800×600 resolution.

To adjust your monitor settings to a lower resolution:

1. *Right-click on your desktop and choose "Properties"; the "Display Properties" dialog box will open.*

2. *Select the "Settings" tab, then "Screen Area."*

3. *Adjust the sliding bar in the section by clicking and dragging on the handle (you can also use the ← key to lower the setting and the → key to raise it after you're done capturing).*

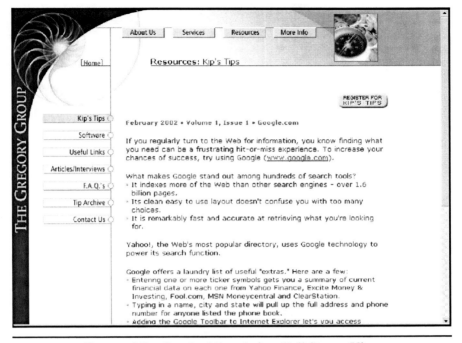

FIGURE 5.3   Standard Resolution, Full Screen View

TIP: *MultiRes* (http://www.entechtaiwan.com) is a free utility for quickly changing monitor resolution settings with a couple of mouse clicks within your taskbar.

Capture Browser Images in Full Screen Mode

Take another look at Figure 5.3. See how clean it is? That's because it was captured in "Full Screen" mode in Internet Explorer. "Full Screen" mode removes the menu and icon bars normally displayed, leaving room for more of the page displayed in the browser window. Figure 5.4 captures the same page, but inside an Internet Explorer (IE) window frame. See the difference?

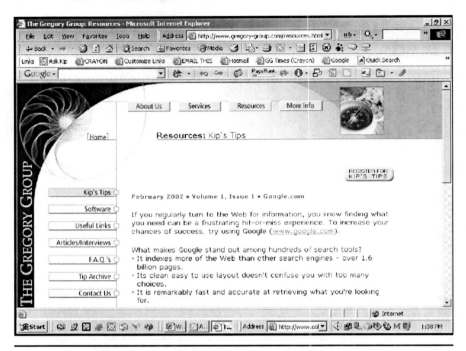

FIGURE 5.4   Standard Screen View

 To switch back and forth between normal and full screen mode, press *F11*.

 TIP: Word, Excel, and Acrobat all have a "Full Screen" view. To activate it in Word or Excel, select Vıew, Full Screen; in Acrobat press *Ctrl + L*. Pressing the *Escape* key in any of the three will return you to the previous view.

Highlight Text

One way to draw people's eye to specific text on a Web page, document, or spreadsheet in your presentation is to highlight it. Word includes a highlighting tool ( ) on its "Formatting" toolbar (near the right edge) that you can use to apply any of 15 different colors to selected text. Excel offers a similar function on its Formatting toolbar called "Fill Color" (⊞). To highlight text on a Web page, you're going to want the Microsoft's *Web Accessories for IE 5* free download mentioned in Chapter 1.

TIP: Add a designer's touch to slides with highlighted text by capturing two images of the chosen page: one without and a second one with highlighting. Apply a "Random Bars" or "Wipe" transition to the second slide and the highlighting will magically appear, drawing the audience's attention where you want it.

Frame the Content the Audience Should Focus On

Another easy way to draw your audience's attention quickly to a section of a screen shot is with shapes (a circle, oval, square, rectangle, star, etc.) around the information you want to highlight. You will find a number of choices on the Draw menu.

To create an animated frame:

1. *Select the shape you want from the "Draw" menu.*
2. *Click and drag your mouse to size the shape around the outside of the information you want to highlight.*
3. *Move the shape behind the text by selecting the shape and then selecting Draw, Order, Send Backward (you may have to do this several times).*
4. *Adjust the appearance of the object by right-clicking on it, choosing Format Object.*
5. *Animate the object using the Custom Animation option on the Slide Show menu.*

TIP: To create a perfect circle or square using the Rectangle (▫) or Oval (▫) icons on the Draw menu, press the *Shift* key while you click and drag your mouse to create the object.

Consider Buying a Screen Capture Program

The "Print Screen" button is a good basic tool, but if you create screen shots frequently consider a program like *HyperSnap-DX Pro* (http://www .hypersnap.com) or *SnagIt* (http://www.techsmith.com). Both let you insert pictures automatically into a specific PowerPoint file without having to switch back and forth between programs. Each also lets you save a series of screen-shot images quickly as separate image files, and each lets you apply special effects to the images you capture.

TIP: Inserting graphic images into PowerPoint files can bloat the file's size, especially ones that are in the .tif format. You can use your screen-capture program to save pictures with a .gif extension before inserting them into PowerPoint, which will keep your files as small as possible.

TIP: If you make a lot of changes to a PowerPoint file, you can compact its file size and eliminate unnecessary space by periodically using the "Save As" option (press *F12*) to resave your file (you can save the file with the same name).

Repurposing Content

If you've been using PowerPoint for a while, you probably have a library of older files you draw from regularly in creating new material. Here are three suggestions for cutting down on the time and effort it takes to develop each presentation.

Use "Slide Finder" to Create and Keep a Library of Frequently Used Slides

Do you routinely lose time searching for slides to copy into a new presentation? Try this: Collect the slides you use often in a single file (call it "Frequently used slides.ppt") and bookmark the file using the "Slide Finder" feature (select *I*nsert, Slides from *F*iles to open the "Slide Finder" dialog box). "Slide Finder" includes a "Favorites" tab that works just like "Favorites" in Internet Explorer, a way to get right to the PowerPoint files you want. Once open, "Slide Finder" lets you insert selected slides or entire file contents into what you're working on.

Accent Technologies' *PowerSearch* plug-in for PowerPoint (http://www .accent-technologies.com) is another great timesaver. It lets you search presentation files stored on your hard drive for slides containing specific text. As it locates slides that include your search terms, it copies each one into a new PowerPoint file, along with a link (and the path) back to where the original is located. Use it to locate what you want to put in your "Frequently used slides" file.

TIP: If you want the ability to inventory and manage a large collection of slides or presentation files, consider Accent's *Presentation Librarian* (http://www.presentation-librarian.com).

Title Your Slides So You Know What's on Them

Without titles you won't know what you're working with when you're setting up a Custom Show, using the "Slide Navigator," or working in the "Outline View." If you don't want the title to be visible on the slide itself, as when you're using a full-size screen shot, select and drag the title object above and off the slide; it will still show in the Custom Show and Navigator lists.

TIP: Ever had to skip ahead in a presentation because time ran short? To avoid fumbling with the "Slide Navigator" to jump ahead in your slides, type up and print out a numbered list of slide titles and keep it by your laptop while you're presenting. If you need to move to your final slide or a question is raised about one you've already covered, you can type its slide number and press *Enter,* and go right to it.

Use the "Replace" Feature to Find and Change Text Automatically

If you customize certain slides with the name of the groups you present to, clients, prospects, or others, the "Replace" feature is an excellent, fast tool for making the change.

 Activate PowerPoint's "Replace" feature by pressing *Ctrl + H.*

Looking Good in Print

The printed material you leave behind can make an impression on people long after you have finished presenting. Here are some ideas and products to help you make the most of that opportunity.

Brand Everything You Distribute

Make it easy for attendees to contact you later by including your name, phone number, e-mail, Web site, and company logo. As with a business card, you never know where it might circulate.

To add your information to each page of your PowerPoint handouts, select View, Header and Footer, and in the dialog box that opens choose the "Notes and Handouts" tab (presentation title in the Header, the other information in the footer). Review how it looks by choosing the "Print Preview" option. You may need to adjust the size and positioning of the header and footer text boxes in the Handout Master (by selecting View, Master, and then Handout Master) so that everything fits properly.

TIP: For a professional-looking logo designed inexpensively, check out *The Logo Factory* (http://www.thelogofactory.com) or its affiliated service, *Logos in a Box* (http://www.logosinabox.com).

Set Your Print Options to the Format You Use Most Often

If you consistently print your slides a certain way (1, 2, 3, or 6 to a page, in color or in gray scale), configure PowerPoint to use those settings by default. From the main menu, select Tools, Options, and then the "Print" tab to make your choices.

TIP: Number your handout pages! It's annoying to leaf through pages that aren't paginated.

If You're Printing in Black and White, Make Sure Your Slides Look "Clean"

Before printing, look at your slides in the "Grayscale" view to ensure they'll look right on paper (select View, Color/Grayscale, Grayscale). You may find dark shapes where you expected to see text, a diagram, or other feature. Adjust the "Grayscale" settings for that object by highlighting the object and choosing Grayscale Setting on the shortcut menu.

TIP: Some objects requiring adjustment may be on a master slide. To change those, select View, Master, and then Slide Master (be sure to change your View from "Color" to "Grayscale," as just described) and make the necessary adjustments.

Consider a Printing Utility Program

ClickBook (http://www.clickbook.com) lets you create PowerPoint handouts in booklet form (ClickBook also works with Word, Excel, Acrobat, and other Windows programs). It gives you the ability to print trifold brochures, table tents, wallet cards, or CD-case inserts on any printer. Pick the layout you want to publish and the software will make the necessary adjustments to your printer automatically.

TIP: Creating 5.5-in. × 8.5-in. booklets requires a special stapler to bind your material. The makers of ClickBook sell two staplers that will fasten up to 25 sheets. Check them out at http://www.bluesquirrel .com/clickbook/staplers.asp.

CREATING POWERPOINT HANDOUTS IN WORD

Newer versions of PowerPoint give you more options than ever in printing out your slides. One thing you can't do is annotate your handouts with sidebar comments (as when you might want to elaborate on a graph. Your only option is to create a separate slide with the desired text and place it just before or after the slide on which you wish to comment.

Here's an alternative: transfer the slides to Word where you can insert additional text wherever you like. To do that, select File, Send To, Microsoft Word. Once the slides are in Word, you can resize them (and the table containing them) to suit your needs.

(continued)

TIP: *Handout Wizard* (http://www.mvps.org/skp/how/) gives you additional control over PowerPoint handouts, allowing you to choose which slides to print, in what order, how many per page, margin spacing and slide titling, and numbering. It also allows you to include different layouts in the same handout file.

Preparing "Digital" Handouts

Suppose you want to share an electronic version of your presentation. You can send people a copy of your PowerPoint file, but that requires them either to have PowerPoint or a PowerPoint viewer installed on their computer.

The most widely used solution is to send copies of your material in portable document format (PDF) format, which can be opened and viewed on any computer equipped with a PDF viewer. *Adobe Acrobat* (http://www.adobe .com/products/acrobat/) is the best-known tool for creating PDFs. You can either buy the full Acrobat program or subscribe to Adobe's *Create Adobe PDF Online* service (https://createpdf.adobe.com), which lets you convert Microsoft Word, Excel, PowerPoint, and Publisher files over the Internet.

 TIP: Adobe's *Acrobat Reader* (http://www.adobe.com/products/acrobat/ readstep2.html) is a free PDF viewer. Make sure any of your clients you communicate with via e-mail have a copy. It's not only good for viewing presentation files, but can be used to review copies of account statements and other information published as PDFs as well.

Publishing with Acrobat enhances your material and your image in four ways:

1. *Consistency.* Converting a presentation file to PDF ensures that people viewing your work will see it as you intended, with the colors and fonts you built it with—not fonts or color schemes substituted by the recipient's PCs, which throws everything out of whack.

2. *Portability.* Creating an Acrobat version of your material (slides or handouts) allows you to send it anywhere quickly and easily (via e-mail

or on disk) without having to worry whether the recipient has the right version of PowerPoint to view your work.

3. *Security.* If you have information you want others to see or print out but not modify, you can use Acrobat's security settings to restrict their access.

4. *Professionalism.* You convey a more professional, more solid impression when you create materials that can be downloaded or e-mailed and read by anyone anywhere.

TIP: To speed up the conversion of PowerPoint, Word, and Excel files to PDF, use the PDFMaker macro Acrobat adds to those programs when it's installed. The macro flags any hyperlinks embedded in the file you're converting and retains these links in the PDF version. That means you can send out proposals, e-books, and e-brochures that are interactive (i.e., letting the reader go to what interests them most using a table of contents at the front of the file). Using PDFMaker is an easy way to create polished, customer-friendly proposals.

CatchtheWeb (CTW) (http://www.catchtheweb.com) is a handy tool for sharing and annotating Web pages with others. Files created with CTW can be viewed off-line (i.e., without having to be connected to the Internet). The program lets you highlight text and add sticky notes to any page before you capture it, allowing you to draw viewers' attention to specific content and comments.

PowerPRESENTER from *PresentationPro* (http://www.presentationpro .com) is actually a collection of three tools available individually or as a set: PowerCONVERTER, EmailPRESENTER, and OnlinePRESENTER. Each lets you convert PowerPoint files into "Flash" presentation format, which can be e-mailed to others, posted at a Web site, or copied and distributed on CD.[2] PresentationPro's PowerVOICE service lets you add professional narration to your slides.

Setting Up to Present

A key piece of presenting a professional image is making sure the presentation itself goes off without a hitch. Below is a ten-point checklist to help you achieve maximum impact and avoid problems:

- Keep a backup of your final presentation file on CD (if your laptop has a CD-R drive) or stored on a Universal Serial Bus (USB) storage device in your computer case.

- Stock a presenter's survival kit consisting of fresh markers, fresh batteries (for your remote), masking tape (to hang signs or mark the floor), duct tape (to avoid tripping over cables), an extension cord, and a surge protector/power strip.

- Check in upon arrival with your host (if you're being sponsored) as well as the facility manager. Make sure any equipment you've requested is in place.

- Provide the person introducing you with a brief, typed introduction (no more than one minute) they can read aloud to introduce you.

- Position your laptop as a teleprompter waist-high in front of your speaking area (not behind a podium), so you can move around the room and still see it.

- Plug in your remote control, start up your PC, and make sure both are working properly; open your presentation file and any other programs or files you plan to use.

- Adjust the PC's power profile to "Always on" and disable your screen saver.

- Check your sound and sight lines. Confirm that attendees sitting at the back of the room will be able to see and hear you. Adjust the room lights if necessary to improve visibility. After the sound check, mute or turn off your microphone until you are being introduced.

- Mark your territory. Use masking tape on the floor to signal areas where feedback in the sound system is triggered by your mike, or where you interfere with the image projected on the screen.

- Get yourself a glass of water, take a sip, and wait for show time.

 TIP: Most LCD projectors include a menu option that will tell you how many hours the bulb has been in use. Check your owner's guide to see how long they last. Keep a backup bulb on hand, especially when the one in use is nearing the end of its useful life. You can get a replacement for most models at *Bulbman* (http://www.bulbman.com) or *Super Warehouse* (http://www.superwarehouse.com).

TIP: Create a snapshot of your room requirements and provide it ahead of time to organizations for which you'll be speaking. It will make everybody's job easier if you lay out your needs clearly.

DON'T LET THIS HAPPEN TO YOU

Make enough presentations and eventually you're going to encounter the unexpected; it's not a question of if, but when. Several years ago I was scheduled to speak after lunch at a sales conference in San Diego. Although my computer had been working fine all morning, when I set up for my talk during the lunch break I could not get PowerPoint to start.

Quickly finding my hosts, I explained the situation and asked if they had a computer I could borrow and if I could swap spots with the next presenter. Fortunately they did and thankfully the next presenter agreed to jump ahead of me on the schedule.

Skipping the gory details, let's just say that Murphy's Law was alive and well that day. Eventually, I was able to transfer my presentation file to the other machine and fix enough of the differences in fonts and slide layouts to go on when the other speaker finished.

I bought my first CD burner the next day and have been sticking with standard fonts ever since.

Delivering Your Message

You've researched your audience, developed a strong presentation, created impressive handouts, and set the room up. Everything's primed and ready. Here are some bits of advice to help you make the most favorable impression possible.

Stand tall, shoulders straight. Remember to smile; establishing and holding eye contact with individuals around the room (for at least 3 seconds) will help. Many will nod and smile at you; smile right back. Don't stare at your screen or look over the audience at the back wall, it's the people in the seats you want to connect with.

Move regularly and with confidence. Three good places to speak from are front and center (for your opening and closing, and to emphasize major points), left-center (the audience's left, your right; to provide variety), and rear-center-left near the screen (when you want to point out slide content). When pointing something out on the screen, speak facing your audience, not your slide. Point and gesture broadly and smoothly. Similarly, if you're going to use a flipchart or board, write large and clearly.

When shifting to speak to someone, turn and face them, shoulders squared. In your anchor positions, pivot slightly occasionally to address different parts of the room. Don't fall prey to "lighthousing" (the continuous semicircular rotation of your head or body) or any other unconscious nervous motion: pacing, rocking back and forth, or the like. In the same vein, if you carry a remote use it subtly, don't wave it around like a wand.

Be enthusiastic, it's contagious. Let the passion you feel about your topic be conveyed to your audience. Interact with them. Ask their opinions. Get them to answer your questions. Engage them in an exercise. The quickest way to rapport is through dialog. Use humor. You don't necessarily have to tell jokes; you can win an audience over by finding what's funny about everyday life. Self-deprecating humor is best; audiences warm faster to speakers who don't take themselves too seriously.

BREAK FREE FROM THE PODIUM . . .

Interlink Electronics (http://www.interlinkelec.com) manufactures a number of radio frequency (RF) remote controls and other devices that can be very useful as presentation tools. RF remotes give you more latitude in working a room of attendees than infrared ones, because you don't need to point the remote directly at the projector to advance your slides. You can be 100 feet away from your laptop and still control your slides.

. . . AND GIVE YOUR AUDIENCE A HANDS-ON EXPERIENCE

Interlink also markets RF keyboards and mice, which give you complete control of your computer without having to stand over it at the front of the room. Plug in the wireless USB keyboard, hand it to a seminar attendee, and invite that person to test drive your Web site, an illustration system, or any other program you want to demonstrate to the audience. Short of renting out a computer lab or training center (which can be very costly), you're not going to get a better chance to let people try things for themselves.

You've heard it before: the camera doesn't lie. If you're serious about improving your presentation, video tape it. You'll be amazed at how much you see yourself doing that you were never aware of while on stage.

The best counsel I can give you is to be yourself. When you're speaking you own the stage; command the space just as if you were hosting your audience in your home. If you're nervous in front of a group, remember your audience wants you to succeed; if you bomb, what does that say about their decision to be there? Forget about seeing them naked; imagine them all lined up to buy what you're selling.

And don't forget the most important thing: Ask for the order.

Help with Public Speaking

Want to read more on public speaking? The following sites are worth bookmarking. They offer many useful articles, tips, and worksheets.

Virtual Presentation Assistant (http://www.ukans.edu/cwis/units/coms2/vpa/vpa.htm) is run by the Communication Studies Department at the University of Kansas. It provides a good, well-organized, succinct refresher on the basics: topics like determining your purpose, selecting and researching your topic, analyzing your audience, outlining your points, and using visual aids.

Advanced Public Speaking Institute (http://www.public-speaking.org) is maintained by Tom Antion, a professional speaker and trainer. The site offers over 100 articles on improving your public speaking skill and a helpful preprogram questionnaire you can use to lay out what you know (or need to) about any group you will be addressing.

Allyn & Bacon's public speaking Web site (http://www.abacon.com/pubspeak/) offers interactive exercises you can use to define your audience, focus your research efforts, and organize your material.

 TIP: The *Google Directory* includes two lists of public speaking–oriented sites that can be found under Business > Business Services > Public Speaking > Education and Training, and Science > Social Sciences > Communication > Public Speaking.

A Proven Approach for Sharpening Your Skills

Looking for feedback on your presentation skills that doesn't cost a fortune? Try *Toastmasters International* (http://www.toastmasters.org). Its 200,000 members participate in thousands of clubs around the world. To see what groups operate in your area click on the "Find a Club" link and search by country, state, city, and so on, or just enter in your area code or city. If you work for a large firm, check if the company already has an in-house chapter you can join.

TIP: The *National Speakers Association's Academy for Professional Speaking* at http://www.academyforprofessionalspeaking.org offers a slate of meetings, workshops, and networking opportunities designed to help those who want to pursue speaking at a professional level.

The Value of Feedback

One of the biggest oversights presenters fall prey to is failing to get audience feedback. Some speakers scoff at the notion that you should ask your audience to tell you how you did, saying it's nothing more than a thinly veiled ego stroke. But that's not what I'm talking about.

What I mean is taking full advantage of the opportunity you have while in front of a group to obtain information about them and to open a dialog. Not everybody attending your presentation is going to buy or make an appointment that day. Why not get their permission to stay in touch over time?

My feedback form is a single sheet that includes space for a person's contact information, check boxes for several free premiums (more about those in a minute), a place to score the presentation and offer comments, check boxes to indicate areas of interest, and a section to request contact on specific issues.

The form is introduced early in the session. I tell attendees that we will be covering a number of sites and tools, and strategies for how to use them. If they'd like to receive a recap of the presentation by e-mail that includes the ideas discussed and links to the sites mentioned, all they have to do is fill out the form and check a box. They can also sign up to receive my *Kip's Tips* newsletter (http://www.kipstips.com) and a free assessment questionnaire.

To them, there are several benefits: they don't have to write down a bunch of lengthy Web addresses (and risk misspelling them), they get a reminder/refresher within several days of the session, and they have the opportunity to learn about other tools that can help them over time, all for free.

At the same time their information helps me tailor future communications with them, I can use their feedback to make improvements, and I can get some great testimonials. Toss in the word-of-mouth advertising I get if they like what I send them enough to pass it along to others and you get a very powerful marketing strategy. All for the price of developing a couple of e-mail messages that can be broadcast as easily to thousands as they can be to a single person.

TIP: If you want to pursue the sponsored seminar route (speaking for organizations to their employees or members), summarize the feedback you receive from each event you do and create a file of those summaries. They can be a potent marketing tool.

ACTION STEP

What questions should you be asking your audience to qualify them as prospects for your services? What premiums might you offer to send them following your presentation? Write your ideas in the space below.

Useful Resources

There's no lack of excellent help available online when it comes to Power-Point. Equipment manufacturers, resellers, and consultants have all created sites containing tips, training and tools to improve your effectiveness with the program. This section outlines resources worth knowing about. To take advantage of the content they offer,

- Ask your assistant or intern to review them and provide a summary of key takeaways from each article.

- Copy instructions and snippets of information into your knowledge journal or use *SurfSaver* (http://www.surfsaver.com) to keep copies of articles you find useful for later reference.

- Use *HydraLinks* (http://www.hydralinks.com) to keep a list of the pages you want to go back to, so that you can get through the tables of contents before you bog down in individual articles.

Some of the best sites are maintained by PowerPoint Professionals Most Valuable (MVPs), people who voluntarily contribute answers to Microsoft's official PowerPoint newsgroup, providing answers and guidance to users all over the world.[3] Six are listed below.

Steve Rindsberg's PowerPoint FAQ List (http://www.rdpslides.com/pptfaq/) is usually my first stop for PowerPoint information. It offers an exhaustive set of questions and answers on the program. Beyond the virtual encyclopedia of free information he provides, Rindsberg also sells a number of add-ins under the brand name PPTools. You can read more about them at http://www.rdpslides.com/pptools/.

Geetesh Bajaj has written a large number of excellent tutorial and product review articles on PowerPoint that are cataloged at his site (http://www.indezine.com), which also includes a search tool that queries the leading PowerPoint MVP support sites simultaneously for information on your keywords.

Sonia Coleman (http://www.soniacoleman.com) offers tutorials and 28 sets of professionally-designed templates you can download for free. She also sells *PowerLink™ Plus*, a program that lets you use PowerPoint files as digital business cards you can send to clients and prospects on a CD.

Shyam Pillai (http://www.mvps.org/skp) specializes in developing add-ins for PowerPoint. The Handout Wizard mentioned earlier is one of them. Others worth checking out are Color Scheme Manager, Image Importer Wizard, Live Web, and Word/Phrase Search.

TAJ Simmons offers hundreds of custom-designed backgrounds and templates that can be purchased on CD or downloaded from his site, *Awesome PowerPoint Backgrounds* (http://powerpointbackgrounds.com). A free sample is available for the price of an e-mail address and location. You can also order custom-made backgrounds inexpensively.

Tushar Mehta (http://www.tushar-mehta.com). Mehta is an MVP, but for Excel, not PowerPoint. He's here because he's put together a very helpful tool that you may want to own, the PowerPoint Slide Show Timer. The Slide Show Timer puts a digital clock display on your slides that can be set to show how much time has elapsed since your presentation began, how much time is left, or just the time of day. It's a helpful tool for staying on track and finishing on time.

 TIP: You'll find a very helpful list of Web sites maintained by Microsoft's MVPs at http://mvps.org/links.html. Every Microsoft product in this book is on it.

The five free sites below offer technical articles and instructions, guidance on presentation development and delivery, as well as templates and graphics. Some also maintain communities where you can get your questions answered.

Presenters University (http://www.presentersuniversity.com) is maintained by InFocus, a manufacturer of digital projection equipment. The site is divided into three main sections: self-study courses (i.e., articles), free downloads, and a bulletin board for posting questions called "Ask the Professor."

Presenters Online (http://www.presentersonline.com) is sponsored by Epson, another equipment manufacturer. Training content is divided into "Presentation Fundamentals" (a collection of 75+ articles on delivery, message, and visuals) and "Putting it Together" (which includes over 80 step-by-step tutorials, most addressing common questions on and practical uses of PowerPoint).

PowerPointers (http://www.powerpointers.com) provides articles on communicating effectively, building and planning a presentation, and communicating within your specialty. Register at the site and you can use a helpful "My PowerPointers" function to bookmark articles for later viewing. You can also sign up for a twice a month newsletter: "2thePoint."

Presentations magazine's site (http://www.presentations.com) is organized into four sections: Creation, Delivery, Technology, Resources, and Buyer's Guide. You will find more than 100 articles on PowerPoint, if you type *PowerPoint* on the Advanced Search page and then select "All available dates." You'll find practical, quick advice on issues like organizing your message, gauging your audience, and handling room setup.

PowerPointAnswers (http://www.powerpointanswers.com) offers a number of helpful, brief articles on using PowerPoint more effectively. You can also get inexpensive consulting help on PowerPoint-related issues using the site's PowerPointCustomAnswers feature.

Two Tools for Dressing Up Your Presentation

CrystalGraphics (http://www.crystalgraphics.com) offers an array of add-ins for PowerPoint under the name "PowerPlugs for PowerPoint" that can give presentations a more professional, more polished multimedia look. I have used the slide transitions product for years with great success. Check the site for a full description of their products.

Ever wanted to illustrate investment formulas on your slides? You can if you install the Equation Editor that comes with Microsoft Office. If you need a program that's more sophisticated, take a look at *MathType* (http://www.dessci.com/en/products/mathtype/).

Presenting Over the Internet

Talk about giving a presentation, and most people immediately envision standing at the front of a conference room or on a platform in an auditorium addressing an audience. But that's not the only way to deliver your message. The Internet has opened up a whole new frontier for communicating with people, whether they are across town or across the globe.

Do you have clients who have relocated, people you'd like to hang onto but can't justify meeting with in person because of the time and expense of getting to them? Or maybe you wish you were able to act on introductions and referrals clients give you outside your local area, *without* having to jump in your car or on a plane? Web conferencing can be a mechanism for achieving either goal.

Whether your primary concern is client retention, new client acquisition, or collaborating with strategic partners, conferencing over the Internet can be a helpful tool of getting you in front of your audience. It's not going to eliminate the need or desire for face-to-face meetings, but it can change the frequency and nature of your interaction with clients, prospects, and others.

The number one benefit Web conferencing offers is convenience; no one has to leave their desk. Beyond that, you can interact with your audience in ways that would cost a fortune to create in a meeting room setting.

Used properly, Web conferencing can be an effective sales tool, training vehicle, and even relationship builder. As high-speed connectivity continues to take root, it will become a day-to-day tool for more people. Here's how you can get up to speed on this remarkable technology.

Understand the Concept

Simply put, Web conferencing uses the Internet to link two or more people via computer so that information can be shared and discussed between them as if they were sitting together in a room looking at the same computer screen.

As presenter, you upload a PowerPoint presentation file to a central server, which is then broadcast to your audience in a "virtual" meeting room. Invited participants are sent an e-mail ahead of time confirming the date and time and containing a link to your conference sign-in page. Once logged in, they are able to view your presentation as you deliver it over their monitor (voice communication can either be done over the Web or by conference call).

As an audience-participation tool, the technology offers some great benefits, including the ability to:

- Poll your audience.
- Open and share software applications on your computer.
- Give a tour of selected Web sites.
- Field questions by phone or via chat (i.e., typing responses with your keyboard).

TIP: Web conferencing is a fast-moving technology. If you want up-to-date information on what services are available and how they compare, check out *Conferencing on the Web* (http://www.thinkofit .com/webconf/), or search *PC World* or *PC Magazine* for current articles and service reviews.

Look at the Leading Providers

A number of companies have developed conferencing platforms and hundreds more market those services as resellers. Seven of the best-known manufacturers/product providers are:

- Centra (http://www.centra.com).
- Genesys (http://www.genesys.com).
- MeetingPlace (http://www.meetingplace.net).
- Microsoft Office Live Meeting (http://www.microsoft.com/meetlive).
- Netspoke (http://www.netspoke.com).
- Raindance (http://www.raindance.com).
- WebEx (http://www.webex.com).

If you plan to do a lot of Web conferencing, collaborating on projects, or demonstrating software or Web sites, WebDemo (http://www.linktivity.com) is another tool worth considering. Unlike the services just mentioned, Web Demo is a software program you buy and install on your Web server. The up-front cost of purchasing the program is higher than what you'll pay to occasionally rent an online meeting room, but the long-term savings can be dramatic if you plan to conduct virtual meetings and presentations regularly.

TIP: Ask your top product and service vendors if they have a conferencing capability and how you can utilize it.

Learn from Others

The best way to understand Web conferencing is to experience it firsthand. All the providers just listed offer regular, scheduled live demos. Many also sponsor presentations by outside experts. Sit in on some sessions to get a feel for how the process works.

Use Free Trial Offers to Test Various Services

Again, most of the vendors listed offer them. When you're ready to actually see how conferencing works, take a test drive.

Decide What Service, Approach, and Pricing Best Meet Your Needs

Most services now offer both pay-per-use and flat-rate plans. Pay-per-use is metered; you're charged for how long the session lasts and how many people participate. Flat-rate plans let you use a certain number of "seats" as often as you want for a specified period: monthly, quarterly or annually.

TIPS FOR CONDUCTING BETTER WEB CONFERENCES

Most of the same rules for successful presentations discussed earlier apply when you're presenting using the Internet. Here's a quick rundown of suggestions for how to make the most of the opportunity, gathered over five years of doing Web-based presentations.

When developing your presentation:

- *Build interactivity into your session.* The more you can engage your audience, the better. Polling makes participants feel involved, and can give you important insight into their needs.[4] Tours of Web sites are another way to maintain interest.

- *Practice, practice, practice.* You're going to depend far more on your voice than you do when presenting in person. Smile, show enthusiasm, and use inflection. What sounds normal to you will sound monotonous to them. Listen to radio talk show hosts and reporters for an idea of how to present well without video.

- *Consider using a script,* or at minimum outline the key points you want to make on each slide. The network anchors all use one—why shouldn't you?

Before your event begins:

- *Buy a high-quality telephone headset* to leave your hands free (don't ever use a speaker phone). *Hello Direct* (http://www.hellodirect.com) offers a wide range of choices.

(continued)

- *Arrive early.* You never know what last-minute problem you'll encounter. I've had to reload presentation slides at the last minute when unanticipated slide problems cropped up. Get to your meeting 30 minutes or an hour early to get yourself organized.

- *Forward or unplug phones in your office* that might ring and disrupt or distract from your delivery.

- *Deactivate call waiting if you have it* to ensure you don't get any beeps or clicks that interrupt. Try pressing *70 after the dial tone; consult your phone service provider if that doesn't work.

- *Turn on a sound machine to block out background noise.* Ambient noise in your office can detract from your delivery. Buy a white-noise machine like the "Sound Soothers" sold by *Sharper Image* (http://www .sharperimage.com).

- *Familiarize yourself with the speaker console/controls.* Each service has a "control board" for presenters and moderators where audience questions appear, highlighting tools can be accessed, and so on. Be sure you know what's on it.

- *Open applications you'll be sharing in advance* to whatever screen or file you plan to use, to save time. Size the window (using your mouse or by pressing *Alt + Spacebar*) to shrink or enlarge it to be whatever dimension you want.

During the event:

- *Stand and deliver.* Getting up out of your chair frees you to make the gestures and movements you would if you were presenting in person. Even though the audience won't see you making them, they will hear your enthusiasm.

- *Keep up a steady pace*—not too fast and not too slow. Don't let more than a minute go by without changing the information that appears on the screen.

- *If you're presenting to more than five people, work with a partner.* Let your partner moderate, field questions, and handle any technical difficulties so you can focus on presenting. For larger groups, your conferencing vendor may provide someone who can play that role. Provide a brief written introduction beforehand. If you're planning a Q & A session, ask the moderator to read questions submitted by the audience via "chat out loud."

- *Start on time and end a few minutes early.* Use a clock, stop watch, or timer.

After it's over:

- *Get feedback.* Ask a colleague or coach to sit in and critique your session. Post a survey at a site like *Zoomerang* (http://www.zoomerang .com) or send a quick e-mail to solicit audience feedback.
- *Use what you learn to improve your sales effectiveness.* Word your presentation survey questions well (both those during and after the event) and you can get a long way down the qualification path by analyzing and acting on the responses.

Presentation opportunities are all around you. Not just the ones you create for yourself (sales calls, seminars, and client appreciation events), but those offered by organizations and companies looking for good speakers and content to put on the agenda of their training sessions, meetings, and conferences. Combine the techniques laid out in this chapter with the strategies you learned about in Chapters 3 and 4 and you can pinpoint your best prospects, find out what they are concerned about, lay out a plan for connecting with them, and present your story persuasively when given the opportunity.

Notes

1. Read the section on templates in Chapter 6 to learn how to locate templates stored elsewhere on your computer.
2. MacroMedia's free Flash Player is a popular multimedia viewer browser plug-in. You can download it at http://www.macromedia.com/software/flashplayer/.
3. You can access the Microsoft PowerPoint newsgroup from the Google Groups site (http://groups.google.com). Type in *public.microsoft.powerpoint* in the search box.
4. Check with your vendor to see if they can provide you with a "postshow" report that details individual responses to questions.

Automate Time-Consuming Tasks

Applying the Speed-Dial Principle

It's the survival of the fastest, not the fittest.

—Alvin Toffler

In a world that measures success in microseconds, knowing how to leverage your computer to save time is a big advantage; it's one of the biggest reasons we're drawn to technology in the first place.

This chapter outlines a number of practical ways to recapture the time you're losing every day to "administrivia," such as handling e-mail, locating content you've already created (and want to repurpose in e-mails, letters, presentations, and proposals) and processing large mailings to clients and prospects—even routine, redundant activities such as reformatting reports downloaded from product or service suppliers.

None of these activities sound very sexy. That's the point—they aren't. But right now, you're probably spending hours every week mired in them, and that prevents you from doing the stuff that's really exciting (and critical): meeting and working with clients and prospects, moneymaking.

Consider this: According to a survey by the Insurance Advisory Board, advisors spend nearly twice as much time on office administration and preparation and follow-up on sales calls as they do actually in front of clients and prospects; about a 2:1 ratio. Move 10 percent of your time from those first activities to getting in front of more people and you'll increase your selling time by 25 percent.

157

> **TIP:** Do you have someone on staff whose job it is to "make you look good" by ensuring that information gets to clients and others STP (sooner than possible)? Make sure they read this chapter!

Tame Your Inbox

Is your Inbox a mountain of messages? Do you regularly handle the same e-mail more than once? Have you forgotten to follow through because an important message was "lost"? You're not alone; staying on top of e-mail is a universal struggle. E-mail is a double-edged sword: the convenience and immediacy are great, but its gravitational pull is like a black hole. Here are three things you can do to keep from getting totally sucked in.

Set Up Rules to Direct Incoming E-Mail to the Right Folder

Rules, which some programs call "filters," act like a traffic cop. When you set up a rule, you tell your e-mail program to watch for messages from certain people or with specific content and do something with them: move them to a separate folder, delete them (like spam), or notify you with a special message. To set up a rule in Outlook, select Tools, Rules Wizard. You will have the choice of working from a predefined template or starting a blank rule. I find it easier to work with blank rules and build from the bottom up, but you may like using the templates. Either way, the Wizard will walk you through a process involving four steps:

1. Deciding which conditions you want to check for.
2. Telling Outlook what to do with the message.
3. Identifying any exceptions.
4. Giving the rule a name (and activating it).

Be sure a check appears in the box next to your new rule, and you're ready to go.

> **TIP:** Back up your rules so you don't have to rebuild them from scratch if something happens to your PC. To create a backup file, select the Options button in the lower right-hand corner of the Rules Wizard's opening screen. Next, select Export Rules. Name the file (it will be given an .rwz extension) and remember where you save it so you can go back to that folder and copy it to a CD when you're done.

Flag Messages from Important People in Different Colors

If you want e-mails from specific senders (clients, top prospects, etc.) to stand out when they hit your Inbox, tell Outlook to change the color of the message headers from those people. By default, Outlook's message headers are black, but they can be changed to any of more than a dozen colors.

To adjust the color, open the Organize feature under Tools on the main menu; a section will appear above your Inbox messages titled, "Ways to Organize Inbox." Click on the "Using Colors" link on the left side, then on a message from whomever you want to flag and choose a color to assign to that person. Click on "Apply Color" and you're done.

TIP: Keep your color code simple. Use one color for clients, a different one for prospects, and a third for your boss or coworkers. Add more if you need them.

Shield Yourself from Spam

According to Ferris Research, unsolicited commercial e-mail (UCE)—what most of us call spam—cost U.S. businesses more than $10 billion in lost productivity in 2003 alone.[1] Ten billion! The situation, having reached epidemic proportions, now has rivals Microsoft, AOL, and Yahoo collaborating to come up with solutions to the problem and Congress passing legislation to eliminate it. So in the meantime what can you, as an individual, do to protect yourself more effectively from it? Five things:

1. *Guard your e-mail address carefully.*

   Never give it out to anyone you don't know and trust. Think twice about providing it to any merchant online whose policies for use aren't crystal clear. Forget about including it in any public directories online unless you're looking for trouble.

2. *Create a separate account for newsletters and nonessential information provided to you by others (i.e., the Hotmail option described in Chapter 3).*

   One of the best ways to cut down is to segregate essential from nonessential messages. What's essential? Clients, prospects, your boss, your team. What's not? Everything else.

3. *Learn to use the rules/filters just outlined.*

Familiarize yourself with what protections your e-mail provider has in place and look for instructions at their site on how best to employ them. It's probably a safe bet that messages containing names of body parts, any of George Carlin's seven dirty words, the terms "hot fox" or "Viagra," or the phrase "can't miss marketing opportunity" aren't coming from your top clients or prospects. Flag them and send them right to the trash (Deleted Items). If you already have a spam problem, spend a few days reviewing messages looking for word patterns in the Subject line or body of the message that are consistent; then add those words and phrases to your filter list. You may have to experiment a little to get them right, but it's worth the trouble.

4. *Keep track of what's happening by occasionally visiting PC World and PC Magazine.*

Until the spam problem is solved, it's going to remain in the headlines; both publications periodically run feature stories summarizing the latest developments. As the problem gets worse, expect more such articles.

5. *If necessary, install antispam software.*

Many antispam programs employ a so-called *white list* strategy (the opposite of *blacklisting* a sender), where only those addresses that you specify are allowed to send messages directly to you. Everything else is filtered through a one-time permission screen where the sender has to request the recipient's OK to have messages delivered. Messages from senders without approval are blocked.

Again, consult *PC World* and *PC Magazine* on which programs are currently receiving the highest marks and what the pros and cons of each option are.

TIP: Develop the habit of handling messages once. Schedule times to deal with e-mail each day. Scan senders and subjects to identify messages requiring your action and put them in a separate folder so you can respond as soon as you finish sorting. Forward whatever you can delegate to others for follow-up. Create a rule to divert chronic junk directly to your Deleted Items folder.

ELIMINATING THE BACKLOG

If your Inbox is overflowing with old messages, here's how to clean it out.

1. *Create a backup of the messages you have before doing anything.* By default, your messages are stored in a file called "Outlook.pst." Copy that file and any other personal files you have created (they also have a .pst extension) to a CD so you have an archive if you need it. Not sure whether you have any other .pst's? Use the Windows search function (press ⊞ + *F* to activate it, then type **.pst* in the "Search for" field) to find out.

2. *Delete messages that require no action.* Scan the message header list for e-mails you know don't need to be saved, replied to, forwarded, or otherwise acted upon. Highlight any you find and press *Ctrl + D* to delete them.

3. *Delete older, redundant messages from message threads.* If I send you an e-mail, you respond, and then I reply back to you, all using Outlook's Reply function (versus creating a new, blank message each time), a thread is created. The second message from me in your Inbox contains the complete "dialog," which means you can safely erase the older one. You can locate and eliminate those duplicate messages quickly by sorting messages by conversation topic (View, Current View, By Conversation Topic).

4. *Create "Do It" and "Delegate It" subfolders in your Inbox.* As you locate messages requiring action by you or someone else, move them into the appropriate folder. To create the folders, right click on "Inbox" in the Folder List and select "New Folder." To move a highlighted message, press *Ctrl + Shift + V* to open the "Move Items" dialog box, then select which folder you want to move it too.

 TIP: You can assign different follow-up flags to messages (by date or by action) by right-clicking on them and selecting Follow Up, then choosing a category from the drop-down menu or typing in your own. Flagged messages can be organized and prioritized using the View menu.

(continued)

5. *Archive messages in separate folders organized by subject.* If you want to keep messages you've dealt with handy for later reference, put them in a separate personal folder arranged by client, project, newsletters, or the like. That not only keeps your Inbox clean, it will keep you under any size limits your firm imposes on individual e-mail account storage (in Outlook itself .pst folders over 3 GB in size won't function properly).

> **TIP:** To set up a new personal (.pst) folder, select File, New, Outlook Data File, Personal Folders File.

6. *Process the messages in your "Do It" and "Delegate It" folders.* Start with the most recent messages first. If there are too many to do in one sitting, schedule an hour a day to review and deal with their contents until the files are cleared out.

> **TIP:** If you delete or move a large number of messages from a personal folder, be sure to compress the .pst file when you're finished to recapture disk space. Right click on the .pst folder you want to compress in the Folder List in Outlook, choose "Properties" from the shortcut menu, select "Advanced," and then "Compact."

Keep Contact Information Up-to-Date

If you maintain a database of client and prospect contact information, you *know* one of the most time-consuming activities in your (or your assistant's) routine is keeping that information current. Having to manually copy and paste, or re-key, new e-mail addresses or changes to street addresses or phone numbers can chew up a lot of time. And what about when someone moves or decides to change e-mail providers and doesn't tell you? You only find out when the letter or e-mail you send bounces back undeliverable, triggering a scramble to get the new information.

Two services that can alleviate that burden are *GoodContacts* (http://www.goodcontacts.com) and *Plaxo* (http://www.plaxo.com). Both use the Web to automate the process of keeping contact information up-to-date.

Here's how they work. After signing up for either service, you download and install their software applicaton on your computer. You then identify which people in your database you want to e-mail a contact update request to. You draft a brief cover message (which is personalized for each recipient), make sure your own contact information is correct (it is included in the message you send out), and hit "Send."

When your message is received, if a contact wants to respond, he or she clicks on a link to open a form containing fields for the information you are requesting (the form is prefilled with any contact information you already have in your database for that person). The recipient OKs the information as is, or makes the necessary changes, and then clicks a button to send it back. The vendor then e-mails that information to you so it can be synchronized with your database.

To streamline the process even further, both services will *automatically* update information between subscribers any time it is changed by either one. In other words, if a client decides to sign up for the same service you are using and subsequently updates their own contact information with that service, you can set your software to process their update automatically.

You can purchase GoodContacts software for Outlook, Outlook Express, ACT!, and a variety of enterprise (i.e., corporate) customer relationship management (CRM) software programs. Plaxo is free and works with Outlook and Outlook Express.

Manage Frequently Used Content

Do you ever find yourself hunting through the text of old messages, letters, or proposals for content to paste into something you're currently working on—a description of your services, answers to routine questions, or just the directions to your office? Paging through messages one at a time or opening and closing multiple files until you put your finger on what you need is very time-consuming. Here are three ways to avoid that task.

Create AutoText in Word

Store boilerplate text you use repeatedly in letters, proposals, or reports in Word's *AutoText* library. AutoText allows you to add a phrase, paragraph, or page's worth of content instantly to whatever you're working on just by typing a few keystrokes.

To see how it works, open a blank Word document and start typing *To Whom It May Concern*. By the time you've typed "To W," a small box will pop up next to the text inside which will appear "To Whom It May Concern:

(Press ENTER to Insert)." You can either press the *Enter* key to accept/insert the AutoText, or continue typing (in case what you were actually wanting to write was "To William," for example).

You will find the AutoText function under <u>I</u>nsert on Word's main menu. Most of the default contents relate to the opening or closing of a letter or e-mail, but you can add whatever you want: background on you or your firm, responses to frequently asked questions, or even a table of columns comparing popular investments.

To add new AutoText, type the text you want to include in your AutoText library, highlight it, then press *Alt + F3*. You can accept the name offered (the first few words of what you've typed) or give it a different one.

If you create your own AutoText entries, be sure to make a backup of your "Normal.dot" template file (you can read more about templates in a few pages). That's where AutoText content is stored. If you don't back it up and something happens to the file, Word will create a new Normal.dot and your work will be lost.

TIP: If you use Microsoft Outlook and have configured it to use Word as your e-mail editor, you can use AutoText when composing e-mail messages.

TIP: If you've started adding material to your knowledge journal, take a minute now to see what content you might want to include in your AutoText library.

Use AutoFill and Custom Lists in Excel

The AutoFill feature in Excel (not to be confused with the AutoFill function built into the Google Toolbar discussed in Chapter 3) gives you a way of entering cell labels and formulas without having to type them in. It's a similar time-saver to AutoText. AutoFill looks for a pattern in the data in whatever range of cells you select, and will continue that pattern across any additional cells added to the selection when you drag the AutoFill handle.

The AutoFill handle is the small box at the lower right-hand corner of the border surrounding a selected cell or range of cells. You trigger the feature by clicking on and dragging that box. For example, if you type the figures 10, 20, and 30 into the three adjacent cells, select those cells and then click and drag the AutoFill handle across seven additional cells, the numbers 40, 50, 60, 70, 80, 90, and 100 would appear automatically.

AutoFill works in the following three ways:

1. If cell content is numeric, AutoFill will *build on* whatever sequence it identifies (e.g., the 10, 20, 30 example just given).

2. If cell content consists of formulas, AutoFill will *duplicate* the formula, making adjustments in the cell references contained in the formula(s).

3. If cell content is text labels (including numbers as labels), AutoFill will *repeat* the data contained in the cells, unless you have created a Custom List that Excel recognizes.

The *"Custom Lists"* feature lets you add text you use frequently in your spreadsheets using the AutoFill function. It's similar to Word's AutoText. Four entries are included by default: abbreviated days of the week (Sun, Mon, Tue, etc.), full days of the week, abbreviated months of the year (Jan, Feb, Mar, etc.), and full months of the year. You can add more: names of clients, products, ticker symbols, locations, time frames (Q1, Q2, etc.; Month 1, Month 2), positions, vendors, and so on.

Custom Lists are inserted into a spreadsheet using the AutoFill feature. To see how they work, type *Monday* into a cell and *January* into the cell right below it. Then click and drag the AutoFill handle across some additional columns to the right of those cells. The days of the week and months of the year will appear automatically.

To add a Custom List to your AutoFill library using the existing contents of your worksheet, follow these steps.

1. *Select (highlight) the cells in your worksheet that contain the labels you want included in the Custom List.*

2. *From the main menu, select Tools, then Options, then the "Custom Lists" tab.*

3. *Select Import, then OK.*

You can also type the information you want to include into the List entries field on the "Custom Lists" tab.

Take Advantage of Templates

If you often create letters, proposals, e-mails, spreadsheets, or presentations with virtually identical content and you're not using templates to prepare them, you're working harder than you have to. Templates are files that contain specific text or formulas, customized formatting, or layout settings that you can duplicate as needed. Word, Excel, PowerPoint, and Outlook all offer an extensive selection of templates, which you can use "as is," or modify to suit your needs. Follow these three suggestions to make better use of them:

1. Take an Inventory of the Template Files You Already Have. Word, Excel, and PowerPoint all copy templates to your hard drive during installation. To find out what you've got on your computer, select File, New within each program and look at the templates listed, or do a file search by selecting Search from the Start menu, then For Files and Folders. In the field labeled "Search for files or folders named" in the dialog box that opens, type the appropriate information listed here:

If you want to locate templates for	*Type in*
Excel	**.xlt*
PowerPoint	**.pot*
Word	**.dot*

 Remember you can press ⊞ + *F* to open the Windows "Search" feature.

When you find a template, open it and investigate how it's been set up. You can modify it using the steps outlined under "Build your own" below.

2. Look Online for Other Examples. *Microsoft Office Template Gallery* (http://office.microsoft.com/templates/) includes templates for all of the Office programs organized into various categories. In particular, take a look at Stationery and Labels, Marketing, and Meetings and Projects.

TIP: Want to see what other templates might be available that meet your specific need? Try Googling **template** together with other terms that describe what you want (*spreadsheet, presentation, sales letter,* etc.). And don't forget to ask the companies you work with what templates they make available.

3. Build Your Own.   Any Word, Excel, or PowerPoint file can easily be turned into a template. Here's how to do it with a Word document (follow the same steps with the other programs):

1. *Locate and open the file you want to base your template on. "Genericize" the file by removing specific names, addresses, dates, figures, or other information that are changed each time a new version of the file is created.*

2. *Select "File," "Save As" (or press F12) to open the "Save As" dialog box. Select "Save as type" at the bottom of that dialog box. On the list, look for the "template" option and select it.*

3. *Give the template a name you'll recognize and save it.*

TIP: Back up any templates you create. Templates from Microsoft can be reinstalled if something happens to your PC, but unless you have a copy of yours, they will be lost, and you will be stuck recreating them unnecessarily.

Consider creating a template if you prepare any of the following materials:

- Monthly newsletters
- Quarterly or annual statement cover letter
- Seminar handout materials
- Spreadsheets used with clients or prospects
- Proposals for prospective clients
- Articles for publication
- Booklets and brochures

Streamline Your Marketing

Systemization is the foundation of long-term marketing success. How many times has a really good idea for connecting with an audience occurred to you, only to slip through your fingers because you can't figure out how to execute it with limited resources? This section outlines inexpensive ways to act on those opportunities when you find them, so you can get the word out.

Learn to Do Mail Merges

Mail merging allows you to turn a mass mailing into personal correspondence. It combines information about intended recipients (e.g., names, addresses) with the contents of a template to create an individualized end product for each reader. If you're not familiar with how the process works, take a few minutes to explore Word's mail merge capabilities using a step-by-step set of Wizard screens. Here's how it works in a nutshell:

1. *Select Tools from the main menu, then choose Letters and Mailings, and then Mail Merge Wizard.*
2. *Following the Wizard, select the document type and set up.*
3. *Select the "Recipients."*

    You can create a recipient list from an existing list (including Excel files), by incorporating your contacts from Outlook or by typing a new list from scratch.
4. *Select or create the document content to be merged.*

    To add content from your list of contacts, place your cursor on the screen where you wish to enter the information and then click on the appropriate item to be merged from the contact file (address book information, a greeting line, electronic postage, postal bar codes, or the like.)
5. *Preview and Print.*

    Preview your merged documents and make any changes necessary. Finally, complete the merge and print.

 TIP: There are a number of ways you can merge information to personalize communication. To explore what they are, search on *mail merge* in Word's Help.

Outsource Fulfillment

If you work alone or with a small staff, processing marketing campaigns, seminar flyers, or annual statement mailings can bring everything else to a standstill. Here are five resources that can reduce the burden so you don't get sidetracked stuffing and stamping envelopes.

NetPost Services (http://www.usps.com/netpost/). Surprisingly few people are aware that the U.S. Postal Service entered the Internet age several years ago. Today they offer automated fulfillment for mailings of all sizes through NetPost. With it, you can have letters, booklets, flyers, and postcards mail-merged and delivered to one or thousands without ever touching a piece of paper. Your pieces are processed and mailed the next business day from one of four mailing centers nearest each recipient: either California, Illinois, Florida, or New York.

The site offers step-by-step guidance to completing a mailing in five steps:

1. Selecting your document.
2. Selecting a mailing list.
3. Adding a return address.
4. Choosing your mailing options.
5. Paying for your order.

Once you are familiar with how to set up a mailing, NetPost's Express option gives you a dashboard of choices that let you quickly select which options you want to employ.

 TIP: The site's Help section includes tutorials on creating documents, mail lists and address books, uploading files, reviewing mailing information, and deleting documents and mailing lists that you've stored. Review these and the Getting Started section if you want to better understand how the process works.

NetPost provides a cost estimator to help you budget for and plan your mailings (http://www.usps.com/mailingonline/quickcal/). For example, a one-page black-and-white letter on 28-lb (stationery) stock, mailed first class in a regular No. 10 envelope sent to each of your top 100 clients would cost you a little more than $50, including postage. The site even breaks out the production and postage costs separately.

 TIP: You can request samples of five different mailers: one-page personalized letter, one-page flyer or self-mailer, full-color postcard or black-and-white postcard. Order one of each to gauge which would be most appropriate for your audience.

You can find additional authorized providers of NetPost's online direct-mail fulfillment services at http://www.usps.com/directmail/.

 TIP: Check out *Microsoft's Office Marketplace* (http://office.microsoft .com/marketplace/) for a listing of third-party vendors that offer automated fulfillment programs that integrate with Word and Outlook.

Kinko's (http://www.kinkos.com). Kinko's maintains more than 1100 stores in nine countries across the globe, mostly in the United States. If you have print needs for seminars, sales calls, client-appreciation events, or other meetings, it's likely you can transmit what you want printed electronically and then pick it up or have it delivered. Kinko's will accept files created in portable document format (PDF), or if you don't own Adobe Acrobat, you can use their File Prep Tool.

When I'm traveling, I use Kinko's electronic services to have workshop handout materials printed and delivered to my hotel, so they are waiting for me on arrival. It's a remarkably convenient service whether going across town or across the country, and because it often helps me avoid the cost of shipping materials, it practically pays for itself.

Keyboard Shortcuts

A *shortcut* is a fast way of getting something done. Every program has them, commands that are triggered by pressing different combinations on your keyboard. This section includes all the shortcuts described elsewhere in this book, along with many others: for Windows, Excel, PowerPoint, Word, Internet Explorer, Outlook, and the Google Toolbar. I would recommend reviewing it while sitting at your computer, and dog-earing this page for easy reference later on.

THE GREAT DEBATE: KEYBOARD VS. MOUSE

Which do you use more often to control your computer: your keyboard or your mouse? When starting out, many prefer the mouse; you don't have to memorize anything, you just have to point and click on icons on the screen. But as you grow more comfortable and confident about what to do, taking your hands off the keyboard to navigate slows you down. Over time those seconds add up; that's why it's worth learning what's here.

Windows

There are certain tasks you perform so often on your computer, you probably don't even think about them. The following shortcuts will help you do those things faster. They work the same way no matter what software application you're working in.

When you want to	*Press*
Minimize all the windows you have open on your PC in order to click on a desktop icon (remember "D" for desktop)[2]	⊞[3] + D
Open the "My Computer" window to view files and folders on your hard drive (remember "E" for explore)	⊞ + E
Open the "Search" dialog box so you can locate files and folders using their name (all or part of it), text content, file type, or date created (remember "F" for find)	⊞ + F
Activate the Start menu	⊞ (or *Ctrl* + *Esc*)
Cycle through all open applications running on your computer using a small icon window that appears in the middle of the screen	*Alt*[4] + *Tab* + *Tab* (as needed)

See which applications are running on your computer and switch between them	*Alt + Esc*
Cycle through all open applications running on your computer using program buttons in the taskbar	⊞ *+ Tab*
Type an address in the Address bar within the taskbar (especially useful for launching Web pages from your desktop without opening IE)[5]	⊞ *+ Tab, Tab*
Close a Windows Explorer window, or individual windows in many programs without exiting the program itself (remember "W" for window)	*Ctrl + W*
Copy highlighted text, files, or folders to the Windows Clipboard (remember "C" for copy)	*Ctrl + C*
Cut (remove) what's highlighted from its current location and place it in the Windows Clipboard (think of "X" for eXtract)	*Ctrl + X*
Paste the contents of the Windows Clipboard where the cursor is positioned (think of the "V" as an "insert here" symbol)	*Ctrl + V*
Undo your last action on the keyboard (in some programs, this can be done repeatedly)	*Ctrl + Z*
Close the currently active application	*Alt + F4*
Close a window within an application (without closing the program itself)	*Ctrl + F4*
Copy an image of the entire computer screen to the Windows Clipboard	*Print Screen*
Copy just an image of the currently active window to the Windows Clipboard	*Alt + Print Screen*
Maximize the current application window so that it fills the screen	*Alt + Space bar, X*
Activate a program's Help function	*F1*
Move to the beginning (or end) of a file	*Ctrl + Home* or *Ctrl + End*

> **TIP:** Many programs include a description of their shortcuts in the Help file. Press *F1* to open it, locate the tab labeled "Index" and in the search box on that tab, type ***shortcut*** or ***keyboard shortcut*** to see what's listed.

Microsoft Office (Excel, PowerPoint, and Word)

The following shortcuts work in all three Microsoft Office programs: Excel, PowerPoint, and Word.

When you want to	Press
Save the document you're currently working on	*Ctrl + S*
Open a file saved on your computer or network	*Ctrl + O*
Start a new document, message, presentation file, or spreadsheet	*Ctrl + N*
Print what you're currently working on	*Ctrl + P*
Select text one word at a time	*Ctrl + Shift + arrow keys (⇆)*[6]
Bold selected text	*Ctrl + B*
Underline selected text	*Ctrl + U*
Italicize selected text	*Ctrl + I*
Search for text within a file (opens the "Find and Replace" dialog box to the "Find" tab)	*Ctrl + F*
To replace text, formatting or special characters within a file using "Find and Replace" (opens the "Find and Replace" dialog box to the "Replace" tab)	*Ctrl + H*
Check spelling within the file (and grammar usage, if activated)	*F7*
Move the cursor through text one word at a time	*Ctrl + ⇆*
Activate the main menu of the program (also called the "menu bar")	*F10*

Select the next (or previous) toolbar	*Ctrl + Tab* or *Shift + Ctrl + Tab*
Display a menu of commands that can be applied to the selected text	*Shift + F10*
Choose an option from a drop-down menu	*Alt + underlined letter,↓↑*[7]
See a pop-up box description of what a chosen command does (also called "context-sensitive help")[8]	*Shift + F1*
Insert/remove a hyperlink	*Ctrl + K*

Excel

When you want to	*Press*
Edit the contents of an active cell	*F2*
Cycle through absolute cell reference options for any cell included in a formula[9]	*F4*
Recalculate all sheets in the workbook (file)	*F9*
Recalculate the active worksheet	*Shift + F9*
Define a name	*Ctrl + F3*
Insert a name into a formula (if you're a longtime spreadsheet user, you may refer to it as a *range* name)	*F3*
Enter today's date into a cell	*Ctrl + ;*
Enter the current time into a cell	*Ctrl + Shift + :*
Hide (or unhide) selected rows	*Ctrl + 9* or *Ctrl + Shift + 9*
Hide (or unhide) selected columns	*Ctrl + 0* or *Ctrl + Shift + 0*
Start a new line within the active cell	*Alt + Enter*

Change the format of selected cells using the "Format Cells" dialog box	*Ctrl + 1*
Apply the "General" number format to selected cells	*Ctrl + Shift + ~*
Apply the "Currency" format to selected cells	*Ctrl + Shift + $*
Apply the "Percentage" format to selected cells	*Ctrl + Shift + %*
Apply the "Number" format to selected cells	*Ctrl + Shift + !*
Select the entire range of cells within any section of a worksheet that's bordered by blank rows and columns	*Ctrl + Shift + **
Extend a current selection of cells right (or left), one cell at a time	*Shift +* ⇆
Extend a current selection of cells down (or up), one cell at a time	Shift + ↑↓
Extend a current selection to the last (or first) cell containing data in a row	*Ctrl + Shift +* ⇆
Extend a current selection to the last (or first) cell containing data in a column	*Ctrl + Shift +* ↑↓
Extend a current selection to entire column(s)	*Ctrl + Spacebar*
Extend a current selection to entire row(s)	*Shift + Spacebar*
Go to the bottom right-hand cell of the worksheet	*Ctrl + End*
Move one screen to the right (or left) in a worksheet	*Alt + Page Down* or *Alt + Page Up*
Move to the next (or previous) worksheet in the workbook	*Ctrl + Page Down* or *Ctrl + Page Up*

PowerPoint

When you want to	*Press*
Cycle forward (or backward) through objects on a slide in the Normal View	*Tab* or *Shift + Tab*
Insert a new slide into a presentation	*Ctrl + M*
Move between panes in Normal View clockwise (or counterclockwise)	*F6* or *Shift + F6*
Switch back and forth between the "Slides" and "Outline" tabs in Normal View	*Ctrl + Shift + Tab*
Duplicate a selected slide (in the "Slides" tab of the Normal View or in Slide Sorter) or selected object (within the Normal View)	*Ctrl + D*
Show (or hide) gridlines (press it again to hide)	*Shift + F9*
Change grid settings	*Ctrl + G*
Copy the formatting of an object	*Ctrl + Shift + C*
Paste (apply) that formatting to another object	*Ctrl + Shift + V*
Increase (or decrease) the font size of selected text	*Ctrl + Shift + >* or *Ctrl + Shift + <*
Change the case of selected text (cycles between capitalized, all caps and lower case)	*Shift + F3*
Center a paragraph	*Ctrl + E*
Left align a paragraph	*Ctrl + L*
Right align a paragraph	*Ctrl + R*
Promote (or demote) a paragraph, when working in Outline View	*Alt + Shift + ⇆*
Move selected paragraphs down (or up)	*Alt + Shift + ↑↓*
Group (or ungroup) selected objects	*Ctrl + Shift + G* or *Ctrl + Shift + H*

Run a presentation in Slide Show View	*F5*

The last five shortcuts apply when you're working in the Slide Show View (i.e., when presenting or viewing a presentation in full-screen mode).

Hide/display the arrow and navigation button	*A*
Display a blank *black* screen (press it again to redisplay the current slide)	*B*
Display a blank *white* screen (press it again to redisplay the current slide)	*W*
Go to the next hidden slide in the presentation	*H*
Go to a specific slide within the file	*That slide's # + Enter*

Word

When you want to	*Press*
Copy the formatting (bold, italics, spacing, etc.) of selected text	*Ctrl + Shift + C*
Apply copied formatting to other text	*Ctrl + Shift + V*
Increase (or decrease) the font size of selected text	*Ctrl + Shift + > or Ctrl + Shift + <*
Change the case of selected text (cycles among capitalized, all caps, and lowercase)	*Shift + F3*
Center a paragraph	*Ctrl + E*
Left align a paragraph	*Ctrl + L*
Right align a paragraph	*Ctrl + R*
Indent a paragraph (or remove a paragraph indentation)	*Ctrl + M or Shift + Ctrl + M*

Apply a Heading 1, 2, or 3 style	*Alt + Ctrl + 1, 2, or 3*
Promote (or demote) the Heading styles (1 to 2, 2 to 3, 3 to 4, etc.)	*Alt + Shift + ⇆*
Apply the "List Style" (i.e., put bullets next to each paragraph you've selected)	*Ctrl + Shift + L*
Apply "Normal" text style (i.e., to remove any special formatting)	*Ctrl + Shift + N*
Apply a style by activating the "Style" box	*Alt + Ctrl + S*
Create AutoText using selected text	*Ctrl + F3*
Enter text from the AutoText library	*Enter, after the AutoText bubble appears*
Insert a page break	*Ctrl + Enter*
To move the cursor to the end (or beginning) of a document	*Ctrl + End or Ctrl + Home*
To move the cursor to where you made the last change in a document (you can go back to the last four revision points)[10]	*Shift + F5*
Select text one line at a time (down or up)	*Shift + ↑↓*
Select text one paragraph at a time (down or up)	*Ctrl + Shift + ↓↑*
Select text one screen at a time (down or up)	*Shift + Page Down or Shift + Page Up*
Select text from the cursor to the end (or beginning) of a document	*Shift + Ctrl + End or Shift + Ctrl + Home*
See how your document will look when printed (Print Preview)	*Ctrl + Alt + I*

Switch to Outline View (useful when you want to rearrange contents in your knowledge journal)	*Alt + Ctrl + O*
Switch to Page View	*Alt + Ctrl + P*
Switch to Normal View	*Alt + Ctrl + N*
Split a document into two panes, so you can look at different sections of it simultaneously	*Alt + Ctrl + S*
Switch back and forth from one split pane to the other (press it repeatedly)	*F6*
Display (or hide) nonprinting characters (paragraph marks, etc.) ·	*Shift + Ctrl + **
Find the next occurrence of contents you typed into the "Find" dialog box	*Alt + Ctrl + Y*
Update a table of contents (make sure the cursor is within the table)	*F9*
Enter today's date into a document	*Alt + Shift + D*
Redo or repeat an action (the opposite of undo)	*Ctrl + Y*
Open the "Macros" dialog box to run a macro or create a new one	*Alt + F8*
Get statistics on the current file (number of pages, paragraphs, word count)	*Ctrl + Shift + G*

Internet Explorer (IE)

When you want to	*Press*
Open an additional browser window	*Ctrl + N*
Open a link on a Web page in a new window	*Shift + left click*
Put your cursor in the Address bar so you can type in a new Web address	*Alt + D*
Fill in the http://www... and .com at the beginning and end of what you've typed into the address field	*Ctrl + Enter*

Search the currently active Web page for specified text (very useful for quickly locating search terms on text-heavy or long pages)	*Ctrl + F*
Go to the home page designated on the "General" tab under Internet Options	*Alt + Home*
Organize your Favorites	*Ctrl + B*
Move a selected Favorite up (or down) in the list while in "Organize Favorites" dialog box	*Alt + ↑↓*
Go back to the previously viewed page	*Alt + ←*
Go forward to the next page viewed (if you have moved backward)	*Alt + →*
Close the active browser window	*Ctrl + W*
View a Web page without the menus and toolbars (i.e., full screen), especially useful when doing a screen capture (press *F11* again to return to normal view)	*F11*
Look at Web addresses you've previously entered into the Address bar	*F4*
Move to the beginning (top) or end (bottom) of a Web page	*Home* or *End*
Display a menu of options for any link on a Web page	*Shift + F10*
Select all of the contents of a Web page (for copying to the Clipboard)	*Ctrl + A*
Add the current Web page to the bottom of your Favorites list	*Ctrl + D*
Scroll down or up the page one screen at a time	*Page Down* or *Page Up* (*Spacebar* or *Shift + Spacebar*)
Refresh the contents of the current Web page (useful for pages that are updated frequently, such as news headlines and stock quotes)	*Ctrl + F5*

Outlook

When you want to	Press
Reply to a message	*Ctrl + R*
Reply to everyone who received the message you're responding to	*Ctrl + Shift + R*
Send messages and check for new mail	*Ctrl + M*
Search messages for specific text	*F3*
Search for text within an open message	*F4*
Find the next occurrence of the text you are searching for	*Shift + F4*
Move one or more item(s), like messages, to another folder	*Ctrl + Shift + V*
Create a new folder	*Ctrl + Shift + E*
Copy item(s) to another folder	*Ctrl + Shift + Y*
Go to another folder	*Ctrl + Y*
Switch to your Inbox	*Ctrl + Shift + I*
Switch to your Outbox	*Ctrl + Shift + O*
Expand (or collapse) a selected folder containing subfolders	→ or ←
Open your address book	*Ctrl + Shift + B*
Move to the next (or previous) item in a list	*Ctrl + Shift + > or Ctrl + Shift + <*
Mark an item as read	*Ctrl + Q*
Flag an item for follow-up	*Ctrl + Shift + G*
Accept (or decline) a meeting for your calendar	*Alt + C or Alt + D*
Create an appointment in your calendar	*Ctrl + Shift + A*

Create a new contact	*Ctrl + Shift + C*
Create a new journal entry	*Ctrl + Shift + J*
Create a request for a meeting	*Ctrl + Shift + Q*
Create a new task	*Ctrl + Shift + K*
Create a request for a new task	*Ctrl + Shift + U*
View a single day schedule in your calendar	*Alt + 1*
View your schedule by week	*Alt + −*
View your schedule by month	*Alt + =*

Google's Toolbar

When you want to	*Press*
Put your cursor in the Google toolbar's search field	*Alt + G*
Generate a list of search results in the same Internet Explorer window	*Enter*
Open your list of results in a new window	*Shift + Enter*
Go directly to the top result in the search, in the same window (the "I'm Feeling Lucky" feature)	*Alt + Enter*
Go directly to the top result, but in a new window	*Alt + Shift + Enter*
Use Boolean connectors AND, NOT, and OR	+, -, |
Get current news, pricing, and performance information on any publicly traded security	Type *stock:* then the ticker symbol
Generate a list of sites that link to a specific URL	Type *link:*name of URL (no spaces)

Use Google to search within a site for specified keywords	Type *site:*name of URL (no spaces)
See what other pages have information similar to a specific Web page	Type ***related:*** name of URL (no spaces)
Search for a specific type of file (PDF for Acrobat, doc for Word, xls for Excel, ppt for PowerPoint, and rtf for Rich Text Format)	Type keywords then ***filetype:*** type of file (no spaces)
Search just within page titles for specified	Type ***allintitle:*** keywords
Search just within the text of pages for specified keywords	Type ***allintext:*** keywords
Search just within a Web page's URL for specified keywords	Type ***allinurl:*** keywords

In Chapter 2, you learned how to assign a keyboard shortcut to launch your knowledge journal. Below are suggested assignments for popular programs. To use them, go to the Programs menu on the "Start" list, find the desired program, then right-click on it and choose "Properties." In the shortcut key field, enter the combination you want to trigger that program to launch.

 TIP: When setting up shortcuts to launch programs or files, use the first letter of the program's or file's name; it'll make remembering the shortcut easier.

To Launch	I Press
Excel	*Alt + Ctrl + Shift + E*
Internet Explorer	*Alt + Ctrl + Shift + I*
Knowledge Journal	*Alt + Ctrl + Shift + J*
Outlook	*Alt + Ctrl + Shift + O*
PowerPoint	*Alt + Ctrl + Shift + P*
Word	*Alt + Ctrl + Shift + W*

Let Macros Do the Work

Macros are the ultimate keyboard shortcuts. A client of mine calls them Speed Dial for her computer. A macro records what you do on your keyboard or with your mouse, stores those actions as a set of instructions, and replays them (very quickly) at the touch of a button. Just like Speed Dial for phone numbers you call frequently, macros work best on repetitive tasks. If there are things you do on your computer the same way every time (and you do them often), they are worth knowing about.

TIP: Review the workflow worksheets you created in Chapter 2 to identify where you (or someone else) might build a macro to automate your most time-consuming tasks. You or an assistant can build the simple ones and you can hire somebody to build the others (college interns, for example).

Types of Macro Software

Each Microsoft Office program (Word, Excel, PowerPoint, Outlook, and Access) lets you create macros (under <u>T</u>ools, <u>M</u>acro), but unless you're familiar with Microsoft Visual Basic (VB), you won't be able to edit the ones you record. The tool I use is called *Macro Express* (http://www.macros.com). I like it because it's simple; you don't have to know how to write or understand any special programming codes.

Some of the ways I use macros include:

■ Copying and pasting text (repeatedly) between programs.

■ Inserting frequently used text without typing (a la AutoText).

- Applying specific formatting to selected contents of one or more files.
- Updating information in a contact database.
- Making a change to a sequence of slides in a presentation.
- Adding or removing password protection to a file before sending it to others.
- Moving or renaming files.

> **TIP:** *AutoMate* (http://www.unisyn.com/automate/) is another low-cost macro writing program worth looking at.

Getting Started

Macro Express includes a number of "Quick Wizards" instructions for simple, common tasks (e.g., working with text, connecting to the Internet). One of the first things you should do after buying the product is to click through a couple of these instructions to see how they work.

Dissecting someone else's macro is another good way to understand how macros get built. You will find a number of them to choose from (for free) on the Shared Macros page at the Macro Express Web site (http://www.macros .com/share.htm). Download them to your computer, open up Macro Express and use the program's Scripting Editor to see how they were created.[11]

When you're ready to try creating a macro from scratch, follow these five steps:

1. *Make a list of tasks you (or your staff) perform frequently on your computer.*
2. *Pick one that takes five steps or less to work through and understand the process.*
3. *Write down each key (or combination of keys) you press on your keyboard to complete that task.*

   Writing things down reduces the chance of making and recording a mistake. List commands one per line to avoid confusion (use the *Macro Worksheet* in Appendix B). If a program has a keyboard shortcut for a command (*Ctrl + O* to open a file), use it; otherwise write down the keystrokes used to complete the task.

4. *Open Macro Express and select the "Capture" command.*

Click on the Capture icon in the bar on the left side labeled "Actions"; a dialog box labeled "Add Macro" will appear on your screen. Assign a "Hot Key" combination (i.e., a keyboard shortcut to trigger the macro) and then click on the Capture Macro button. Type in a name for your macro, choose the scope (i.e., run it in any program, or a specific program), and then click on "Start Capture."

TIP: When assigning keyboard shortcuts to your macros, use combinations that begin with *Alt + Ctrl + Shift,* or the Windows key (⊞) + *Alt, Ctrl* or *Shift;* none of those are used by other programs in this book, which means you won't unknowingly override a useful shortcut embedded within a particular program.

---

5. *Switch to the program you want the macro for and complete the task as you normally would.*

Take it slow to minimize the risk of hitting the wrong key. When you're done, press *Alt + Ctrl + Shift + X* to stop recording/capturing.

When you're finished, press the Hot Key combination you assigned to test what you recorded to ensure it works correctly. If your macro doesn't work the way it's supposed to, use the Scripting Editor to make adjustments.[12]

TIP: Write a brief description of what each macro does in its "Notes" tab as a reminder in case you forget later on. (And, trust me, you *will* forget.)

Don't be intimidated by how many options Macro Express offers; you will do most of your work with the five below. Here's what each one does.

- *Text Type* is used for recording keystrokes or for inserting blocks of text into a file

- *Speed* lets you adjust how quickly your macro runs (if your PC can't process the commands fast enough and you need to slow it down a little) and whether to add a pause in the middle of the macro that lets you take some action or make a choice.

- *Activate/Launch Programs* tells Macro Express on which program(s) to launch or activate (e.g., when you're copying text from one program and pasting it into another).

- *Repeat Options* is for when you need to complete the same series of steps more than once, as when making the same adjustment to a series of slides in a presentation.

- *Remarks* lets you embed comments within your macros to jog your memory about what certain commands do.

 TIP: Macro Express offers a feature like Word's AutoText called "Short-Keys." The benefit of using it over AutoText is that you can use your ShortKey entries in any type of file, not just Word: a presentation, a spreadsheet, or even a database.

Add-Ins for Excel and Word

In Chapter 5, I described a number of add-ins created to enhance Power-Point's basic functionality. Let's close this one with two tools you can use to beef up Excel, Word, and Outlook: *JWalk's Power Utility Pack (PUP) for Excel* (http://www.j-walk.com/ss/pup/) and *DataPrompter* (http://www.wordsite .com), which works with Word and Outlook.

Developed by John Walkenbach, PUP is a collection of more than 60 add-ins for Excel. If you do *any* amount of work with Excel, you are going to love PUP. I use it all the time. Here are some ways you can put it to work in speeding up routine spreadsheet tasks:

- Clean up inconsistent text in downloads (sign-up forms at your Web site, reports from your broker dealer or custodian, etc.) that you would otherwise manually correct by changing the case or adding/deleting spaces or characters by column, row, or range.

- Combine the contents of two or more columns/rows into a single column or row (like first names in one column with last names in a second).

- Lock or hide cells or protect sheets based on the contents of those cells or sheets (for when you want to protect formulas from accidentally being erased), so that you don't have to individually select each cell, range. or sheet to modify it.

- Copy an exact formula from one cell to another without having to edit the formula in its new location to adjust relative cell references.

- Export a range of cells within a spreadsheet to a .csv (text) file, as when you want to import selected spreadsheet information into a contact management database.

- Adjust the values of all cells in a specified range without having to write a formula for each one (e.g., increase the value of each cell by 50 percent).

- Print the same batch of ranges, worksheets, or entire files on a recurrent basis without having to open each one.

In addition to PUP, Walkenbach also offers a free download called the "Enhanced Data Form," which picks up where the Form tool built into Excel's Data menu leaves off. If you or anyone in your office routinely inputs data into a spreadsheet, Walkenbach's form tool will save you from having to constantly jump around the file to enter that information.

Finally, the site also includes a very helpful collection of links to products, consultants, and publications that can enhance your effectiveness with Excel. You'll find the links at http://www.j-walk.com/ss/excel/links.

TIP: The *Google Directory* includes an extensive list of Excel add-ins under Computers > Software > Spreadsheets > Excel > Add-Ins.

DataPrompter allows you to choose which text to insert from a menu that it adds to Word's main menu. It's a terrific way for you to create highly customized proposals, annual account summaries, or quarterly reports, that is, by organizing the content you use regularly into separate subject-oriented directories.

Once you've assembled those pieces, you can customize your content even further. *DataPrompter* prompts you for any data that needs to be changed (e.g., names, investments, dates) and then instantly updates that data throughout your document.

TIP: Go to Google and type in **add-in** or **add-on** or **add on** and the name of the software and see what add-ins might be offered for the programs you use.

Notes

1. Ferris Research (http://www.ferris.com/Welcome.html) June 19, 2003.

2. You can restore those windows to their original size by pressing it again.

3. The ⊞ key (the "Windows" key) is generally found near the Ctrl (Control) and Alt keys, to the left or right of the spacebar on a standard keyboard.

4. Press and hold the *Alt* key while pressing the *Tab* key repeatedly.

5. To activate the desktop Address bar see "Add an Address bar to your desktop" on page 89 in the section titled "Turbocharge Your Browser" in Chapter 3.

6. Use *Ctrl + Shift +* → to select text to the right of the cursor or *Ctrl + Shift +* → for text to the left of the cursor.

7. ↓ represents the down-arrow key, ↑ the up-arrow key.

8. This is generally a faster way of getting an explanation of a chosen function than opening the full Help file. Try it first.

9. For more information on how absolute and relative cell references work in Excel, consult its Help file.

10. *Tip:* Use this shortcut to go right to the last change you made in any Word document saved on your hard drive. Pressing it after opening the file will bring you directly to your last edit.

11. To download them, right-click on a link to any one of them and choose "Save Target as," then select where you want to store the file on your hard drive (set up a folder called "Downloads" and within that, another folder labeled "Macro Samples").

12. I frequently find macros don't work because my computer processes their instructions too quickly—the PC essentially trips over itself in trying to do what it's being told. Slowing down the keystroke speed within the macro solves the problem.

7

Get the Help You Need to Succeed

Delegating Your Way to the Top

Leadership is the art of getting someone else to do something you want done because he wants to do it.

—Dwight Eisenhower

One of the most common fears among those in business for themselves is losing control. They confuse accountability for achieving a result with being personally responsible for doing all the work. The thing that distinguishes successful entrepreneurs and executives from the pack is that they figure out what they are good at, what only they can do, and then they focus on those things as much as possible. They learn to accomplish everything else necessary to achieving their goals through other people.

How effectively do you delegate responsibility to those around you? How well have you equipped those people with the tools and knowledge they need to get the job done systematically?

The acid test is to ask, "What would happen to my business if I disappeared from the scene for a week, a month, or a year?" For too many advisors, the answer is it too would disappear, because the business has no value apart from them. They *are* the business. They are what gives it life and keeps it going. They are indispensable. And that's a problem.

Whether you are responsible only for yourself or you lead a group, knowing how to identify and capitalize on the human and technological resources available to you is essential. Chapter 2 laid out an approach for achieving systematic breakthroughs; this chapter is that one's corollary, outlining ideas on how and where to find the people you need to accomplish those breakthroughs.

Resources Hiding in Plain Sight

If you're saying to yourself, "But my problem is I work alone, and I don't know where to find the people or tools I need," relax. Even (in some ways, especially) if you are a one-person operation, there is all kinds of assistance you can draw on—regularly or as needed. Here's a list of some of the alternatives:

People

- Virtual assistants (VAs)
- College interns
- Freelancers
- Your broker–dealer or custodian
- Product partners/wholesalers
- Software vendors
- Study groups
- Business coaches
- Professional tutors
- Family and friends
- Strategic partners
- Clients

Education/Learning

- Adult education classes
- The Internet
- Computer-based training (CBT)
- Trade associations
- Books

Let's start by talking about the first one on the People list, virtual assistants.

Virtual Assistance

The Internet has revolutionized many businesses, but there's at least one that it created single-handedly: virtual assistance. In the past decade, thousands of former executive assistants and support professionals have traded corporate jobs for entrepreneurial opportunity, providing services to clients whom they may never meet in person.

VAs are independent contractors who set their own hours and work from home. That means no employee, no tax burden, and no need for extra space. While some accept project work, most VAs seek long-term client relationships and price their services on a retainer basis, charging $30–$35 per hour and up. They are highly trained professionals who take advantage of technology wherever possible (computers, phones, faxes, scanners, e-mail, instant messaging) to stay accessible and deliver what's needed.

How do you find them? One way is to ask someone who's already working with one. Another is to Google the search phrase "*virtual assistance*" (with the quotes included) along with the state or city you live in. A third is to consult Google's Directory, which includes a list of Secretarial Services and Virtual Assistants (look under "Office Services" in the "Business Services" section of the "Business" category).

One of the resources listed in the Google Directory is *AssistU* (http://www .assistu.com), a company that has trained and certified thousands of VAs. I first utilized its services to find a VA after reading about the company in a magazine.

You can post your position (for free) at AssistU. The company provides a comprehensive questionnaire that's useful in defining your needs, regardless of whether you decide to post the position there or not (e.g., What's happening in your business that leads you to consider a VA? What activities do you need to delegate to give yourself more time?) If you do choose to post at AssistU, you should begin hearing from interested VAs by e-mail within hours. From there, you can set up phone interviews with those who sound like they might be a good fit.

Other sites that offer directories of VAs you can contact regarding your needs are:

- International Association of Virtual Office Assistants (http://www .iavoa.com).
- International Virtual Assistants Association (http://www.ivaa.org/).
- Canadian Virtual Assistant Network (http://www.canadianva.net/).
- Virtual Assistants for You (http://www.va4u.com).
- VA Certification (http://www.vacertification.com).

A good VA can provide a wide range of services including:

- Preparing correspondence/reports (letters, e-mail).
- Developing creative materials (brochures, newsletters, flyers).
- Designing and maintaining Web sites.
- Transcribing meeting and conference notes.
- Entering data and building spreadsheets.
- Preparing presentations (PowerPoint slides and handouts).
- Researching on- and off-line.
- Managing and maintaining contact databases.
- Planning meetings, preparing seminars, and arranging travel.
- Sending out mass mailings and information packets.
- Invoicing and paying bills.
- Answering phones and maintaining your appointment schedule.

Virtual assistance is an avenue worth considering if you need to routinely delegate follow-up to others, but aren't prepared (or don't want) to hire an employee. Good VAs can be much more than an extra set of hands for your business; they can act as a sounding board and give you the freedom to focus on the things that really matter in taking your business to its next level of success.

Interns: Affordable Workers, Eager to Learn

Another strategy that doesn't require bringing someone on permanently is hiring a college or graduate student to complete routine office tasks. You'll be drawing from a pool of well-educated, Web-savvy workers eager to learn and gain experience, and who are available at a fraction of what you'd have to pay a "professional" worker.

In most cases, you can post directly with the career centers of local schools at no charge. To find out what schools are near you, visit *Braintrack* (http://www.braintrack.com). If you want to advertise at several schools simultaneously, think about broadcasting a posting at *MonsterTRAK* (http://www .monstertrak.com) or Experience's *eRecruiting* (http://www.experience.com). Thousands of students and alumni comb their listings daily looking for job opportunities. Follow these steps to get your position posted:

1. *Map out what and who you're looking for.*

   Brainstorm a list of tasks you'd like to delegate. Use that list to pre-pare a position description and copy for an ad. No one likes to be stuck at the copier all day; be sure to season your position with some project-oriented, challenging work.

2. *Scan ads to get ideas on improving the way your position is "packaged."*

   To make sure your posting is in the right ballpark financially and oth-erwise, take a look at what other companies in your area are offering. Ask career centers at your target schools if you can log onto their site, or ask the posting vendors for sample ads. Check out your local paper, the *Washington Post* (http://www.washingtonpost.com/jobs/), the *New York Times* (http://www.nytimes.com/pages/jobs/) or the *Los Angeles Times* (http://www.latimes.com/classified/jobs/) for ideas.

3. *Advertise when the time is right*

   Real estate is all about "location, location, location." Hiring college students is about "timing, timing, timing." You will have the most suc-cess if you post two to three weeks before a new term starts and five or six weeks before the year wraps up. Don't expect much response once students are a few weeks into the term and their schedules are set.

 TIP: For summer hires: run ads starting in late March. For fall hires: start running ads in mid-August. For spring semester: place ads in late December.

---

4. *Start with the top tier schools in your area; expand your search only if you have to.*

   All college students are not created equal, and there's nothing more frustrating than being stuck with an unmotivated one. You're looking for the best combination of talent, drive, discipline, and good personal chem-istry you can find. If you have a choice of schools in your area, post at the most academically demanding ones first.

5. *Alert professors in related departments that your position is open.*

   Depending on your needs, students pursuing chosen majors or schools can be very helpful (e.g., journalism if you need someone to do a lot of writing; marketing if you need to research new markets; information sys-tems if you need programming expertise). Advising professors in those departments that you're looking may lead you to a higher-quality pool of applicants. Visit the schools' Web sites to review faculty bios and follow up by phone or e-mail with those who teach about related disciplines. Or call the department secretary, explain your situation, and ask for a recommendation on which professors to contact for guidance.

TIP: If you're interested in students who are pursuing a financial planning degree, visit the *CFP Board of Standards'* site to review a state-by-state list of schools with board-registered programs (http://www.cfp.net/become/programs.asp). Each listing includes the name of the school, the degree or certificate granted, contact e-mail address, contact person, mailing address, and phone number. Some also include a link to the school's site.

Streamlining Interviews and Selection

Interviewing job candidates can be a time sink. One of the easiest ways to avoid that problem is to create an information-gathering process where your candidates shoulder the follow-up responsibility. How? Send those who pass your initial screen a list of questions inviting them to tell you more about themselves.[1] Here's what I use; feel free to borrow from it.

Dear [CANDIDATE NAME]

Thanks for responding to my posting for the marketing assistant position. I appreciate your interest.

Please reply to the questions below, which will help make subsequent conversations we might have more productive. Your answers are an opportunity to describe what you've done, what you're looking to do, and why you'd be a good fit for this role. Specific examples detailing skills, responsibilities, and accomplishments help most.

If your answers indicate you're well-suited to the position, I'll contact you to arrange a convenient time to talk further. I look forward to hearing from you.

Thanks very much,

Kip Gregory

P.S. I've included more information on the company and the job, along with a job description/contracting agreement to give you a better sense of what's involved.

QUESTIONNAIRE

Please respond to the following questions, highlighting how your experience would help you in this position. Resumes provide a general description of job duties; what I'm looking for here are **specifics**—answers that show **how** you've developed/applied skills and accomplished goals.

1. How does this position relate to your career goals/aspirations?
2. What work-related projects have you organized and coordinated?
3. In what ways have you interacted with clients/customers in other jobs?
4. What are the most important things you learned from those experiences?
5. Provide some specific examples of business-related research you have conducted, how you have done it, and the tools you have used.
6. What software have you used regularly; which programs are you most proficient with?
7. How would others you've worked with previously describe you?

THE COMPANY

The Gregory Group coaches clients on how to use technology and the Internet to win more business. We work with financial services organizations and individual advisors across the US and Canada. Our workshops, seminars, and coaching programs are delivered in person and over the Web.

We are looking for people hungry to learn and to assist in providing exceptional service to our clients. Our work is challenging, fun and rewarding; the atmosphere casual but professional. We are located in Washington, DC (less than 10 minutes on foot from the Metro's Red Line).

THE POSITION: MARKETING ASSISTANT
(15–30 HOURS/WEEK)

The primary requirements of this position are to provide marketing and administrative support and to assist in maintaining clear, well-documented office procedures. Job duties include managing a contact database, doing research on the Internet, keeping projects running smoothly and on time, completing proposals and customizing materials for client programs, arranging programs/scheduling travel itineraries, maintaining our Web site, etc. Routine support like filing, copying, answering the phone, making follow-up phone calls, and running business errands (FedEx, Kinko's, Post Office, etc.) is expected.

Though there are other aspects of the job, its main thrusts require excellent organizational skills and attention to detail, strong interpersonal skills, and highly efficient, effective computer work.

THE SUCCESSFUL CANDIDATE

We are seeking someone who is responsible and results-oriented, who can work as well independently as they do on a team, and who has demonstrated the ability to get the job done in past assignments. Proficiency with [list the programs you regularly use here], and Internet research are strong pluses . . .

Is all that a lot to throw at someone right at the beginning? Perhaps, but experience has borne out several things:

- *Being clear about what's expected in the job appeals to the kind of person you want to hire.* The college students you want desire that type of job on their resume; it makes them more marketable.

- *It weeds out the curious from the serious.* It doesn't take much these days to shotgun a résumé, especially using the Internet; a couple of clicks and material is delivered to thousands of potential employers. This approach puts the ball back into the applicant's court right away.

- *It saves a lot of unnecessary back-and-forth message exchange.*

Expect 25 to 50 percent of those you send the questionnaire to return it. You will cut that group down again by half in reviewing their responses. Schedule a brief phone interview or in-person meeting with each remaining person. Using these steps, you can reduce a group of 100+ applicants to a handful of very strong candidates in a matter of days, without spending more than a few minutes on each one.

TIP: Have replies sent to your secondary e-mail account, so your primary mailbox isn't overrun with responses that distract you from pressing business. And asking for e-mails only (no faxes or mailings) will save having to scan or retype the information.

Finding Freelancers

Maybe you don't need someone long-term, or located in your office. Perhaps you have a project that requires specific skills for a limited time, and all you really want is to find someone who can do what you need at a reasonable price with no strings attached. One place to find them is *Elance Online* (http://www.elanceonline.com), a marketplace for all kinds of professional services, including Web design and development, programming expertise, accounting and bookkeeping, graphic design, and administrative support.

At Elance Online you can browse descriptions and ratings of providers within any category or search across categories for those who meet specified criteria. You can post a project description for free using Elance's *Basic Marketplace*, or for a small fee (refundable once the job is awarded) within Elance's *Select Marketplace*, where vendors have gone through a verification screening process. You can even customize your view of Elance by setting up a "My Elance" page if you plan to utilize the service regularly.

A second source is *AllExperts* (http://www.allexperts.com), a free service launched in 1998 (which bills itself as the "oldest & largest Q&A service on the Internet"). AllExperts is narrower than Elance; more research-focused than a marketplace of buyers and sellers. To see what the site's roster of experts looks like, drill down by subject area or search by keyword. You can also check out the site's "Top Experts of the Month" spotlight. AllExperts offers a profile of each expert, along with ratings from others who have used their services. The only downside: you can't view previous questions and answers to get a first-hand sense of how well each expert performed.

One site that does post responses provided by their screened researchers is *Google Answers* (http://answers.google.com). Google Answers provides access to researchers who work in one or more of ten categories: Arts and Entertainment, Business and Money, Computers, Family and Home, Health, Reference, Education and News (all one), Relationships and Society, Science, Sports and Recreation, and Miscellaneous.

After registering at the site, you can pose your question and assign a price you're willing to pay for an answer (between $2 and $200 plus the 50¢ processing fee Google charges on top of that). Google Answers tilts the playing field in the buyer's favor; you don't have to pay until you're satisfied with what you learn. Often, you will hear from researchers almost immediately, either with an answer or a request for clarification.

TIP: Many of the questions that go unanswered at Google Answers fall on the low end of the scale. Consider what the right answer to your question is worth to you when setting the price you're willing to pay.

You can (as of this writing) look at every question and answer that has been posted at Google Answers without paying. The answer database is searchable by keyword, and your search results can be sorted by Relevance, Date, or Price. Check it first to see if what you're interested in has already been addressed. (Some of the better answers tend to be the ones provided for higher-priced questions, so it may be worth sorting by price.)

Success in using any of these services depends on knowing how to ask a question the right way. Here are two sample postings. Which do you think is better framed?

"Where can I buy lists of e-mail addresses for high net worth investors over the Internet?"

or

"I'm a financial advisor in the Bay Area of northern CA. A large percentage of my clients are wealthy cardiologists and retired airline pilots (i.e., they own investable assets in excess of $2 million). I'd like to know if there are electronic directories available for purchase/download (that can be imported into Goldmine via a text file) which contain lists of people in either group and include name, address, phone number, and e-mail information. What are my options?"

You still may not get the answer you're looking for with the second one, but you will give yourself a much better shot by being specific.

The last resources covered in this section are *reference librarians* and *independent research professionals*. Both can be great online information sleuths, and most have access to proprietary information sources you don't.

Here are several ways you can leverage their expertise:

- Call the library reference desk at your alma mater and ask for guidance.
- If your school isn't nearby, take a look at the list of academic libraries maintained at *LibWeb* (http://sunsite.berkeley.edu/Libweb/) to find ones that are.
- Contact your local public library and ask for a business reference librarian's help. To locate the public libraries in your area, check out *Libweb's Directory of USA Public Libraries* (http://sunsite.berkeley.edu/Libweb/Public_main.html).

Independent information brokers represent another avenue. You can hire them to help you with almost any research project. Fees vary; some charge by the hour, others by the project. One place to find them is the *Association of Independent Information Professionals* (http://www.aiip.org).

Leveraging Vendors

There's increased emphasis today on delivering value-added services. It's no longer enough to offer a good product or service—that's just the ante to get into the game. Broker–dealers, mutual funds, insurance companies, and other providers are trying hard to distinguish themselves by offering a range of additional support. Ask the ones you work with the following questions to understand what their capabilities are:

- What preapproved materials (direct mail, newsletter articles, seminar presentations, etc.) and marketing programs does your firm make available electronically?
- Which of those are advisors in your territory using most successfully, and how?
- How do I get them (on CD, download from the site, by e-mail, etc.)?
- What other value-added support can you and your firm offer?
- What expertise do you personally offer that can save me time or make me money?
- What features of your Web site would be most helpful to me?
- Who do you know that is leveraging technology especially well in their business and what exactly are they doing?

- What business management and business development training do you offer?
- How can you help me improve my productivity in the following areas (be prepared to list the three to five that matter most)?
- What can you do to help me develop my staff?

A few firms are developing solid value-added programs, but many either dismiss them or are focusing on the wrong issues, especially when it comes to technology. The problem, as mentioned earlier, is that providers are selling one-inch drill bits when their customers are looking for one-inch holes. I've heard it countless times from people in information technology (IT), training and development, sales management, even senior executives: "We're doing great things, and we're making progress, but we're still not getting nearly the utilization we want."

Why? If you're an advisor or a field wholesaler, you already know the reason: You're not predisposed to explore all this stuff, and even if you were, you don't have the time, and no one has ever shown you what to do in a way you can relate to.

In 2002, I wrote a piece, "With Technology, the Training's the Thing" (see box), for *Financial Planning* magazine on the subject. After its publication, I heard from more than 100 people across the industry, mostly advisors, but surprisingly, CEOs and senior managers at some of the largest organizations in the business as well. All said essentially the same thing: *Kip, your observations are right on the money.*

Ironically, what many company executives miss is *that* they are today's technology providers. Sure, they are called broker–dealers, fund companies, life insurers, banks, and other things, but an increasing chunk of what they provide (and most of how they operate) depends on technology that they've spent millions to develop; technology they are hoping you will use.

WITH TECHNOLOGY, THE TRAINING'S THE THING

For all the talk of technology's benefits, there's surprisingly little dialogue on the specifics of making it work. Everything you read and hear says build a Web site, implement a contact management system or publish an e-mail newsletter, but rarely are you given details on how to do it.

At the same time, companies that spend millions on technology wonder why utilization isn't higher. Product providers invest heavily in their Web sites, broker dealers build sophisticated back office automation tools and software developers continue to crank out more creative, more "feature rich" programs. But as creatures of habit, advisors remain largely unaware of these resources.

Most technology providers miss the fact that advisors use a fraction of the technology they own because they have too many choices, too little time and no idea where to start. Not that planners aren't keenly interested in solutions; "keeping up with technology" or "operating more efficiently" consistently rank high on their list of challenges. Many recognize their chief obstacle is they don't know what they don't know and are hoping someone will show them the right path to follow.

Therein lies the opportunity for companies interested in generating more assets, getting planners to adopt their technology or strengthening the loyalty of their best advisors. If you're in any of those categories, my advice is make planners aware of solutions to common problems, help them (and their staff) develop the skills to use those solutions and then coach them on applying that knowledge to improve results. In the process, you'll not only create more than satisfied customers, you'll build business partnerships.

Why don't more companies do that? Usually because, like the advisors they serve, their sales and support teams can't teach what they don't know. If those teams don't use (and appreciate the value of) technology, trying to coach others on connecting the dots is a difficult exercise.

Yet opportunities are everywhere. Take client communication for example. Every advisor wants to do a better job using technology to stay in touch with clients—whether by e-mail or through a Web site or in desktop publishing a newsletter. And while figuring out how to implement an automated communication strategy isn't brain surgery, it's time consuming—it requires learning what's out there, understanding how it works, and doing the work of integrating it into your business.

Product and service providers could easily create programs that outline the how-to's of marketing electronically to clients by bundling what they offer with the standard tools (like Microsoft Office), training and techniques necessary to do the job. That's the essence of value-added support. And done properly its benefits are measurable, its appeal powerful.

To be fair, some companies offer support of this kind. But typically it's packaged in a glossy brochure that ends up in a desk drawer, not ingrained

(continued)

in the daily activity of their field sales team. E-wholesaling programs have also begun to spring up where staff trained on the company's technology and Web site walk planners through what's available. But most of those efforts don't go far enough; they focus on proprietary solutions and are primarily a way to reduce field marketing costs.

The answer to the industry's technology challenge is education. And provider companies should take the lead in delivering it. Here's a radical suggestion: forget about developing yet another proprietary software solution next year. Instead, invest that money in advisor (and wholesaler) training on the tools you already offer—and they already own.

Planners don't need more choices; they need help in understanding how to use what they have. Give them hands-on assistance and you'll get their attention, their loyalty, and their business.

The companies that will win the mindshare/market share battle will distinguish themselves through the creative use of tools and skills like those outlined in these pages. If you want to benefit from their effort, ask your vendors how they can help you implement the strategies we've been discussing. (And if you're a product provider looking for clues on how to do it, read "Using Technology to Build a Better Sales Force" in Appendix A.)

Learning Resources

Okay, suppose you're not someone who can sit down and figure things out on your own, technological or otherwise. What are your options? There's a hierarchy of alternatives; I call it the Learning Pyramid. It has five levels:

1. Hard knocks
2. Self-study
3. Study group
4. Classroom
5. Coaching

Hard knocks is where you probably are today. I want to talk briefly about the other options, each of which represents an easier, more efficient way to acquire knowledge.

Let me be clear: I'm not suggesting you retool your life to spend your day at your computer. It's a mistake to think of these options solely in personal terms; consider them as ways you can help your *business* acquire corporate competencies. You may not need (or want) to sharpen your own skills further, but someone on your team needs to if you hope to create and keep a competitive edge.

Self-Study

If you're disciplined enough to stick with a routine, there are many options. A simple one is the weekly routine of exploring programs on your PC described in the Introduction ("Getting Started"). Another alternative is to sign up for an online course. *Google's Directory* lists a number of sites that offer courses under Reference > Education > Distance Learning, including *CyberU* (http://www.cyberu.com).

If you just want an online tutorial, *Find Tutorials* (http://www.findtutorials.com) offers over 400 of them, all free, on Microsoft Office and other applications. You can also pay an annual subscription fee and get access to other courses offered at the *Find Tutorials* site.

TIP: The Google Directory has a tutorial resource list under Computers > Education > Internet > Help and Tutorials.

Study Group

The study group concept has been a part of the financial services landscape for a long time. It's proven to be a great way to share best practices for those who actively participate in them.

If you're already part of a study group, consider adding something on technology to your meeting agenda, at least occasionally. And (to the point made earlier), how about getting your assistant or someone else on your team involved in a group that's focused *specifically* on office technology? Other advisors do what you and your staff do every day and could be working more efficiently, more profitably, and more successfully by leveraging the very same tools that are sitting on your desktop. Wouldn't you like to find out what they're doing (and how)? A study group can give you the platform.

Classroom

One of the simplest and cheapest ways to climb the curve is to enroll in an adult education course. Community colleges are a good option, offering inexpensive courses at beginner, intermediate, and advanced levels. To find one check your local classified ads, or scan the *Community College Directory* (http://www .community-college.org) for schools in the United States (or *Community College Web* (http://www.mcli.dist.maricopa.edu/cc/info.html) for a United States/international directory).

Coaching

Great sales managers are great coaches, gifted at spotting talent and developing it. The problem is there just aren't enough good sales managers to go around, especially if you're independent (you may not even *have* a manager). That's partly why so many "coaches" have sprung up in the past few years.

If you haven't seen it and are considering a coach, look at Ed Morrow's book *Personal Coaching for Financial Advisors* (http://www.financialsoftware .com). It can help you assess if coaching is right for you, what your choices are, and how to select the right individual or organization.

Many advisors are skeptical about coaching. They like the idea; it's the people doing it they're not sure of. There are the "egos" whose message boils down to "Look at me, look how great I am; you can be just like me, for 10,000 bucks I'll show you how," and the "therapists" who listen and offer golden rule advice (write down your goals, keep a to-do list, etc.), but rarely provide specific suggestions for making improvements. Don't misunderstand; there are also people and firms in the market doing great work. You just have to find them.

Here are some suggestions on how to determine whether a coaching relationship might work for you:

- Talk to someone who has worked or is working with a coach and find out what tangible benefits they've gotten from the time and money invested.

- Visit the industry magazine sites listed in the next chapter. Look at the columns, many are written by industry coaches, or search the article archives on *coach* or *coaching*.

- Visit Internet sites devoted to executive coaching. Google's Directory includes a long list of them under Business > Management > Consulting > Executive Coaching.

- Make contact with the coaches you're considering and find out if the fit is right. Ask questions, determine what specific outcomes you will realize, and don't be afraid to pass on a situation that just doesn't seem right.

Five things to look for in selecting a coach/consultant are:

1. Good chemistry; you relate well to each other.
2. You speak the same language, and they understand and have addressed the challenges you face.
3. Their approach is proven and built on simple, well-defined processes that allow you to measure how well you're progressing.
4. You see clearly how you will accelerate toward your goal faster with them involved.
5. They understand the relationship has a finite life span and they have planned their obsolescence into the timetable and process they follow.

Note

1. Very special thanks to Carol and Mark Sheer (http://www.marksheer.com), who shared their hiring process with me when I was first getting started, and on which I based the approach outlined here.

Assembling Your Toolkit

What Else You May Need and Where to Find It

Do not wait; the time will never be "just right." Start where you stand, and work with whatever tools you may have at your command, and better tools will be found as you go along.

—Napoleon Hill, *Think and Grow Rich*

One of today's great myths is that you have to have the latest technology to succeed in business. Hijacking the notion that speed is critical, vendors prod you into buying their wares so you can do everything *faster* (though in reality not necessarily any *better*). It's a classic case of buying the sizzle and choking on the steak, and it's a big part of why people are generally cynical about technology.

The truth is that most people already own *most* of what they need; they just have to learn to use it more effectively. But beyond the tools already covered, what exactly should you consider equipping yourself with? That's what this chapter is about. In addition to covering the need-to-have and nice-to-have programs, it will answer two questions I encounter frequently:

1. Where do you find all the stuff you talk and write about?

2. What guidance can you give me about buying/upgrading hardware and software?

You may have the bases we're going to cover taken care of, though I meet people all the time who don't. The tools highlighted here are designed to protect you from disaster, make you more productive, or improve the operation of your computer. The disaster-prevention tools are essential; the others are optional depending on your requirements, your comfort level with the technology, and how much you have to do for yourself that can't be delegated or outsourced to others.

Avoiding Disaster

Keeping your equipment and your data out of harm's way is essential to staying in business. A good disaster-prevention plan addresses four areas of risk: damage from e-mail viruses, permanent loss of data by any cause, protection from attacks by hackers, and disruption and data loss caused by electrical outages. Let's talk briefly about each one.

Virus Protection

Using e-mail and the Web without anti-virus software is worse than playing Russian roulette. Viruses can delete critical operating system files, erase your priceless data, or render it inaccessible—before you even know it. Virus protection is the first of four cornerstones in an effective disaster-prevention/ recovery strategy.

It's not enough to install and run the software regularly, you have to keep it up-to-date; new viruses surface every day. The two leading programs are *Norton AntiVirus* (http://www.symantec.com/avcenter) and *McAfee* (http://www.mcafee.com), about $30 each. Each monitors and protects against over 60,000 viruses. *Whatever product you use, set it to check new e-mail messages as they arrive, establish a schedule for scanning your hard drive automatically at least once every other week, and be sure to reinoculate your PC continually by configuring the software to retrieve updates (called "virus definitions") automatically from the company's Web site.*

A File Backup System

Not creating data backup files is just as dangerous as not shielding your PC from harmful viruses. It's something everyone knows they should do, but few ever act on. If your system fails for any reason, the result can be devastating: your data can be lost, and you may be put permanently out of business. Forget about terrorist attacks, your computer could be stolen, your home or office flooded or consumed by fire, you could be hit with an electrical power surge during a storm, or you might just accidentally spill coffee on your PC some morning. To avoid irreparable harm, regularly save copies of your data files and keep them in a safe, separate place.

Onsite. When backing up, you have a number of choices, the first is whether to do it onsite or online (i.e., over the Internet). If you choose to back up onsite, you need specific equipment: either a CD (or the newer digital video disk (DVD)) drive that allows you to burn (i.e., copy) files to blank CDs or DVDs, a Zip drive for copying to Zip disks, or a storage device that plugs directly into your PC through a universal serial bus (USB) port or PC card slot.

There are pros and cons to each option. For pure backup, the small USB storage devices marketed today are tough to beat (search the magazine sites mentioned later in the chapter for *USB miniature storage* for the latest information). I recommend using CDs because, in addition to providing you with a backup mechanism, they can also be used to create and distribute materials to clients and others. CD drives are available in two "flavors": CD-R (recordable) and CD-RW (rewritable). The difference: you can copy over files on a rewritable CD, but not on a recordable one. CD-Rs are much less expensive, and are available at pennies per disk when you buy in bulk.

Many PCs today come factory equipped with a CD burner (i.e., drive). If yours didn't, you can buy one as an accessory. Visit your computer manufacturer's Web site to see what they offer or check out Clnet's *Shopper.com* (http://www.shopper.cnet.com) or *mySimon* (http://www.mysimon.com) to comparison shop (equipment prices vary depending on the burner's speed (i.e., how fast it copies) and other factors). You will also need software for copying data from your hard drive to your CDs. Roxio's *Easy CD Creator* (http://www.roxio.com) is one of the leading products in the category. Check the Web for others.

TIP: When shopping for any computer hardware, keep in mind you will find the best balance between cost, longevity, and functionality on models that were leading-edge six to nine months ago but have since been replaced by something newer.

One other backup tool worth having is *GoBack* (http://www.symantec.com/goback/). GoBack takes snapshots of your computer's file configuration every few minutes and stores them on your hard drive so that if your PC has a problem, you can return the machine to working order quickly and easily.

Online. If you prefer to back up files using the Internet, you will need dependable high-speed access to the Web; a dial-up connection won't cut it. There are a number of Web-based services to choose from, ranging from basic ones like *Yahoo's Briefcase* (http://briefcase.yahoo.com) to more sophis-ticated (and expensive) options like *@Backup* (http://www.backup.com) or *Connected* (http://www.connected.com). Cost, storage space, security, and ease of use are all things worth considering.

> **TIP:** If you work for a large company, contact your computer help desk to find out what automated backup procedures are in place. If there aren't any, or not all of your critical files are covered by the process, back up what you need separately.

An Internet Firewall

The third piece of a good disaster prevention strategy is blocking hackers from breaking into your PC and stealing your data. You may think you're an unlikely target, but hackers don't discriminate; they scan the Internet looking for unpro-tected computers or networks they can penetrate. I was shocked to come face-to-face with that reality several years ago after having a *digital subscriber line* (DSL) connection installed in my home office. One day I noticed my modem's transmission light flickering, though I wasn't actively online at the time. Alarmed, I shut down my PC—only to get a message in the process that six other users were accessing my system. I immediately called my computer sup-port guy, who the next day set up a firewall. It was a frightening experience that taught me I wasn't immune to the problem.

Today, a number of inexpensive hardware and software products will make your PC invisible on the Internet. On the hardware side, *Linksys* (http://www.linksys.com) and *D-Link* (http://www.dlink.com) are leading manufac-turers. For software, *ZoneAlarm* (http://www.zonelabs.com), *Norton Person-al Firewall* (http://www.symantec.com/sabu/nis/npf/), and *McAfee Firewall* (http://www.mcafee.com) will all give you added protection.

> **TIP:** To assess how vulnerable your PC is to outside attack, try *Shields-UP!*, a free service offered by *Gibson Research Corporation* (http://grc.com). You will find a link to ShieldsUP! on GRC's home page. Two quick tests will tell you how at risk your PC is, and gen-erate a report suggesting ways to reduce your exposure.

TIP: To ensure you have the latest patches for Windows and Internet Explorer (IE), check *Microsoft's Windows Update* (http://windows update.microsoft.com) routinely. There, you can have your PC scanned and see what updates are available. You decide which, if any, to download and install. Use Windows 98 or later? Look for "Windows Update" on your Start menu to connect to the site automatically.

SMOKING OUT SPYWARE

Ever have browser windows suddenly pop up on your screen with ads for products, services, and Web sites you have no interest in? They are *very* annoying.

That happens for several reasons, the most common one being that you visited a site that secretly loaded a cookie or program on your computer to push those ads at you. Such programs are generally referred to as "spyware."

The easiest way to get rid of them is to download, install, and run Ad-aware from Lavasoft (http://www.lavasoftusa.com/software/adaware/). Ad-aware is a free product that will analyze the files on your hard drive and detect and eliminate any spyware files it finds. When I ran it the first time on my PC, it identified 97 such files that had been installed over time. Now I use it monthly to keep my system clean. It's an easy, no-cost, fast way to eliminate an annoying problem.

Surge Suppressors and Battery Backup

The final cornerstone of disaster prevention is to put safeguards in place to insulate you from electrical problems. The first of those is surge suppression for all your equipment (including your phones); the second is battery backup (what's technically called *uninterruptible power supply* (UPS)) for each computer and monitor in your office. The two are separate and distinct capabilities; you should have them both. Suppressors protect your equipment from sudden power surges that can occur when lightning hits an electrical line or when power is restored after a failure. UPS systems (about the size of a car battery) store enough power to keep your PC and monitor running long enough for you to save your work and shut down in the event your power goes off.

Again, don't kid yourself that the odds of avoiding either a power surge or an outage are in your favor; I learned that the hard way. I can't get a single winning number on a PowerBall ticket but, sure enough, lightning has struck me twice in the same place—my office. When I first set the office up, I mistakenly believed that battery backup equipment I had purchased also shielded against power surges (something most UPS systems now do), so I only bought a UPS system. During a storm later that summer, a lightning bolt hit a power line in my neighborhood and ran right down the block into my office and, poof, like a Looney Tunes cartoon explosion, it cooked an assortment of computer parts.

After replacing everything that was fried, and adding separate surge suppressors, I was thrilled when the same thing occurred again only months later. The culprit this time: the phone line. It turned out that when the phone company installed my DSL connection the previous year, the technicians failed to ground the outside phone line properly, which left the door open to another surge. It was a fluke thing, and unless I'd been a lineman for the county, not something I could have known to look for, but the experience reinforced the importance of trying to anticipate all the possibilities (remember the Danger Zone—you don't know what you don't know?). Be sure any surge suppressor strips you buy also include outlets for phone lines.

American Power Conversion Corp (http://www.apcc.com) is a leading provider of UPS systems and surge suppressor strips; *Tripp Lite* (http://www .tripplite.com) is another.

TIP: If you work from home, consider getting whole-house surge protection. Check with your power company to see if they offer products and programs that will strengthen your overall shield against electrical damage. And if you hit the road with a laptop, pick up a portable suppressor to put in your carrying case.

TIP: Remember to check your surge protectors periodically to make sure they haven't failed. Some will sound an alarm alerting you if they do, but others only have a warning light indicator that can be easy to miss. Make a note to routinely inspect your equipment to make sure it's functioning properly, especially after storms.

Productivity Tools and Utilities

If you had to boil *Winning Clients in a Wired World* down to its essence, one of the things you'd be left with is the notion of productivity enhancement—getting more done in less time with less frustration, in order to have greater impact. Each of the seven strategies revolves around that principle in one or more ways.

There are some tools that didn't fit easily into the seven strategies framework, but which you should know about nonetheless. They are included below in two sections: "Productivity Tools" and "Utilities."

Productivity Tools

Document Imaging (A.K.A. the "Paperless Office"). The move toward electronic filing of client records is underway in earnest, especially among independent advisors. The notion that you can eliminate a chunk of your overhead expense (i.e., file storage) and create a "paperless office" by scanning documents into electronic format has appeal for obvious reasons. To set yourself up, you will need a scanner, document imaging software (make sure it incorporates optical character recognition [OCR] to convert images to actual text), a CD or DVD burner (and a supply of disks), and a person to complete the imaging process for you (an assistant, intern, or temporary worker). There are a number of products you can choose from. Two of the leading companies are *LaserFiche* (http://www.laserfiche.com) and *ScanSoft* (PaperPort) (http://www.scansoft.com/paperport/pro/).

I don't claim to be an expert on the subject, but several people are. David Drucker and Joel Bruckenstein's book, *Virtual Tools for a High-Margin Office* (Bloomberg Press, 2002) covers the issue extensively. You can contact Drucker at http://www.daviddrucker.com.

Fax Broadcasting. As e-mail communication has exploded, faxing has diminished. Still, there are people who prefer to receive material by fax. *WinFax* (http://www.symantec.com/winfax/) lets you send messages to groups of people at the touch of a button. j2's *jBlast* (http://www.j2.com/services/jBlast.asp) is a Web-based service that will transmit generic or personalized faxes for pennies per page to groups of any size.

High-Speed Internet Access. You probably have a lightning-fast, always-on Web connection at your office, but what about at home? If you're limping along with a dial-up account, upgrade to high-speed access via cable, DSL, or satellite dish. Call your cable and phone providers to see what they offer, or visit *Broadband Reports* (http://www.broadbandreports.com) or *Get-*

Connected (http://www.getconnected.com) to investigate your options. Each site gives you a list of providers, the type(s) of plans they offer, setup and monthly fees charged, what type of access it is (cable, DSL, satellite, etc.), and download speeds. You can also read comments from users of the services you're considering.

TIP: Once you're set up with high-speed access, periodically test your connection to ensure it provides the throughput you're paying for. One site where you can check your DSL speed is *Toast* (http://www.toast.net); try *TestMySpeed* (http://www.testmyspeed.com) if you use cable.

TIP: If you need high-speed access when traveling, check out *Geektools'* directory of hotels before making your reservations (http://www.geektools.com/geektels/). The site lists properties in the United States, Canada, and more than 30 other countries.

Signature Software. If you want to include your signature or a handwritten postscript in the electronic letters and other documents you create, take a look at the line of products offered by vLetter (http://www.vletter.com). Send vLetter a sample of your signature and handwriting and the company will convert it to a font that you can install on your computer. You can incorporate all or part of your signature and the custom handwriting font into letters, e-mails, and proposals.

Typing Tutors. Want to know *the* single best way to improve your efficiency with a computer? Learn to touch type, or if you already know how, to increase your typing speed. Until tablet PCs or Dick Tracy wristwatches go mainstream, keyboards remain the primary way information gets from your brain to your computer and vice versa. Knowing how to type proficiently is a prerequisite to making that transfer quickly. (I'm not talking about 70–80 words a minute—I mean the ability to type faster than you write, which probably means 35–40 words a minute.)

Think sharpening your typing skill isn't the best use of your time? Take a lesson from Jack Welch. Here's what he told *Newsweek* magazine in December 2000, while he was still GE's CEO, about his personal introduction to the Internet and how he learned to type.

NEWSWEEK   When did you personally start using the Internet?

WELCH   After the Christmas of 1998. My wife had been using the Internet for three or four years, trading stocks and doing other things. I didn't have time for it. Then everybody in my office started buying Christmas presents online. A few weeks later I went to Mexico with my wife. She started showing me Yahoo investor sites, where people were talking about GE stock. "Jack's a jerk, Jack's great, Jack should do this." My God, it was fascinating. So I started sneaking in from the pool during the rest of the vacation to look at it. When I got home I bought a CD-ROM and spent a weekend learning how to type. It gave you a contest: "You've now got 21 words a minute." So I spent weekends competing at it. I can type pretty well now.[1]

You can buy a tutorial at your local computer superstore or purchase one online. *Typing Instructor Deluxe* (http://www.individualsoftware.com/new/consumer/details/tx7_details.htm) and *Mavis Beacon* (http://www.mavisbeacon.com) are two popular programs.

TIP: You can find out your current typing speed by taking a quick test online at *Typing Pal* (http://www.typingpal.com/test/). When you are done, the site will generate a report giving you your word per minute count, how many errors you made, and what level typist that qualifies you as (beginner, average, or expert).

Voice Recognition.   Another way to achieve greater efficiency is to bypass the keyboard entirely and dictate your notes, letters, or proposals directly into your PC using a voice-recognition program like *NaturallySpeaking* (http://www.scansoft.com/naturallyspeaking/) or *ViaVoice* (http://www.ibm.com/software/speech/). Voice-recognition software lets you program your computer to recognize your spoken words and convert them to text. You can also use it to control your PC (e.g., telling it to start a program or open a file). If you buy one, plan on spending at least 30 minutes "training" your computer to recognize your voice, which you do by reading selected passages into a microphone plugged into your PC (one ships with the software). These programs are remarkably accurate (in the high 90 percent range today), and the more you use/train them, the better the software will get at recognizing your speech patterns.

Utilities

File Compression Software. Ever downloaded or received a file with a name ending in ".zip" and been unable to open it? Those are compressed files, shrunk to make them easier to send or store. They usually require special software to open. The leading utility program for compressing files is *WinZip* (http://www.winzip.com).

File Viewers. Increasingly, companies and individuals are publishing materials in portable document format (PDF). Doing so retains the file's original look no matter where it's viewed or printed. Most PDF files are created using Adobe Acrobat, discussed in Chapter 5. Opening and printing PDFs requires either the full Acrobat program or Adobe's free *Acrobat Reader* (http://www.adobe.com/products/acrobat/readstep2.html). You should at least have the Reader.

Multimedia Player(s). Multimedia players let you watch video files or listen to audio files on your PC. The best known are Apple's *QuickTime* (http://www.apple.com/quicktime/), Microsoft's *Windows Media Player* (http://www.microsoft.com/windows/windowsmedia/), and Real Networks' *RealOne Player* (http://www.real.com). Microsoft's and Apple's software is free (Apple also sells a Pro version of QuickTime). Real Networks' RealOne product is available by subscription only. Start with the Windows Media Player and use it until you find yourself needing more advanced features that are built into the other products you have to pay for.

Quick View Plus. Available at (http://www.avantstar.com/solutions/quick_view_plus/), *Quick View Plus* (QVP) is another utility worth having. QVP is a handy tool for viewing and printing e-mail attachments and file downloads created with software that's not installed on your computer. QVP recognizes 200 file formats and is especially useful if you need to handle files from clients or prospects created with software you don't own. You can copy and paste contents of any file QVP recognizes into the programs you use regularly where you can manipulate the information as needed.

Remote Access. *GoToMyPC* (http://www.gotomypc.com) is a remarkable Web-based service that lets you access and work on another PC over the Internet using any Web browser. After logging on via a secure connection, you can utilize the computer remotely just as if you were sitting right in front of it, not only to copy files from that PC to the one you're working on "locally," but to actually open and run applications on that other computer, regardless of whether your local PC has those same applications installed. Expertcity, makers of GoToMyPC, offers a free trial and individual and corporate accounts (you can subscribe monthly or annually). If you work with a virtual assistant or receive (or provide) support long-distance, it is definitely worth checking out.

System Utilities. *Norton SystemWorks* (http://www.symantec.com/sabu/ sysworks/basic/) includes a suite of programs that helps you fix (and avoid) problems; recover deleted files; optimize your PC performance so that it starts up, runs, and shuts down faster; and protects you from viruses (Norton AntiVirus is included in the product).

Where to Get the Inside Scoop

People often ask, "How do you keep up with everything that's out there?" The honest answer is there's too much for any one person to ever keep track of. Sites, applications, and equipment are in a constant state of flux. I try to stay plugged in several ways: by reading, surfing the Web and using software on my own, and by listening to suggestions clients, presentation attendees, and *Kip's Tip* readers pass along (you can sign up at http://www.kipstips.com, if you want to become one).

My first stop is almost always *Google* (http://www.google.com), or more accurately, the Google toolbar in my browser, either to search for specific sites or to see if there's a *Google Directory* category (http://directory.google.com) on whatever subject I'm exploring. After that, where I go depends on what I need at the time.

General Computing Issues

For general computing information, I look to:

PC World (http://www.pcworld.com).   This companion site to one of the most widely read computing magazines offers a wide array of useful content. There are three things about it I really like. It has a five-year archive of articles you can browse or search, even without a subscription. It provides a well-organized buying guide (e.g., laptops, desktops, personal digital assistants (PDAs)) that's updated regularly and can be very useful when you're considering adding to or upgrading your equipment. Finally, it has a library of thousands of useful software patches (fixes to popular programs) and *shareware* ("try before you buy" software bought over the Web) that you can download.

PC Magazine (http://www.pcmag.com).   This site is associated with the other well-known computing magazine. PCMag.com offers many of the same features as PC World and a few others. You can view the current and previous issues, product reviews, and descriptions/downloads of thousands of shareware programs. PCMag.com also includes a discussion area where you can post questions and get feedback on technology you own or are considering buying. PC Magazine is known for its Editors' Choice awards, given to the top product(s) in each category reviewed. Many consider these awards to be technology's equivalent of the Good Housekeeping seal of approval. See if there's an Editor's Choice award in any category of equipment you're shopping for prior to making a purchase.

Clnet (http://www.cnet.com) and *ZDNet* (http://www.zdnet.com; also owned by clnet).   These sites also offer extensive product reviews and in clnet's case, downloads of various programs (http://www.download.com). Every product listed is scored on a one-to-five star scale based both on an in-house review and reader/user comments.

LangaList (http://www.langa.com).   Fred Langa publishes one of the best newsletters I've ever read; apparently I'm not the only one who thinks so; over 100,000 people worldwide subscribe to it. The feedback and suggestions from readers that Langa includes are a big part of what makes it so valuable. People continually write in with usage tips for common programs and all kinds of useful resources they've found on the Web. Langa offers two versions of his newsletter (both are published twice weekly): the standard one is free, the other (his Plus edition) costs $12 per year and includes content not found in the standard edition, as well as access to a downloadable archive of all past issues. LangaList isn't for everyone, but if you're on the front side of the technology adaptation bell curve, or have someone on staff responsible for keeping your team's computer systems running smoothly, you should sign up.

Windows Users Group Network (http://www.wugnet.com).   WUGNET bills itself as the oldest and largest independent online group for Windows users. Like LangaList, WUGNET's information isn't for the novice, but I would recommend it to anyone who is comfortable with installing or removing software. Two sections stand out: its "Shareware Hall of Fame," which lists programs WUGNET has spotlighted each week for the past several years (many of the things you've been reading about are listed there), and its

"Computing Tip of the Day," which includes suggestions on making better use of Office, IE, and Windows.

The Scout Report (http://scout.wisc.edu).   The Scout Report is one of the Web's oldest weekly e-mail newsletter services, dating back to April 1994. Every Friday, TSR publishes a listing of new and interesting Web sites culled by hundreds of librarians and other researchers across the globe. Newsletter content is organized around five recurring categories; the two I find helpful are "General Interest" and "In the News."

Financial Services Industry-Related Computing Issues

For industry-specific information, I generally start at the leading free publication sites, looking for articles and to see what people are talking about in the communities and on message boards. Articles can give you a good overview not only of what new technologies are out there, but issues in the news as well. *Message threads* (exchanges posted online between two or more people), if they are available, can provide unvarnished insight into how individual users feel about those technologies (and lots of other topics).

Financial services industry sites I find helpful include:

Financial Planning Interactive (FPi) (http://www.financial-planning.com) and *On Wall Street* (http://www.onwallstreet.com).   These sister magazines are owned by Thomson Media. FPi offers a software directory that lists over 150 industry-specific programs grouped into 18 categories (asset allocation, estate planning, fund analysis, etc.). It also moderates several special-interest communities, including one on technology, under the umbrella "Shop Talk." Finally, it has a searchable archive of articles. *Financial Planning* magazine's annual survey of software and guide to the Internet is published every December.

Registered Representative (http://registeredrep.com).   One of more than 80 trade journals and magazines published by Primedia, RR offers an archive of back issues, forums for exchanging messages with other registered users of the site, and a list of "Most Requested Stories."

Financial Advisor (http://www.financialadvisormagazine.com).   One of the industry's newer magazines, *Financial Advisor's* Web-site offerings are limited to an archive of past issues and a calendar of events, which is similar to the one maintained at FPi. Nonetheless, well-written articles and columns make this site worth visiting.

The Journal of Accountancy (http://www.aicpa.org/pubs/jofa/joahome.htm). This is the official publication of the American Institute of Certified Public

Accountants (AICPA). You can find more than six years of articles archived by month, in addition to the current issue. The Journal is a section of the *AICPA*'s site (http://www.aicpa.org), which is an incredibly rich (and dense) source of information on accounting—for CPAs and those who have developed strategic alliances with CPAs (or want to).

The Journal of Financial Planning (http://www.journalfp.net).   The official magazine of the *Financial Planning Association* (FPA) (http://www.fpanet .org), it contains an archive of past articles and a directory of industry resources. (As an aside, the FPA's site itself is a very useful resource for any advisor; it offers online education and communities for exchanging ideas and getting questions answered. Be sure to check it out, too.)

Morningstar Advisor (http://advisor.morningstar.com).   Joel Bruckenstein and David Drucker write regularly for this site on technology issues advisors face and products that can help them. Their pieces are worth a look.

Finally, here's a paid site worth investigating (it even offers a 30-day free trial period).

Horsesmouth (http://www.horsesmouth.com).   One of the richest learning resources for advisors on the Internet, the site caters to the needs and interests of financial professionals, especially advisors on the front line, their support staff, and those who manage sales teams. You will find content on developing business, building knowledge, sharpening skills, computing, and managing a branch. "My Horsesmouth" lets you save and make notes on selected articles. Its discussion area, where you can dialog through message postings with leading industry experts and practitioners, offers suggestions on topics including marketing, business planning, practice management, rookie success, and prospecting. The site also delivers an e-mail update to your mailbox every morning (Daily Oats), which offers a summary of new articles and a digest of overnight market analysis. Check with your firm, your suppliers, or your trade association to see if they provide access at reduced or no cost.

TIP: E-mail newsletters from sites like those just mentioned can be a treasure trove of information, or an unwelcome distraction. Give yourself three issues to judge whether the content is worth reading regularly. If it is, keep the subscription; if not, opt out. And be sure to use your secondary e-mail account to manage those subscriptions so you don't clog your primary inbox.

AN OPPORTUNITY YOU SHOULDN'T OVERLOOK

Most financial services professionals don't realize that there are communities on the Web like FPi, Registered Rep, the FPA, and Horsesmouth that cater to their needs. These groups can be valuable not only in researching technology and other topics but as professional networking vehicles. Sadly, they are woefully underutilized. The industry's leading magazines and associations touch tens of thousands of subscribers and members, yet regular users of these online communities number only in the hundreds at best.

Building traffic at an online community is a chicken-and-egg problem. Companies want to see steady volume before investing significantly in developing content, but advisors won't visit sites repeatedly unless they see something worthwhile.

What's the answer? As a user, the first step is to *realize that these sites are designed for you*. The second is to *visit them* whenever input from others who do what you do in the industry might be helpful. Third, *participate*. Offer advice, leave a reply, or post a question of others to get a conversation started about a topic of interest to you. Online communities prosper when there's an exchange of ideas and value that participants can't get anywhere else, and word of that value spreads, drawing others into the circle.

There's still a wide open opportunity for a forward-thinking organization to become *the* place people in financial services congregate online to trade ideas and share expertise. The firm that eventually captures it will do two things: one, continually deliver worthwhile content, not fluff or product and service sales pitches masquerading as articles; and two, offer an easy, effortless way to get to that content so that participants can exchange (i.e., read, retrieve, and post) messages quickly and painlessly.

Buying Hardware

Here are some tips on buying hardware you should follow to save time, money, and frustration in equipping your office.

1. Define Your Needs on Your Terms

Whether you're shopping in stores, on the Web, or with a catalog, you're going to run into lots of technojargon. Here's a typical description of laptop features seen in an ad from one of the leading manufacturers: "Intel Pentium 4 Processor at 3.2 GHz; 15″ XGA TFT Display; 512 MB DDR SDRAM memory; 60 GB Hard Drive; 32MB DDR Graphics Card."

I do this for a living, and I can't tell you what all that means. When you read technical terms you don't understand, visit *Webopedia* (http://www.webopedia .com) to find out what they mean. Type in the word(s) and search for a definition.

Start by listing your needs as you understand them, then ask a technology consultant or salesperson to translate those terms into the right equipment and features. For example, here are some of the things you'll likely want in a PC: speed (a fast processor); lots of storage (a big hard drive); ability to connect to other PCs and the Internet (a network card, maybe even a wireless card); a drive for copying files to CD (CD-R or CD-RW); lots of "outlets" in case you want to add other equipment (USB or FireWire slots to handle peripherals); a good size monitor that won't cause eye strain.

2. Ask Around

Know anyone who's recently bought equipment you're considering? Ask them how happy they are with it, what else they looked at, and how they did their homework.

 TIP: If you would like to see what people are saying about virtually any equipment you are considering buying, check out *Epinions* (http:// www.epionions.com) where you can read consumer reviews on computers, electronics, and more.

---

3. Shop from a List, Not on an Impulse

Unless you have money to burn, don't buy on a whim. Who do you think spends less on groceries, someone with a list shopping on a full stomach or the one wandering the aisles just before lunch? Write down what you need and why; you'll spend a lot less.

4. Don't Buy on the Bleeding Edge

One feature you *don't* want in your new equipment is the "est," as in fastest, biggest, or cheapest. Pick from the middle of the menu, the stuff that was new 3–6 months ago (savings are often greatest there). And *never* buy the first release of any new technology (unless you want it as a toy to play with)! Let others play lab rat for the developers; your time's too valuable to waste working out experimental bugs.

5. Stick with Name Brands and Spring for a Longer Warranty

Forget the no-name stuff. "You get what you pay for" is all too true when it comes to technology. Firms like Dell, Gateway, Hewlett-Packard, and IBM are your safest bet. Bear in mind that one of the ways PC makers have cut prices in recent years is to scale back on service/support warranties. Many systems today come with only a year of service and 90 days or six months of software support. Spend the extra money for a multi-year package that covers both. Consider it insurance.

6. Shop the Outlets

They don't really advertise them, but each of the major PC manufacturers sell current equipment that's been refurbished, often at savings of $300 or $400 over the same item sold as new. What is "refurbished"? Equipment returned for some reason, often under a money-back guarantee. Usually "refurbs" carry the same warranties "new" PCs do, so check to make sure that any refurbs you might buy do. Here are the Web addresses for some of the leading brands:

Dell	http://www.dell.com
Gateway	http://www.gateway.com
Hewlett Packard	http://www.shopping.hp.com
IBM	http://www.ibm.com

7. Expect to Upgrade Your PC Every Three Years

Thirty years ago, Gordon Moore (one of the founders of Intel) made a prediction that has proven eerily accurate. Moore's Law says that computing power doubles roughly very 18–24 months. If automobile makers could safely double the speed of your car, wouldn't you want to trade it in for a newer model? Your time is valuable; don't be afraid to invest in faster equipment every few years.

Upgrading Software

Wondering when's a good time to upgrade your older software programs? Here are three rules of thumb on when to step up to the latest version of the programs you use regularly (and, yes, you may need to make an occasional exception):

1. *Consider a change when what you use is at least two generations older than the current version.*

If you own version 2, skip version 3 and buy version 4. Companies spend a fortune on ads to convince you the new product is essential to your well-being. It (usually) isn't (note to manufacturers: I said "usually.") Don't think about upgrading until you can identify at least three good, specific reasons why you need the new release. One exception to this rule is Internet security and virus protection software: advances in those programs are worth having as soon as they are available.

2. *Once you are ready to buy a new version, wait until the .1 or .01 release is available.*

One of my favorite sayings is: "The early bird gets the worm, but the second mouse gets the cheese." In the rush to market, companies knowingly overlook dozens, sometimes hundreds of program bugs that they subsequently repair—after the new product is launched. Given that reality, it's worth delaying purchase of a new program until the company publishes a patch file to correct bugs in the program, usually 3–4 months after the new version comes out.

3. *Install the program midweek, in the middle of the day.*

Why? *Hold times.* If you run into technical difficulties and need to talk to someone to get them resolved, you're going to wait longer to speak to a live person if you call first thing in the morning, as the day is ending, or at the beginning of the week.

 TIP: Check manufacturers' Web sites periodically to see if updates/patch files are available for the programs you use. *VersionTracker* (http://www.versiontracker.com) is a free service that publishes a continuously updated list of software upgrades and patches/fixes for over 30,000 applications

---

Resolving Technical Troubles

Let's be honest, the help you get from most technology companies today is lousy. Reaching a live person who can actually answer your question and solve your problem is an exercise in frustration. Long hold times, reps that know less than you about the product, having to pay only to get the wrong answer—it's not a pretty picture.

Stiff competition has driven manufacturer margins through the floor and one of the biggest casualties has been customer service. A recent *Consumer Reports* survey put customer satisfaction with software support "among the lower-ranked services rated in the past 10 years."[2] More and more customers are being pushed to company Web sites for self-service solutions.

So what can you do? Here's what I'd suggest (if you're willing to pay, skip right to number 9).

1. *Start with the program's Help file,* which you can access by pressing the *F1* key.

2. *Try Googling some keywords.*

3. *Ask your assistant or a coworker* if they know.

4. *Contact your internal support desk.* Good internal help desks not only can answer questions about proprietary programs your firm uses, but often can guide you on the commercial applications you have installed.

5. *Check the product's Web site to see if it offers a knowledge base* of technical support documentation on your application and search it.

6. *Search newsgroup postings to see if others have had your problem (and how it's been solved).* The fastest way to do so is at *Google Groups* (http://groups.google.com), where you can keyword search over 20 years worth of postings across tens of thousands of newsgroups.[3] If you regularly revisit the same newsgroup(s) for answers, or want to post questions of your own, get a newsreader program like Outlook Express so you can download, save, and post messages the same way you do e-mail. You will need access to a news server that carries the newsgroup(s) you're interested in; check with your Internet Service Provider (ISP) to see if they provide access.[4]

7. *If you don't uncover an answer, post your own question.* Some manufacturers who host their newsgroups, like Microsoft, let you submit postings using forms at their Web sites. If the newsgroup is independent of the manufacturer, again you will need Outlook Express or another newsreader and access to that group through a feed service.

8. *Call the manufacturer's technical support group.* Avoid Mondays, the first two hours in the morning after they open, the last hour of the afternoon, and Fridays after lunch—those are "rush hour" times.

9. *Try one of the fee-based technical support sites on the Web.* If it's the middle of the night, or hold times are interminable, or you just have no patience for the self-service options, give this option a go. *Tech24* (http://www.tech24.com), and *LiveRepair* (http://www.liverepair.com) are two leading providers. Available 24 hours, 7 days a week, 365 days

a year, the companies' technicians can answer questions on a wide range of popular products, both software and hardware. It's all done through a live chat connection conducted through your browser.

And if you can't get an answer after all that?

10. *Throw your computer out the window.* Just kidding (sort of).

 TIP: The Google Directory maintains several listings of technical support sites. One is under Computers > Software > Operating Systems > Windows > FAQs, Help and Tutorials > Technical Support and Troubleshooting. A second can be found at Computers > Companies > Product Support > Independent Tech Support.

If you want local support for issues like configuring a new PC or network, installing an operating system upgrade, or troubleshooting high-speed connection issues, your best bet is a referral from a trusted source, someone you know, or the local chapter of an industry trade group.

This type of support is often provided by individuals, or very small companies, so be sure to check references thoroughly, especially if you got the name from an ad. Take a look at the *Independent Computer Consultants Association* site (http://www.icca.org) or *Geeks on Call* (http://www.geeksoncall.com), which provides "part-time IT department" support to small and midsized businesses, as well as residential customers through franchises in a growing number of states around the country.

TRY THIS SIMPLE SOLUTION

Depending on the problem, restarting (or *rebooting*) your computer may be all that's needed to get you back on track. Try using the Restart command on the "Shut Down" menu. If your computer is frozen (i.e., not responding to keyboard or mouse commands), press and hold the power button for several seconds, until the machine powers off. Wait a couple of seconds and press the power button again to start the machine.

If you still have problems, try cleaning out your "Temp" folders, both in Windows and in Internet Explorer (where the actual folder name is

"Temporary Internet Files"), and emptying your Recycle Bin. Often, problems crop up simply because the computer runs out of temporary storage space. Taking these steps will give your PC a little breathing room.

Microsoft

Because so much of what's discussed in this book relates to Microsoft products, the support options the company provides merit a closer look. First, some good news: unlike the nightmare scenarios I've often encountered with other vendors, I've consistently found Microsoft technicians to be among the best trained, most personable people I've dealt with. Granted, most of the time I've paid for the privilege of getting through to them, but that's a small price to get on and off the phone quickly and get the situation resolved.

Microsoft offers a range of support options at http://support.microsoft.com. At the site, you will find frequently asked questions (FAQs) for all of the products covered here, a Knowledge Base of 250,000+ articles, downloads of product updates and patches, newsgroups where you can post questions, and a directory of online and telephone-based support options. Each product has its own support center page, which you can get to from a drop-down menu on the FAQs page.

The Knowledge Base is searchable by product, keyword(s), or article ID number. All four of the search methods described in Chapter 4 can be used; you can also type in questions like "How do I . . . ?" or "Where can I find . . . ?" to get a list of results (called natural language searching).

Installation support is available at no charge, both online and by phone 7 days a week. Paid support can be purchased "per incident" for a fee; 5-pack support call packages can also be purchased (saving the need to provide a credit card each time). (*Note:* One or more "free" incident calls are included in the purchase price of many of Microsoft's products, so be sure to ask if you have any you can use when calling.)

TIP: Check the Web sites of software programs you use regularly for a Knowledge Base of articles. Whenever you find one, add it to the Technical Support section of your journal, or bookmark it in a similar section of your Favorites.

ACTION STEP

Go to http://www.winningclientsinawiredworld.com and print out a copy of the *Technology Toolkit Shopping List*. Check off programs and hardware you already own, and those you want to consider adding to your toolkit. Do your homework by visiting the company's site, reading what others are saying about the product(s) you're evaluating at PC Magazine, clnet, or the other sites mentioned.

Notes

1. From "Jack Welch Goes Surfing," *Newsweek,* December 25, 2000; http://www.msnbc.com/news/504447.asp.

2. *Consumer Reports,* September 2003.

3. You will find a list of Office Newsgroups at http://communities2.microsoft.com/communities/newsgroups/en-us/.

4. If your ISP doesn't carry newsgroups, review the list of Feed Service providers in the *Google Directory* under Computers > Usenet > Feed Services.

The Chat Room

Advice from Those Who Have Been There

Would you like me to give you the formula for success? It's quite simple, really: double your rate of failure. You are thinking of failure as the enemy of success. But it isn't at all. You can be discouraged by failure—or you can learn from it. So go ahead and make mistakes. Make all you can. Because, remember that's where you will find success.

—Thomas Watson

I am not discouraged, because every wrong attempt discarded is another step forward.

—Thomas Edison

With the end in sight, I'd like (for a minute) to take you back to the very beginning. At the outset of my research for this book, I asked more than a thousand people for input on what they wanted to see in it. They came from all levels of the industry—advisors, wholesalers, managers, assistants, marketers—and all corners of North America. What they told me is, in large part, why you've been reading what you have.

I also asked them to share what successes they had enjoyed, what challenges they had endured, especially with technology, and what advice they would offer others in addressing those obstacles. What follows are their best bits of advice for integrating technology on the front lines of financial services. Some are general, others are specific; some funny, most serious—but all are helpful.

From: Rick A.

I would encourage new advisors to first get systems established BEFORE beginning to service clients. It becomes more and more difficult to bring on new software and learn new programs once you are in the middle of marketing, serving clients, etc.

Second, condition clients early on to expect the use of e-mail in your delivery of services. It is much more efficient in trying to schedule appointments, send documents, etc. The downside is that, even though clients may give you an active e-mail address, many don't check it for weeks at a time, so sending time sensitive data is a risk.

The paradox in using Web technology that I have found is that, for advisors like me who try to differentiate themselves for the large cookie cutter firms and emphasize close personal service, e-mail, Web sites, etc., can send a message that a client is being "processed" and given the same generic information as everyone else. It is a balancing act to be small and personal as well as use technology in an efficient and effective manner.

Bethesda, MD

From: Harry A.

Be patient, experiment, put a plan/process together. Listen to those that had been on the bleeding edge and survived, hire a consultant—money well spent (oops! I mean invested).

Albuquerque, NM

From: Gene B.

Always seek (on the Net, in print media, at conferences) the next way to be even more useful to your clients without straying from your mission. When you find another way, decide how best to do the job—in house, a contractor, a service, whatever. If equipment must be added, make an effort to find and acquire the best. Put quality before price.

Winter Park, FL

From: Ilene B.

Use the tools available to help increase your efficiency in the office but do not become so dependent on it that you don't apply good reasoning and logic to your advice . . . There are so many tools available that will calculate and project different things for you. I see too many people take the information verbatim and many times it is wrong. You need to add value to what comes out of your computer.

Bethesda, MD

From: Mike B.

. . . The best thing I did was to hire you to help clarify the direction that my business was going and help get back on the path I needed to help the business move forward. The technology was helpful only after I had a clearer understanding of just how the technology and the Web could help me achieve my goals. That use of technology and the Web is still unfolding as I move closer to accomplishing what I set out to do. Get a really clear picture of your business first. A consultant can give one a sounding board to get a clearer understanding of all that is involved in one's business.

Vienna, VA

From: Joe B.

Information is changing all the time. Try to take some time each week to surf the Web. I try to find sites that will help me be more informed or provide value to my clients (by acting as a human filter). About once a quarter I review bookmarks and delete those that are no longer relevant to me. Also, I try to work up a daily and weekly Web site review list that I go to for the next quarter [which] limits the amount of time that I spend on the net doing "mindless surfing."

The industry is changing so fast you can lose advantage if you "over-analyze" cost effectiveness. Try different things; if they don't work, try something else.

West Des Moines, IA

From: Steven D.

Find what works, learn it, and stay with it. Do not scrap it for minor updates and changes. If Word does 99 percent what you want, there is no need to change word processors or even do an update. Wait till there is a real need. If you find something that you may think will help, HIRE someone to implement it and train you. Putting new technologies in place takes you away from your focus and leaves you with a longer learning curve.

Olvia Vista, CA

From: Betsy D.

It takes time to become familiar with the use of technology and the Web, but it's worth it. Don't keep putting it off. If you need to, get someone who is very familiar to sit down with you and show you the basics and some "tricks" that are relevant to you. It will pay off not just "down the road," but immediately, and BIG. Once you experience the ease and speed and vast amount of knowledge available, you'll wonder what took you so long to get started or start expanding.

St. Charles, IL

From: Murielle F.

Embrace technology fully. Dabbling is a waste of time. Make sure you have the right software and hardware for the job. Compromising will only end up costing you more in the long run—both in time and money.

Calgary, AB

From: Barbara F.

I have three words of advice: BACKUP, BACKUP, BACKUP. I laughed this morning as I read 3 articles about the increasing use of hand-held devices, and just this week my palm pilot had a meltdown. I had backed it up last week and also write all appointments on my daytimer, so I survived.

Technology has and will continue to change the way we run our businesses. I couldn't run mine without it. My mantra as far as technology goes is the serenity prayer, and one thing I can't change is my reliance on it.

It seems that the older we are, the more difficult the learning and the use becomes. My 75-year-old dad, an MIT graduate, types things over and over and over because he can't grasp the concept of copy and paste. Meanwhile I overheard a young mother encourage her toddler to do potty training by allowing him to work on the computer. Go figure.

Bethesda, MD

From: Kevin G.

If I had it to do over, I would probably want to learn more about technology in advance as opposed to learning once the need came up.

New York, NY

From: Gigi G.

My best advice is to hold out for a specialist who has *both* technical expertise and vision if you are trying to grow your company to become a
national player. I came to you looking for some minor technical help and
came away with a whole new way of marketing our business.

Tampa Bay, FL

From: Mike H.

Talk to the company(s) you do business with—ask what technology they
offer, why they offer this particular solution, what made them choose one
product over others you may be looking at . . . and most importantly, with
an open mind. Doing so . . . will allow you to leverage all the research
they did before making a decision they implemented (trust me, they gave
it a lot of thought). Then, HIRE SOMEBODY to help you . . . just like you
expect your clients to hire the appropriate professionals to help implement
their financial plan (attorneys, accountants)—seek appropriate professional help!

Des Moines, IA

From: Jeanette J.

Decide who you want to target, look at how they want you to contact/take
care of them, and build systems that are tailored to their needs. You can't
just send out blanket e-mails and believe that clients appreciate it.

Cincinnati, OH

From: Christine L.

Be prepared to commit time in order to put everything in place and then
to explain over and over again how technology works. You cannot let
impatience sabotage your efforts and ultimate efficiency goal for in the
beginning you will be repeating and repeating and repeating. Never
assume that everybody understands after you've explained it once; be
proactive and ask again and again if there is anything you can do to help.
It may seem difficult to get the wheel to roll but when it finally does,
everybody wins.

Montreal, QC

From: Brian M.

The best use of technology for me in the past 3 years is very simple. I have a personal fax machine installed in my office. When proposing an idea to a client it is very easy for me to fax them the supporting information right away. I think it is comforting for them to know that the machine is in my office and that information they send to me goes directly to my desk, rather than float around the office.

Calgary, AB

From: Chris M.

Be skeptical of any messages you get from well-intended friends telling you that they (and now you) have been hit by a virus, and instructing you to remove one or more files from your computer. Your friends have likely been victimized by a hoax; don't you get suckered. Instead, visit Symantec's Anti-Virus Center Hoax Page (http://www.symantec.com/avcenter/hoax.html) and verify what they have reported is really a problem or someone's (bad) idea of a practical joke before you pass it on to others unknowingly.

Washington, DC

From: Lloyd P.

I would encourage anyone early in their practice to buy as much technology as they can possibly afford to buy, because the payoff on it is unbelievably fast and it makes your work so much easier. My only regret with technology is that I didn't do more sooner and we have been early adapters since the mid 1980s, but I wish we would have done it even quicker.

Greenville, KY

From: Rod W.

Go to work for someone else and let them worry about it! Kidding aside . . . Go with the dominant provider (or the standard) almost always. Less bugs, you'll get access to user groups and the companies are (usually) well financed.

Campbell, CA

From: Al Z.

I think it all comes down to attitude. I want to do better and to grow my business. I stay open to the possibilities. You have to believe and know that technology will help you, you can't be afraid of it, and you have to just do it.

Tacoma, WA

And, saving one of the best for last (Deb, did you see the movie *Fargo*?):

From: Deb H.

(After reading your Tip on identity theft) . . . just thought I'd share with you my personal "shredder" solution.

My husband gets so much crap in the mail that in less than 2 years he had burned out 3 "personal shredders"—he puts in envelopes with plastic windows and occasional staples, paperclips, etc. He's an avid gardener & our property is heavily wooded—he bought a BIG outdoor shredder (it will take up to about a 2 inch limb) and shreds all the paper in it & then uses the almost-pulped results as mulch for the flowers. It takes about 15 minutes to do 2 big leaf bags of paper along with some wood for "fiber."

Brevard, NC

Where Do I Go from Here?

The Choice Is Up to You

*The difference between a successful person and others is not
a lack of strength, not a lack of knowledge, but rather a lack
of will.*

—Vince Lombardi, Hall of Fame football coach

If it were true, as has been said, that 80 percent of success in life is just showing up, the answer to the "where do I go from here?" question might be
"nowhere." Having read this far, there would be little left to do now; you
would be pretty much finished. But it's not—not in this business, not in today's
economy. You don't get credit for knowledge, only for what you do with it.

So the real question to ask is, "What's the best way to leverage what I've
learned to improve my results?" The answer depends largely on two things:
what you want to accomplish and your attitude about technology.

I often ask audiences I work with how they feel about technology, inviting
them to raise a hand when they hear the statement they relate to most. The
choices are:

- I live and breathe it.

- I'm usually among the first to try new things.

- If it's practical, fine; otherwise, don't bother me.

- It's right up there with compliance.

- My pen and paperwork are just fine, thank you very much.

In a group, the results invariably look the same: like a bell curve. A few hands go up for each of the first two and the last two choices, but the majority put themselves squarely in the middle category.

Your response says a lot about where you are and where you might go from here. If you're an innovator or early adopter—the first two categories—you may already be well underway. You probably dived in right from the beginning. All I ask is that you write and share your successes; the best way to reach me is kip@winningclientsinawiredworld.com. If you're not one of those people, but you're still eager to proceed, yet unsure how to do so, here's my advice.

First, take advantage of all the low-hanging fruit you can pick: the knowledge journal, browser upgrades, search tips, Web sites, keyboard shortcuts, presentation tools . . . the quick hits, in other words. The stuff you've probably already done, or have asked your assistant to do for you.

But there's another realm, one of long-term improvements; the changes you can make that will result in clients entrusting you with more of their business and more introductions. Things like a solid, dependable communication process, a clear marketing or relationship management plan, and the right systems and staff in place to execute it all.

Achieving those things takes more effort and more time. It's not a matter of just loading a software program. In fact, achieving those objectives is really not about "technology" at all; it's about knowing what outcome you're seeking and how you're going to get there. Technology is just the means to an end.

My advice on that front is to be strategic; develop a game plan and follow it through a step at a time. Identify your imperatives. Let what keeps you up at night guide you in determining what to tackle first. If you need more than that, try downloading two free tools I mentioned earlier: the "Checklist of Challenges" and the "Self-Assessment Questionnaire" (you can find both at http://www.winningclientsinawiredworld.com). Use them to prioritize the issues that are most important and help put into words what you want to achieve in getting to that "next level" of success.

Once you decide what your goals are, match your imperatives with the strategies and tactics in this book that will help you achieve them. Pay special attention to Chapter 2. It may be the least technology-rich chapter in the book, but for my money, it's the most important. You can succeed without a lot of things, but not without a plan. Use the process it describes to build yours.

You may want a guiding hand in formulating and executing a plan, many people do. Figuring everything out on your own can be overwhelming, especially when you have a job to do or a business to run. When looking for help, don't make the mistake of overlooking your staff, even if that's one person.

They may have a far better grasp of the business and what it needs to move forward than you realize.

And if you want outside assistance, I offer a variety of training, coaching, and consulting programs specifically designed for advisors, support staff, sales managers, and wholesalers. All of these programs are built on the strategies, tactics, and tools you've read about here and are designed to help you make more money, create more free time, and increase the franchise value of your business. To find out if you or your team qualifies to participate, visit http://www.kipgregory.com.

I also offer senior executive-level strategic guidance to companies looking to improve sales-force productivity and profitability: product and back-office service providers who want to recruit and retain top producers with something more than payouts; firms that recognize helping their frontline sales people and distribution partners build a successful business is a smart strategy for growing their own. If that's you, please feel free to contact me directly. And be sure to read "Using Technology to Build a Better Sales Force," which follows as Appendix A. It outlines a straightforward framework for leveraging the power of the Internet to improve sales-force effectiveness.

A final word: Don't let your enthusiasm for executing what you've learned dissolve into inaction. You've invested a lot in getting here. Realize that the power to achieve great things is more than ever within striking distance—and seize the opportunity. People spend their lives searching for chances like that; you've got one right in front of you.

Finding and capitalizing on those opportunities is what gives purpose to work. And the reward on the other side of your effort will be great, I promise you.

I wish you every success in realizing it.

Using Technology to Build a Better Sales Force

Note: I wrote this article for the Winter 2002 issue of LIMRA (Life Insurance Market Research Association) International's *Market Facts* magazine. It was adapted from a presentation I delivered to a group of life insurance executives at the organization's 2001 Annual Meeting.

What is your company's Internet strategy? How does it further your firm's marketing, sales, and servicing objectives? Many life companies are finding answers to these questions elusive as they struggle to establish an effective Internet platform.

Integrating the Web into your overall business strategy requires several things: understanding what the market wants, determining what's in it for you to meet that demand, and successfully delivering your solution(s). Address those issues and you're a long way toward implementing an Internet strategy that helps you achieve your business objectives.

Understand What the Market Wants

As the Internet has evolved, corporate conventional wisdom has shifted; once popular beliefs have been proven to be misconceptions. Most life insurance executives now acknowledge that:

- Having a Web site does not mean you have a Web strategy.

- Focusing on consumer marketing (B2C) at the expensive of business-to-business (B2B) marketing has not proved successful for many firms.

- The "Field of Dreams" philosophy (build it and they will come) hasn't worked.

At the same time, some things remain the same:

- The Web continues to be a fascinating, frustrating, and vastly underutilized resource.
- People, including agents and investors, continue to want help in figuring out how to leverage what they offer.
- The demand for help still represents a huge opportunity for those who respond appropriately.

Bottom line: Everybody is looking for help in sorting it all out, but few know where to begin. So how do you fashion a coherent strategy that capitalizes on that situation? Focus your thinking by considering these questions:

- What is your primary method of distribution?
- What is your biggest distribution challenge?
- What are your distributors' biggest problems?

If you sell products directly to consumers, by all means focus your Internet efforts on making your customers' purchase and service experience easier. But if the bulk of what you sell comes through captive or independent agents, you should look first and foremost at how you can allocate your Internet resources to help those agents sell and retain more business. I'm not suggesting it's an either/or choice, you should make resources available to help both audiences—agents and customers. You just need to prioritize the development of those resources appropriately.

With most life insurance products today still sold in the context of a traditional agent/client relationship, it makes more sense to concentrate Internet resources on agent assistance. Given that most life agents aren't on the cutting edge of technology, your first task is to make them aware of the Internet's capabilities as a business-building tool.

You create that awareness by: one, identifying the challenges your agents face (typically, attracting, servicing, and retaining clients); two, showing them how to solve those problems faster, less expensively, and with less frustration, and; three, getting them hooked on the solutions you offer.

Ask most agents what they are using the Web for today and they'll probably answer e-mail, news, maybe a little shopping. Few have grasped its full potential, but all are interested in knowing how they can.

The list of ways to enhance your agents' productivity with Internet technology is almost limitless. Schedule a brainstorming session to identify areas in which agents need help, and time to evaluate, organize, and prioritize the list of possible assistance the Internet (and your company) can provide. Be sure to include some of your agents in the process to get their direct input.

However you approach the task, be careful to avoid the following three common errors:

1. Overlooking the basics—neglecting to show agents practical, immediate ways the Internet can save them time in getting and keeping business.

2. Focusing on proprietary solutions to the exclusion of existing, inexpensive commercial ones—in the name of "differentiation."

3. Failing to create mechanisms that measure and reward agents' commitment to shared success.

Be Clear About What's in It for You

If you're an agent-driven company, and you're not focusing your Internet resources on making them more effective salespeople and relationship managers, you're making a big mistake. But let's say you are already focusing on them. How do you do so in ways that tie agents closer to you?

Create a skill-building program whose price of ongoing participation is continued production of a mutually agreed to volume of business. Offer the program selectively to your best distributors following this five-step framework:

1. Demonstrate ways to use the strategies, concepts, and tools to get more business.

2. Provide agent and team training.

3. Provide participants with a road map to follow to put their learning into practice.

4. Create study groups to establish a sense of community and shared purpose.

5. Blend face-to-face and distance learning to achieve results cost-effectively.

Let's look at each one of those steps briefly.

Demonstrating the benefits to the business is the first step. The big challenge here is focusing on key business drivers, as seen from your agents' perspective. The mistake many product providers make is to focus on (and promote) their proprietary capabilities—product, service, etc.—things that primarily benefit the providers themselves. That's not lost on agents. Don't leave them wondering to themselves, "Who cares? How does that help me?"

Figuring out what's in it for you is easier if you first answer clearly what's in it for them (your agents). You will build credibility and trust much faster that way. Once you do, you will have their attention, and can begin to introduce them to the proprietary capabilities you offer that can make both your lives easier.

Second, in building their Internet skills remember the goal is to simplify, not complicate agents' lives. Don't overwhelm them with the sense that they need to "do it all" themselves. Your message should be that you want to help them improve their businesses' productivity, which means sharpening the skills of their entire team. So include agents' personal assistants in the process, and any others who play marketing, selling, or servicing roles for them.

Providing a road map is the third step in helping them build skills. It's not enough to tell agents all the wonderful things they can do using the Internet. They can get that from a magazine article or reviewing a list of useful links at some of the sites mentioned earlier. You have to help them put the pieces together and lay out specific actions step-by-step so that they don't have to think about what to do. Otherwise, it won't get done.

Fourth is to create a study group environment, which helps accomplish several things: to recognize top producers, or those with the potential to be; to establish a dialog with participants about their pressing challenges, and to act on what you learn so you can continue delivering effective support. Study groups also provide an accountability mechanism when members are responsible to each other for some amount of follow-through.

Schedule regular (monthly) meetings with these groups; split meeting time between building skills and discussing situations where the skills learned can be applied (problem solving).

The fifth and final step is to create both face-to-face and distance learning opportunities for study-group members. You can piggyback events on your existing schedule of producer and advisory council meetings, and supplement those with other in-person meetings and Web conferences. For skill building to be effective, it has to be practiced and refined time and again. Like any training/learning, content should be delivered in digestible pieces and then reinforced with coaching to effect permanent changes in behavior.

Capitalizing on the Web as a virtual meeting space is one of the most cost-effective, convenient ways to deliver training. The mechanics of Web conferencing follow this progression:

1. A presenter invites selected participants to attend a scheduled event.

2. At the appointed time, invitees meet via PC and phone. The phone portion is done by conference call; the PC element by pointing your browser to a private meeting area where the visual components of the presentation (PowerPoint slides, etc.) will be broadcast.

3. Once the conference is underway, the presenter can poll participants (with results instantly displayed for review by the group), tour useful Web sites, respond to questions, demonstrate applications, or collaborate on projects.

There are literally dozens of Web-conferencing providers on the Internet. Two of the leading ones today are *Microsoft Office Live Meeting* (http://www.microsoft.com/meetlive) and *WebEx* (http://www.webex.com).

Remember, two of the things that makes the skill-building process work are the emphasis placed on making the opportunity available selectively (not universally) and the expectation of shared commitment. You don't offer this to everybody, you make the cost of participation (whether hard or soft dollars) clear at the outset, and then you deliver a compelling program.

The benefits you will realize from creating this capability are significant. You will instill greater confidence and increase productivity among your agents. You will improve your communication with them and cut travel and meeting costs at the same time. The expertise you will develop about what works technologically on the front line of sales can be applied across multiple channels. Together, these things will strengthen your company's reputation for innovation, and generate greater interest in your future Internet initiatives.

Get Internal Buy-In Early

Once you decide to implement, you have to establish a plan. Several issues should be addressed in formulating your schedule, or you risk making costly, potentially fatal, mistakes that you may not realize you have made until it's too late.

The first and most important factor is to recognize the critical role your internal sales people will play. Whether you call them wholesalers, field vice presidents, or something else, they are the human glue that will hold your program together. They act as the face on the business relationship between your company and its agents. Having a knowledgeable, enthusiastic person in a guiding role is vital to creating the agent awareness I described earlier.

Keep in mind that if you have multiple layers in your distribution hierarchy, you will have to invest time and energy to enroll each one in your effort.

Think for a minute about the following statements. Which one best describes how you feel about technology?

- I live and breathe it—24/7/365.
- I'm usually among the first to try new things.
- If it's practical fine, otherwise don't bother me.
- I use it reluctantly because I have to.

Odds are you fall into the third category. If so, you are a "pragmatic" user of technology and the Web; well over half the people we survey fall into that category.

But not everybody does. Answers to the question actually fall across a bell curve. One or two in the "live and breathe it" (innovator) category, a few more are usually first to try new ideas (the early adopters), most in the "if it's practical fine" group, and the remainder in the "use it reluctantly" (conservative/resistor) slot.

Excluding the innovators and a handful of early adopters among them, if you want agents and wholesalers to get excited about what the Web can do for them, you have to show them why they should be. If you doubt the importance of that step, ask yourself why so many Internet initiatives across industry have met with limited utilization. Or, in more personal terms, ask yourself why *you* don't take better advantage of the Web. Might it have something to do with not having any time and not knowing where to start?

Creating solutions isn't enough; you also have to invest in promoting those solutions. Doing so requires training your people. Whether or not you train them enough to act as Web-conference facilitators, they at least need to be able to demonstrate knowledge of tools your Web conferences might highlight, and how to use them to solve problems. It's impossible to act as an effective business consultant in today's electronic age without that basic knowledge. Lacking it, you are nothing but a product pusher at the mercy of the market's rate and commission whims.

So the first sale- and skill-building process you need to complete is with your internal group. Show them how the smart use of the Internet (and other technologies) can make them more money, faster, and with less frustration. Get them excited about what it can do for them, and they will enthusiastically carry the message of what it (and your company) can offer to your agents.

Keep these other issues in mind when mapping out your delivery game plan:

- *Learning is a process, not an event.* Set realistic expectations about what you will accomplish and by when.

- *Select participants carefully.* Concentrate on successful agents who are stuck on a production plateau and want to get to the next level of success.

- *Keep content practical and actionable.* Don't require too much thinking on the part of participants. Give them a clear road map for solving common problems quickly and inexpensively.

Transform Your Traditional Relationships

Many companies still think of the Internet as something apart from the rest of their business operation. That's a mistake. Your distribution strategy should drive your Web strategy. If you offer agents solutions that solve their problems, they will come to you for help and answers. When they do, you will have a terrific opportunity to share the proprietary solutions you offer.

Taking that approach, you can transform the traditional producer/product supplier relationship into a partnership where both parties benefit from meeting shared goals. If you think that's going to take work, you're right. We're talking about changing behaviors, and that takes time and effort. But what's the alternative—not doing it? That's not an option in an industry this competitive.

Besides, aren't the outcomes—more production, better communication, and higher levels of performance—what you're trying to achieve?

Worksheets

The worksheets on the following pages are intended for your use. Copies can be shared with your assistant and others on your immediate team; please do not distribute them indiscriminately around your branch office or your company.

Following are the detailed instructions for completing the "Software Inventory Summary" on the next page. Refer to the appropriate sections of the book for information on completing the others; the page(s) related to each one are identified on page 252.

- *The name of each program.* You can find the name of each one you use in one of two places on your PC: the Programs menu, or the "Add/Remove Programs" list. You get to the Programs menu by clicking on the Start button, then Programs. (Most, but not all, of your programs will be on this list.) To capture any remaining names, open "Add/Remove Programs" from your Control Panel, scan *its* list, and add any that are missing.

- *Its version number.* To get the version number for each program, open it, select Help on its main menu, then About; a window will appear containing the version number. In many programs you will also find the *Product ID number* here as well. It's often requested when you call the manufacturer's technical support departments. Record it, too.

- *Any installation codes required to load it onto your computer. Installation keys* are different from product IDs. They are number (and sometimes letter) sequences that must be entered during installation or reinstallation of software. They are generally found on a sticker in (or on) the plastic case installation CDs come packaged in, or are sent to you by e-mail after you purchase a product online. Put those numbers in your summary so you avoid having to hunt them down later on.

- *The number to call for technical support.* The number (and business hours) for a program's technical support can usually be found in the documentation that comes with the software, or in its Help file. Be sure to include the e-mail address as well. There may be one number for free support regarding installation and another one to call for routine usage questions. Include both.

- *The company's Web address.* Record the *uniform resource locator* (URL) for each program you use. If you keep your inventory summary in Word or Excel, you can format the URL as a hyperlink and click on it to open your browser and go right to the company's site to get technical answers, patch files to fix errors with the programs, and so forth.

 TIP: Download and install the free *Berlarc Advisor* (http://www.belarc .com/free_download.html) to get a detailed profile of the software and hardware installed on your computer. It provides within a single Web browser window much of the information described above.

For background on each of the worksheets included in this appendix, refer to the pages shown in parentheses in the following list:

Software Inventory Summary (page 5)

Program Feature Worksheet (page 6)

Work Flow Worksheet (pages 38–39)

The Gregory Group's Online Research Checklist (pages 60–63)

Communication Planning Worksheets 1, 2, and 3 (pages 101–102)

Macro Writing Worksheet (pages 185–186)

Software Inventory Summary

Computer: _____   Review Date: _____

Program	Version	Product ID/Serial #	Technical Support	Web Site

Program Feature Worksheet

Reviewer: _____ Review Date: _____

Program	Command	What It Does	Where to Find It	Shortcut

WORK FLOW WORKSHEET

Process/Challenge: _____   Owner: _____

Step #	Activity	Who's Responsible	Time It Takes	Cost	Tools Used

THE GREGORY GROUP'S ONLINE RESEARCH CHECKLIST

You are more likely to find what you need on the Web faster, and without as many frustrating detours, if you start with a road map. Use this checklist to record where helpful content at useful sites is located.

Site name: _____

Home page URL: _____

☐ Site map _____

☐ Search function _____

☐ Articles/press releases _____

☐ Biographies/history _____

☐ Personalization options _____

☐ Message boards/discussion groups _____

☐ E-mail alerts/opt-in newsletter _____

☐ Staff directory _____

☐ Chapter/branch office listing _____

☐ Event calendar _____

☐ Links/resource list _____

☐ Similar pages (Google) _____

☐ Backward links (Google) _____

COMMUNICATION PLANNING WORKSHEET 1

Client Communication Calendar

Period	Financial	Professional	Personal	Family
January				
February				
March				
April				
May				
June				

(continued)

Period	Financial	Professional	Personal	Family
July				
August				
September				
October				
November				
December				

COMMUNICATION PLANNING WORKSHEET 2

Client Communication Matrix

Topic	In person	1 on 1	Conference Call	Web	Conference	Web Cat/IM	Survey	Listserv	Tape	Letter	Voice Mail	E-mail	Article
_____	☐	☐	☐	☐	☐	☐	☐	☐	☐	☐	☐	☐	☐
_____	☐	☐	☐	☐	☐	☐	☐	☐	☐	☐	☐	☐	☐
_____	☐	☐	☐	☐	☐	☐	☐	☐	☐	☐	☐	☐	☐
_____	☐	☐	☐	☐	☐	☐	☐	☐	☐	☐	☐	☐	☐
_____	☐	☐	☐	☐	☐	☐	☐	☐	☐	☐	☐	☐	☐
_____	☐	☐	☐	☐	☐	☐	☐	☐	☐	☐	☐	☐	☐
_____	☐	☐	☐	☐	☐	☐	☐	☐	☐	☐	☐	☐	☐
_____	☐	☐	☐	☐	☐	☐	☐	☐	☐	☐	☐	☐	☐
_____	☐	☐	☐	☐	☐	☐	☐	☐	☐	☐	☐	☐	☐
_____	☐	☐	☐	☐	☐	☐	☐	☐	☐	☐	☐	☐	☐
_____	☐	☐	☐	☐	☐	☐	☐	☐	☐	☐	☐	☐	☐
_____	☐	☐	☐	☐	☐	☐	☐	☐	☐	☐	☐	☐	☐

Review Date: _____

COMMUNICATION PLANNING WORKSHEET 3

Client Communication Schedule

Month	Topic	Medium	Month	Topic	Medium
January			July		
February			August		
March			September		
April			October		
May			November		
June			December		

Review Date: _____

MACRO WRITING WORKSHEET

Title: _____

Description: _____

Date: _____

Step #	Program	Action	Keystroke(s)

Glossary

Address bar   The place in a browser window where you enter (i.e., type) a Web page URL, directing the browser to display that page.

All keyword search   A type of search where only pages containing all the terms requested are included in the search results displayed (the default method for most search engines).

Any keyword search   A method of search where pages containing any of the terms requested are included in the results displayed.

AutoFill   A feature of the Google toolbar that allows you to enter standard contact information (e.g., name, address, phone numbers, e-mail) into forms at Web sites.

AutoText   1. A feature of Microsoft Word that allows you to insert frequently used text (words, phrases, sentences, paragraphs) into documents by typing only a few keystrokes. 2. A feature in Microsoft Excel that lets you enter certain types of cell contents without typing them in.

Blacklist   A list containing e-mail addresses from which you do not want to receive messages; a standard feature of most antispam programs and services.

Blog (short for Web log)   An online journal used for recording commentary on sites and other information found on the Web.

Bookmark   A shortcut to a Web page URL saved in your browser so that you can return to that page again without having to retype the URL.

Boolean search   A type of search used to pinpoint specific information you seek on the Web using the terms AND, NOT, and OR.

Broadband   The term used to describe high-speed access to the Internet, most often via a cable or DSL connection.

Brochureware   A (disparaging) term used to describe Web site content that offers visitors nothing more than information normally contained in printed marketing material.

Browser   A software program for viewing Web pages on your computer.

Burning a CD   Copying data to a recordable or rewritable compact disk.

CD (compact disk)   A device used to store or distribute information.

CD-R (CD Recordable)   A type of compact disk that data can be copied to (but not overwritten) using a CD burner.

CD-RW (CD-Rewriteable)   A type of compact disk that data can be copied to more than once.

Click   See left-click.

Compact disk   See CD.

Cookie   A file placed on your computer during a visit to a Web site. It contains information used in subsequent visits to that site to tailor the content you see (e.g., registration data or what pages at the site have been previously viewed).

Custom List   A predetermined list of content (text or numbers) you want to include in a range of cells within an Excel spreadsheet (for example, the names of clients).

Dead link   A hyperlink to a Web page that is no longer active; generates the message "Page cannot be displayed" in Internet Explorer.

Desktop   The name given to the area of your computer you see after start-up, but before any programs have been opened, usually containing icons.

Dialog box   A window that appears in your display requesting input.

Dial-up Networking   How you connect to the Internet using a regular phone line.

Digital Subscriber Line (DSL)   A type of high-speed Internet access that utilizes a phone line and a network card.

Directory   A listing of Web pages usually grouped by category and often searchable; a listing of folders or files (or both) stored on your computer or some other storage device.

Docking station   A device used to connect a laptop or handheld computer to peripherals (e.g., a printer) or a network.

Document   A type of file you create using word processing software (most often Microsoft Word).

Double-click   To press the left mouse button twice rapidly, usually to launch a program or file.

Download   To copy a file from another computer to your computer using the Internet.

Drop-down menu   A list of choices that is displayed by clicking on a downward-pointing triangle in a dialog box.

E-mail   An electronic message send by computer to one or more people; the process of sending an electronic message.

E-mail blast (or broadcast e-mail)   A single message (often marketing oriented) that is sent to a large group of people (such as subscribers to an e-mail newsletter).

End task   To shut down a specific program running on your PC by pressing *Ctrl + Alt + Delete* simultaneously.

Exact-phrase search   A type of search where only pages containing a specific phrase are included in the results displayed. Exact-phrase searches are indicated with quotation marks.

FAQ   Frequently asked questions (pronounced "fak"). A page posted at a Web site that answers questions commonly raised by visitors.

Favorite   A term used by Internet Explorer for a Web site bookmarked in your browser.

File   The basic unit of data storage; files come in many types that are distinguished by their extension (.doc for Word documents, .xls for Excel spreadsheets, .ppt for PowerPoint presentations, etc.).

Folder   What files saved on your hard drive or storage media are saved in metaphorically (folders may also contain other folders).

Google   One of the Web's most popular search engines, known for its ability to deliver accurate search results quickly using a very simple interface.

Hardware   The physical technology equipment you use (i.e., computer, monitor, printer, PDA, etc.).

Home page   1. The top page at a Web site. 2. The Web page that loads when your browser opens.

Hovering your pointer   Placing the on-screen pointer directly over an object either to select it or see a description of the object.

HTML   Hypertext markup language. The oldest and still most prevalent coding language programmers use to create Web-page content.

Icon   A small picture used to represent an object (e.g., a file or a window), a command (e.g., copy or paste), or a program (e.g., Excel, Word, etc.) that you can activate by clicking with your mouse.

Icon bar   A row of icons, usually found beneath the main menu of a software program. Many programs group related icons by function (Formatting, Drawing, etc.).

Icon tray   The section of the taskbar (usually at the bottom right corner of the screen) that shows icons for certain programs currently running on your computer.

Installation key   A sequence of numbers (and sometimes letters) required to complete the installation of software on your computer.

Internet Explorer (IE for short)   A Web browser manufactured by Microsoft.

ISP   Internet Service Provider; the company that provides you with access to the Internet. AOL and MSN are two widely used ISPs in the United States.

Keyboard   The device you use to give your computer instructions by typing.

Keyword   A term you want to locate online or within a file using a search tool.

Left-click   To press the left mouse button once.

Link (or hyperlink)   A pointer embedded in a Web page or file that, when clicked on, displays information contained elsewhere within the same page/file or on another page.

Macro   A series of keystrokes or mouse movements automatically executed in sequence by your computer.

Main menu   Where the program commands you use to manipulate software programs are located. On most Windows, the main menu begins File, Edit, View, . . .

MB   shorthand for megabyte (one million bytes, about the amount of text in a short novel); a term used to measure the size of files, RAM, and hard-drive storage space.

Message rules   Instructions you give to an e-mail program that direct the program to handle messages from certain people or containing specific words in a special way.

Message thread   Exchanges posted online between two or more people.

Meta-search   Searching by broadcasting your search terms to multiple engines, done by certain search portals on the Web.

Microsoft Office   A popular suite of business software programs for working with documents (Word), spreadsheets (Excel), e-mail (Outlook), presentations (PowerPoint), and databases (Access).

Modem   A device for connecting a computer to the Internet using a telephone line, cable, or DSL service.

Mouse   A handheld device used to manipulate/control a computer's on-screen pointer in order to select text or graphical commands.

My Computer   A shortcut icon on the desktop that gives access to the Windows' file manager (when you left-click on it), and the System Properties dialog box (when you right-click on it and choose "Properties").

Netiquette   The social "rules" of communicating by e-mail, Web chat, and message postings. An example of bad netiquette is typing a message in all capital letters, which is the equivalent of shouting.

Network card   A device for connecting a computer to a network. The connection can be wireless or via a cable.

Newsgroup   An online bulletin board devoted to a special interest topic (computing, business, lifestyle, and so forth) where visitors post messages with questions, answers, and announcements relevant to that subject.

News Reader   A software program used to download and upload message postings to newsgroups.

OCR (optical character recognition)   A process used by scanning software programs to convert printed text (from handwritten notes, newspapers, magazines, and other documents) to digital form, so that the text can be manipulated electronically and used for other purposes.

Open Directory   The Web's largest human-edited collection of sites, organized into 16 primary categories. The Open Directory, maintained by Netscape, is the basis for a number of other popular Web-site directories, including Google's.

PDF A file extension short for portable document format, most often associated with Adobe Acrobat, one of the programs used to create pdf files.

Peripheral device A supplemental piece of hardware that attaches to your personal computer (for example, your printer).

Portal A popular place of entry to the Internet; a Web site offering a variety of resources including search, news, and content directories. Yahoo is perhaps the Web's best known portal.

Product ID A unique number generated during the installation of software on your computer and used when you call the manufacturer for technical support to confirm that you are using a valid copy of their program.

Program Software you install on your computer that performs certain tasks (i.e., word processing, e-mail, spreadsheet calculations, etc.).

Program menu A section of the Start menu containing shortcuts for launching software installed on your computer.

Rebooting Computer slang for restarting your computer.

Related links Other Web pages that contain content similar to a specified page.

Right-click Pressing the right-hand mouse button once.

Search Attempting to find specific information on the Internet using software or a Web site.

Search engine A program accessed either directly by your computer or through a Web site that scans Web pages for terms you request and lists results.

Shortcut key(s) A key or combinations of keys that triggers a specific action by the computer (e.g., copying text to the Windows Clipboard is done by pressing *Ctrl* + *C* simultaneously).

Shortcut menu A list of frequently used program features that is triggered by right-clicking within a software program.

Signature Standard information you add at the bottom of e-mail messages you send.

Software What you install on your computer so that you can use the computer to perform certain tasks. There are thousands of software applications (also called programs). Some of the more common ones are word processing, e-mail, and Web browsers.

Source code The programming language used to create Web-page content. Examples include HTML, Java, PHP, and XML.

Spyware Software programs or cookies installed surreptitiously on your computer (usually when visiting questionable Web sites) to track your online behavior and usage patterns (e.g., what sites you visit and pages you look at) and report that information back to the program/cookie's creator, or to send ads to your computer that appear (unexpectedly) on your screen while online.

Surf Browsing Web pages indiscriminately (versus searching for something specific).

Surge protection/suppression A way of shielding electronic equipment from damage due to power surges traveling over electrical wiring, usually caused by lightning.

Spam E-mail messages that are sent unsolicited to large numbers of recipients for advertising purposes.

Start button The icon in the lower left corner of your screen (on the taskbar) you click on to open a program, find a file, or change your computer settings. (Pressing the ⊞ key on your keyboard will also activate it.)

T1/T3 A type of high-speed access usually installed in commercial office buildings.

Taskbar The bar, usually found at the bottom of your computer's screen, containing the Start menu and icons for any programs or files that you open on your computer.

Template A master version of a document, presentation, or spreadsheet that contains formatting preferences and is used to create duplicate files that retain those preferences.

Thread/discussion thread A transcript of e-mail messages or bulletin-board postings exchanged between two or more people.

Title bar The bar at the very top of a program window that includes the name of the program being used, and may include the name of the file.

Toggle Using the keyboard to move back and forth between two or more open windows on your computer.

Toolbar A collection of icons, drop-down menus, input fields, and buttons gathered in one place that you use to invoke certain commands within a software program.

UCE (short for unsolicited commercial e-mail) Another term for spam.

Uniform Resource Locator (URL) The technical term for a Web address (pronounced "earl").

UPS Uninterruptible power supply; a battery backup device you can purchase for your computer to provide time for you to save files you are working on and shut down in the event of a power outage.

URL (uniform resource locator) The technical term for any Web address (e.g., the URL for The Gregory Group's Web site is http://www.gregory-group .com).

Vertical portal (or vortal) A portal devoted to a single subject or industry.

Web conference   A gathering of participants from remote locations conducted over the Internet for the purpose of training, presenting information, or collaborating on projects. Sometimes called a "virtual meeting."

White list   A group of e-mail addresses from which you want to receive messages; a standard feature of many antispam programs and services.

Acknowledgments

It's true what people say about writing a book—it's one of the hardest things you'll ever do, at least it was for me. And if it weren't for the help, guidance, and occasional friendly kick in the assets from those around me, you would never be reading this.

At the top of the list are my parents, Martha and Ed Gregory, who shared (among other things) their passion for learning, a solid work ethic, strong faith in God, and enough stubborn Irish genes to persist in what I knew inside was the right thing to do. Their support at every turn over four decades has given me confidence to pursue my own path, and no words could ever adequately express my gratitude.

Right beside them is my wife, Donna, who never dreamed this is what she signed up for back in 1992. She has hung in with me through thick and thin. Thank you, Stone. It's gonna be great.

David Pugh, my editor at John Wiley, who e-mailed me out of the blue one day saying it was time for a serious look at technology and the opportunities it presented and would I consider writing a book on the topic, deserves thanks—for being both a catalyst, and for his patience with a slow writer. Bernice Pettinato of Beehive Production Services and Trumbull Rogers did a terrific job in reviewing, copyediting, and transforming my manuscript into the book you are now holding in your hands (as did Mary Duffy in drafting the index).

Maggie Leyes and Evan Cooper helped me find my stride both in these pages and in the pages of their magazines: Maggie, at *Advisor Today*, gave me a platform for sharing my ideas with NAIFA's 70,000 members through my "BizTech" column; and Evan, whose innovative thinking about delivering value to the advisor on the street gave me a forum for sharing many of these ideas through the Practice Management Institute and my "Working Smarter" column in *On Wall Street* magazine.

Gigi Guthrie and George Wolff stepped in near the finish line to provide me with incredible support and feedback on the manuscript. They were the voice of the audience and have my enduring appreciation.

My assistants and interns, especially Liz Drapa (the fifth member of our family) and LeeAnn O'Neill, kept me running smoothly and between them logged thousands of hours of research and effort on my behalf.

Hans Carstensen, my boss for 11 years at GNA and then GE Capital, and more importantly, the best friend I've made in business, sparked a flame of curiosity about computers that turned into a burning passion. (Maury, I'm still looking for an appropriate way to pay you back.)

Lawrie Blonquist and Kathleen Hosfeld, two other GNA colleagues and great friends, spent hours talking with me about starting a business to share these concepts when my road unexpectedly forked in the woods back in 1997.

Thanks are due as well to a host of generous people in influential roles: Bud Elsea, at the Financial Planning Association (and the IAFP before that) gave me my first shot at a big audience; Jerry Mason while at NAIFA opened lots of doors; Ed Morrow at IARFC; Chris Davis at the Money Management Institute; John Bowen of CEG Worldwide; and Kevin Sheridan, former publisher of *Advisor Today*.

One of the wonderful things you discover when you leave the corporate track to do your own thing is that the world is full of genuinely good people ready to lend a helping hand—out of nothing more than charity: Jay Jagoe (who's made me a better writer and a better person), Fr. Bill Byron SJ (whose quiet guidance helped immeasurably in navigating my journey), Sally Gardner, Carol and Mark Sheer. Thank you all.

To BW, Uncle Buck, and Mr. Mean—you guys are the best; thanks for your encouragement, and for keeping me laughing. Also to my extended family and friends, your unwavering support along the way made a difficult path easier to travel.

To my former colleagues (and still friends) at GNA and GE who became clients: Eric Miller, John Howard, Pat Welch, Buzz Richmond, Randy Ciccati, Larry Carr—thanks for your support in helping me make this dream a reality.

To all who have ever solved a problem or posted a fix online, I say a special thank you. Your willingness to share knowledge freely, for no other reason than to give back and to save others you'll never meet time and frustration, astounds me. Your generosity of spirit is something we should all emulate.

And to the thousands of financial service professionals I've worked with over these past five years: it has been, and continues to be, an honor to collaborate with and learn from you.

Index

Note: Entries with an associated Web site are italicized. Visit http://www .winningclientsinawiredworld.com for a complete list of links to those sites.

Printed in the United States
117031LV00004B/85-213/P